# SOCIAL SERVICES IN SCOTLAND

# SOCIAL SERVICES
# IN SCOTLAND

*Edited by*
**JOHN ENGLISH**
and
**F.M. MARTIN**
Department of Social Administration and
Social Work, University of Glasgow

1983
**SCOTTISH ACADEMIC PRESS**

Published by
Scottish Academic Press Ltd.
33 Montgomery Street
Edinburgh, EH7 5JX


*Second Edition* 1983


ISBN 7073 0345 1

Printed in Great Britain by
Clark Constable (1982) Ltd., Edinburgh

# Contents

# Contributors

The contributors are members of the following departments at the University of Glasgow:

| | |
|---|---|
| John English | Department of Social Administration and Social Work |
| James G. Kellas | Department of Politics |
| Alan McGregor | Department of Social and Economic Research |
| Robert Mair | Department of Politics |
| F. M. Martin | Department of Social Administration and Social Work |
| Kathleen Murray | Department of Adult and Continuing Education |
| Eric Wilkinson | Department of Education |
| Dorothy Wilson | Department of Social Administration and Social Work |

# Introduction

The purpose of this book remains the same as in 1979 when the first edition was published: to provide an introduction to social services in Scotland. Although there were a good many research studies and a few books dealing with particular topics, no overview of the field was available. The editors, together with colleagues at the University of Glasgow, sought to fill the gap; and the reception which the book has received encouraged them to believe that it met a real need. The second edition has been extensively revised: all the chapters have been brought up to date and many have been largely rewritten. In addition the structure of the book has been changed to some extent. Perhaps the most significant addition is a chapter on social security: although there is little relating specifically to Scotland that can be said about a service which is provided on a uniform basis throughout Britain, experience has shown that its omission was a shortcoming in a basic textbook. There is also a new chapter on mental health services. Pressure on available space has meant that, unfortunately, some chapters which seemed of less relevance to most social administration students have had to be dropped.

The proper scope of a book on the social services is to some extent a matter of judgement, but there are chapters on the five services which are commonly included in the definition: social security, health (and mental health) services, housing, the personal social services and education. Central and local government, children's hearings, manpower services, and services for the elderly and physically handicapped are also covered.

It is clearly impossible within one book of reasonable length to deal comprehensively with the social services, and suggestions for further reading are provided at the end of each chapter. Issues in the social policy field, such as universalism and selectivity, and the important economic context have not been covered at all. Many of these issues and constraints on public expenditure are, however, similar throughout Britain (and even beyond), and it is assumed that readers will make use of the extensive literature in the field of social policy and administration that has been built up, especially in recent years. Some more general books which are not primarily focused on particular services are listed below.

## FURTHER READING

A. Gordon, *Economics and Social Policy*, Martin Robertson, 1982.
An introduction to economic issues as they relate to social policy.

P. Hall, H. Land, R. Parker and A. Webb, *Change, Choice and Conflict in Social Policy*, Heinemann, 1975.
A discussion of how social policy develops, together with case studies.

K. Jones, J. Brown and J. Bradshaw, *Issues in Social Policy*, Routledge and Kegan Paul, (second edition) 1983.
A discussion of a variety of topics of importance in social policy.

J. Le Grand, *The Strategy of Equality*, Allen and Unwin, 1982.
An investigation of the impact of social service spending on different income groups.

R. Mishra, *Society and Social Policy*, Macmillan, (second edition) 1981.
A review of contending theories of social welfare provision and its effects in capitalist and socialist societies.

P. Thane, *The Foundations of the Welfare State*, Longman, 1982.
A study of the development of social policy in Britain between 1870 and 1945.

P. Townsend, *Sociology and Social Policy*, Penguin, 1976.
A wide-ranging collection of articles relevant to social policy.

# 1

# *Central and Local Government*

The provision of social services in Scotland is in important respects different from that in the rest of Britain. The reason for this difference is to be found in the history of Scotland and in the special characteristics of its institutions. Many of these institutions are concerned with the machinery of government, and it is through this machinery that decisions are taken which continue to mark Scotland off from the rest of Britain. Thus, to understand social services in Scotland, it is necessary to examine the institutions of central and local government in their Scottish forms. Although Scotland is an integral part of the United Kingdom, it has its own political institutions at both central and local government levels.

## HISTORICAL BACKGROUND

The reason for the existence of these institutions can be traced to the Act of Union between Scotland and England in 1707, for it was at that point that the foundations were laid for the present system of government in Scotland. What happened in 1707 was that a division was made between the activities of government which were considered to be peculiarly Scottish in nature and those which could now be considered to be British. In essence, the Scottish sphere was defined with reference to the important social institutions which had grown up in Scotland before the union: the Church of Scotland, the legal system and the educational system. These were given perpetual guarantees in the Act of Union, so that Scotland did not have to adopt Anglicanism, the English legal system and so on. Thus important differences between Scotland and England would remain despite the fact that Scotland had now ceased to have a parliament and a government of its own. These differences have had to be taken account of in the passage of legislation through the Westminster parliament and in the decisions of the British government.

At this time, such social services as existed, if this term can be used at all, derived mainly from the activities of the church. Thus education and poor relief were offshoots of religious activities, and were effectively controlled by the Church of Scotland and other denominations. The fact that Scotland had its own religious establishment meant that views and practices in such matters marked it off from England, and kept social policy firmly in the hands of Scottish decision-makers. A philosophy of educational opportunity was

3

prevalent which owed much to the founding fathers of Scottish Presbyterian-ism, with its emphasis on an educated population and a career open to talents. A less liberal approach was adopted in social welfare, and Scotland was to operate a more austere poor law system than that south of the border.

By the late nineteenth century the church had shed most of its control over education and poor relief to the state, in particular to the agencies of local government. Poor relief was handed over to parochial boards in 1845, and school boards took over the parish schools in 1872. The system of local government in Scotland remained distinct from that of England after the union of 1707, and at that time consisted mainly of royal burghs. Other types of burgh also grew up, and the system was rationalised to some extent in the 1830s; then county councils were created in 1889. At central government level, poor relief was the responsibility of the Board of Supervision (1845-94) which also acquired public health functions. This was replaced by the Local Government Board for Scotland (1894-1919) and subsequently by the Scottish Board of Health (1919-28). After 1872 education in Scotland was supervised by the Scotch (from 1918 Scottish) Education Department.

Looking to history, then, it is easy to see why Scotland is today different from England in many areas of social administration. The traditions coming down from the past in religion, education, law and local government are still of considerable importance. Central government, after 1707 largely removed to London, was not really interested in these until the late nineteenth century and even then it did not seek to impose a uniform system throughout Britain. It is only with the advent of the welfare state and modern party government in the twentieth century that the pressures for uniformity have become strong, so that people have demanded equal rights throughout Britain.

CENTRAL GOVERNMENT

*The Scottish Office*

Many Scottish institutions of a governmental or quasi-governmental nature had, as we have seen, continued to operate after the union. Nevertheless, there was a campaign to establish a separate department which would speak for Scotland in the United Kingdom government. The Scottish Office was set up in 1885, headed by the Secretary for Scotland (since 1926 the Secretary of State for Scotland). He was effectively in charge of the various boards and departments (such as the Scottish Board of Health) although they were separate legal entities. Parliamentary procedure was reformed in 1894 with the establishment of the Scottish Grand Committee to examine Scottish bills.

In 1928 most of the boards with outside members were replaced by departments headed by civil servants, though they remained nominally separate from the Secretary of State.[1] The Scottish Office in its modern form dates from 1939 when the departments were abolished except as administrative divisions of a single organisation. At the same time the bulk of Scottish civil servants moved from London to the newly built St Andrew's House in Edinburgh. The functions of the Scottish Office are now split between five main departments and a Central Services Department (Figure 1.1). Not only does the Scottish Office continue to have the traditional functions of Scottish government which it obtained in 1885, but it has added numerous new ones such as agriculture and fisheries, electricity and economic development.

The Scottish Office departments have much more of a separate identity than do the divisions of most other ministries, reflecting its wide range of responsibilities which cover a large part of domestic affairs. Three of the departments are of particular importance to the social services: the Scottish Home and Health Department (SHHD) is responsible for the national health service (though not social security) in Scotland; the Scottish Education Department (SED) for most educational provision, except the universities, and for the personal social services through the Social Work Services Group (SWSG); and the Scottish Development Department (SDD) for local government and housing.

By the 1960s it had become evident that the Secretary of State was being held responsible by voters and by MPs for the health of the Scottish economy. This was somewhat awkward for him since he did not possess any powers over the economy other than those deriving from local government, electricity and agriculture. He was able to obtain many new economic powers in the 1960s and 1970s, so that the Scottish Office is now an economic department in an executive as well as planning capacity. In particular, it can give grants to industry and has the function of laying down guidelines for the Highlands and Islands Development Board (set up in 1965) and the Scottish Development Agency (dating from 1975).[2]

If one had to explain why the system of Scottish government has grown over the years the answer would probably come in two parts. First, there are technical reasons. The whole scope and activity of government has grown dramatically in this century, and many new functions are performed which were never undertaken before. Thus, Scottish government has grown along with the expansion of government generally. But why *Scottish* departments rather than *British* ones? The technical answer is that, because of the differences in Scots law, the Scottish local government system, Scottish education and so on, these functions could only be placed under the Scottish Office. No London department would have known what to do with such Scottish 'peculiarities'. London departments were not staffed with Scots lawyers, and their administrators were used to dealing with the different forms of local government in England and Wales. So the functions had to be placed under Edinburgh administration.

But there is a second reason: Scotland is a nation as well as an administrative system. Many Scots want some kind of 'home rule', and a constant theme running through Scottish history is that of nationalism. Thus

FIGURE 1.1    Structure and Functions of the Scottish Office

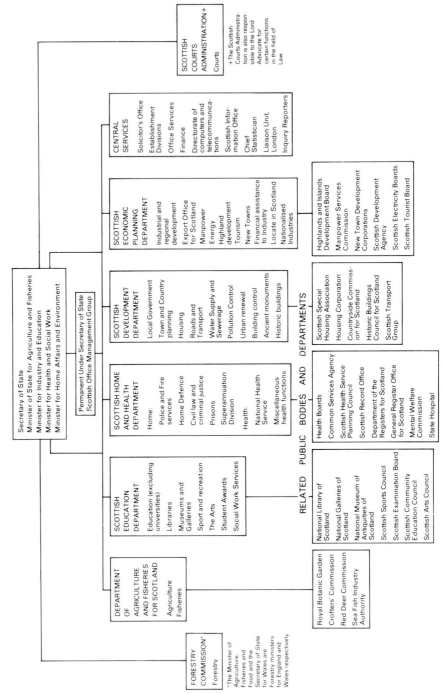

the establishment of the Scottish Office was accompanied by a strong nationalist or home rule campaign. The economic powers given to the Scottish Office in the 1960s and 1970s must be seen against the background of the contemporary electoral successes of the Scottish National Party. Devolution to Scotland came on to the agenda of British politics more as a result of nationalist pressure than through a desire to establish 'good government'. There are therefore both technical and emotional reasons for the growth in the powers of the Scottish Office.

## The Lord Advocate

The Lord Advocate is the government's chief law officer for Scotland and a minister in the United Kingdom government. Unlike the Secretary of State for Scotland, the Lord Advocate has had a continuous existence since before the union of 1707, a clear indication of the importance of Scots law for Scottish administration.

Today the Lord Advocate has two main functions. Assisted by the Solicitor General for Scotland and the Crown Office, he is in overall charge of public prosecutions in Scotland. Unlike the situation in England and Wales where the police prosecute, in Scotland prosecutions are undertaken by the Lord Advocate (in the most serious cases) or local procurators fiscal.

The other function of the Lord Advocate relates to advising government ministers about legislation affecting Scotland and other legal matters. The Lord Advocate's Department which undertakes this function also includes the Scottish parliamentary draftsmen. Law reform, the appointment of judges, sheriffs and justices of the peace, arrangements for the provision of legal aid, and the relationship of the government with the legal profession are all effectively in the hands of the Lord Advocate, although the Secretary of State, as a cabinet minister, also deals with many of them.

## United Kingdom Departments

The Scottish Office and the Lord Advocate's Department are not the only departments of the central government which operate in Scotland. Others, which have responsibilities throughout Britain (or the United Kingdom), include the Department of Health and Social Security (DHSS), the Department of Employment (and the Manpower Services Commission), the Inland Revenue and the Ministry of Defence. There are also substantial numbers of Scottish-based civil servants in departments such as Customs and Excise, Environment and Trade. In fact, far more civil servants are employed in Scotland by these departments than by the Scottish Office. Public sector employees as a whole, including those in the nationalised industries, the national health service and the armed forces, as well as central and local government, account for a third of the employed workforce in Scotland.[3]

The DHSS is responsible for cash benefits (but not health and personal social services) in Scotland, which apart from those paid under section 12 of the Social Work (Scotland) Act, 1968 are uniform throughout Britain. The Manpower Services Commission, which is responsible for job finding services and industrial training, is also particularly important from the point of view of social policy. It should be borne in mind, however, that even here the existence of the Scottish legal system and the Scottish Office are powerful influences. Industrial injuries, for example, in the case of which the DHSS is responsible for paying benefit, often involve a recourse to Scottish courts and are partially subject to Scots law. The Scottish Office is the senior department of government in Scotland and its functions cross-cut with those of other departments. For example, social work is closely connected with social security, and the promotion of industry with unemployment.

### LOCAL GOVERNMENT

Scotland has always had a distinctive system of local government, though the present one was established only in 1975 (see Table 1.1 and Figure 1.2). The new arrangements were based on the recommendations of the Royal Commission on Local Government in Scotland (the Wheatley report),[4] which were implemented by the Local Government (Scotland) Act, 1973. The system is a two-tier one, except for three all-purpose islands authorities (Orkney, Shetland and the Western Isles). It should be emphasised that the different tiers of local government are quite separate from one another, both politically and administratively. Districts are not subordinate organs of the regions of which they form a part, but rather each tier is responsible for different services (see Figure 1.3). The district determines the level of the district rate, just as the region fixes the regional rate. Rates are collected by regional authorities on behalf of districts, so that demands are made up of two components.

### Regional Councils

The upper tier consists of nine regions which range in population from two and a half million (in Strathclyde) to 100,000 (in Borders). Even smaller than Borders are the islands authorities (Orkney has less than 20,000 people). The regions are responsible for most of the more important local authority services, and their functions include education, social work, police, fire, roads and strategic planning.

### District Councils

The lower tier consists of 53 districts, which have populations of nearly 800,000 (in the City of Glasgow) at one extreme to less than 10,000 (in Badenoch and Strathspey) at the other. District functions are somewhat limited but include housing, local planning, libraries, environmental health and public conveniences.

TABLE 1.1

Population of Regions, Districts and Islands Authorities

| | Estimated Population Mid-1981 (000s) | | Estimated Population Mid-1981 (000s) |
|---|---|---|---|
| SCOTLAND | 5,159.5 | | |
| Borders | 100.5 | Lothian | 746.1 |
| Berwickshire | 18.2 | East Lothian | 79.8 |
| Ettrick and Lauderdale | 33.1 | Edinburgh | 446.4 |
| Roxburgh | 35.1 | Midlothian | 82.2 |
| Tweeddale | 14.1 | West Lothian | 137.7 |
| Central | 273.0 | Strathclyde | 2,398.5 |
| Clackmannan | 48.0 | Argyll and Bute | 64.2 |
| Falkirk | 144.6 | Bearsden and Milngavie | 40.1 |
| Stirling | 80.3 | Clydebank | 52.4 |
| | | Clydesdale | 56.7 |
| Dumfries and Galloway | 144.2 | Cumbernauld and Kilsyth | 61.7 |
| Annandale and Eskdale | 35.6 | Cumnock and Doon Valley | 44.0 |
| Nithsdale | 56.1 | Cunninghame | 136.0 |
| Stewartry | 22.6 | Dumbarton | 78.1 |
| Wigtown | 29.9 | East Kilbride | 82.9 |
| | | Eastwood | 54.4 |
| Fife | 340.2 | Glasgow City | 767.5 |
| Dunfermline | 125.8 | Hamilton | 108.8 |
| Kirkcaldy | 148.2 | Inverclyde | 100.9 |
| North-East Fife | 66.2 | Kilmarnock and Loudoun | 81.7 |
| | | Kyle and Carrick | 112.4 |
| Grampian | 483.0 | Monklands | 110.1 |
| Aberdeen City | 212.5 | Motherwell | 149.9 |
| Banff and Buchan | 81.9 | Renfrew | 209.2 |
| Gordon | 63.7 | Strathkelvin | 87.5 |
| Kincardine and Deeside | 42.6 | | |
| Moray | 82.2 | Tayside | 396.8 |
| | | Angus | 92.5 |
| Highland | 192.0 | Dundee City | 185.6 |
| Badenoch and Strathspey | 9.5 | Perth and Kinross | 118.7 |
| Caithness | 27.2 | | |
| Inverness | 56.4 | Islands Councils | 75.3 |
| Lochaber | 19.2 | Orkney Islands | 18.9 |
| Nairn | 9.9 | Shetland Islands | 25.9 |
| Ross and Cromarty | 46.1 | Western Isles | 30.6 |
| Skye and Lochalsh | 10.4 | | |
| Sutherland | 13.1 | | |

Source: The Registrar General for Scotland, *Annual Estimates of the Population of Scotland 1981*, HMSO, 1982.

FIGURE 1.2　Local Government Areas in Scotland

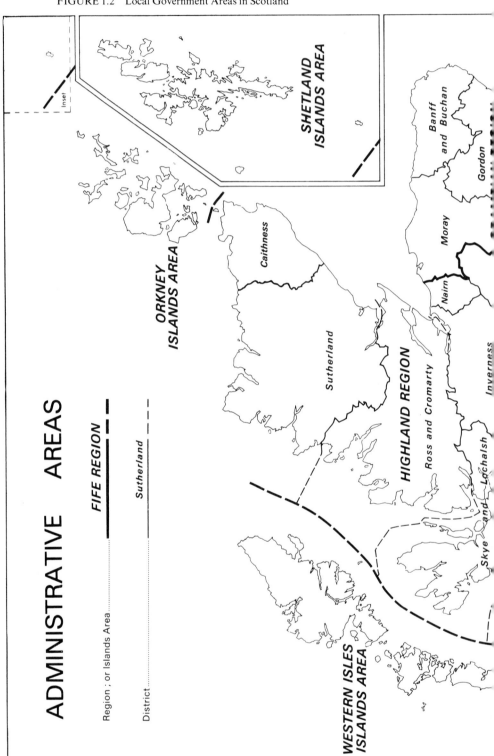

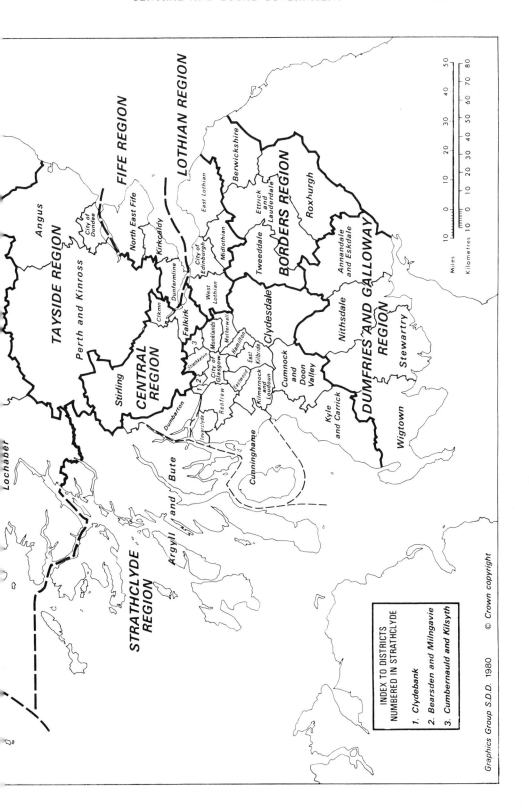

LOTHIAN REGION

FIFE REGION

TAYSIDE REGION

Angus

City of Dundee

North East Fife

Perth and Kinross

Kirkcaldy

Dunfermline

Clkmn

Falkirk

Stirling

CENTRAL REGION

Dumbarton

Inverclyde

Renfrew

Strathkelvin

City of Glasgow

Monklands

Motherwell

Hamilton

East Kilbride

Eastwood

Kilmarnock and Loudoun

West Lothian

City of Edinburgh

East Lothian

Midlothian

Berwickshire

Ettrick and Lauderdale

Tweeddale

BORDERS REGION

Roxburgh

Annandale and Eskdale

Nithsdale

Clydesdale

Cumnock and Doon Valley

Kyle and Carrick

DUMFRIES AND GALLOWAY REGION

Stewartry

Wigtown

Cunninghame

Argyll and Bute

STRATHCLYDE REGION

Lochaber

INDEX TO DISTRICTS NUMBERED IN STRATHCLYDE

1. Clydebank
2. Bearsden and Milngavie
3. Cumbernauld and Kilsyth

Miles

Kilometres

Graphics Group S.D.D. 1980      © Crown copyright

FIGURE 1.3    Main Local Authority Functions

| Regional Councils | District Councils |
|---|---|
| Education | Housing |
| Careers Service | Local Planning |
| Social Work | Development Control* |
| Strategic Planning | Libraries* |
| Roads | Environmental Health |
| Lighting | Refuse Collection and Disposal |
| Public Transport | Health and Safety at Work |
| Water and Sewerage | Licensing (Liquor, Betting and Gaming, |
| Police | Taxis, etc.) |
| Fire | District Courts |
| Civil Defence | Public Conveniences |
| Consumer Protection | Tourism |
| Rating | Leisure and Recreation |
| Registration of Births, Deaths | Museums and Art Galleries |
| and Marriages | Parks |
| Industrial Development | |

*Except in Highland, Borders and Dumfries and Galloway regions where the function is regional. The three islands councils are responsible for all functions, but police, fire and aspects of education and social work are shared with Highland region.

## Community Councils

There are also a large number of community councils which are not strictly local authorities. They do not administer services but are intended to represent the interests of relatively small areas.

## The Convention of Scottish Local Authorities

The entire local government system in Scotland is represented by the Convention of Scottish Local Authorities (COSLA), in contrast to the situation in England and Wales where there are separate associations for the different kinds of local authority. Thus local government speaks with a single voice to central government in any negotiations which take place, for example on the rate support grant. The convention operates as a kind of employers' association in the affairs of local government, and it often stands between the individual authorities and the government or the trade unions.

Despite the combination of regional and district authorities in COSLA there has been strain between the two levels, and the overwhelming domination of Strathclyde region (containing nearly half the population of Scotland) in the system makes the smaller authorities feel powerless. In addition, COSLA has a very small staff and yet is expected to carry the weight of representing the whole local government system.

CENTRAL-LOCAL GOVERNMENT RELATIONS

There are at least two constraints on the actions of local government. First, local authorities may only do what is authorised by parliament, either through general legislation or through private acts promoted by specific local authorities. (Perhaps less importantly in practice they also have various duties placed on them by statute that ostensibly they must perform.) Second, there is the constraint of available resources which in recent years has become crucial. On average local authorities receive more than half their revenue from the exchequer through the rate support grant (RSG) and much of the remainder from local rates, though the relative importance of these sources varies widely from area to area.

Central and local government may speak with different voices, not only on desirable levels of expenditure but also on specific policy issues. Regional, district and islands councils are democratically elected bodies, and are generally committed to the policies espoused by the political party holding a majority of seats on the council. Some of these policies may be significantly at variance with those of the government of the day. When a Labour government was anxious to push ahead with comprehensive education it faced opposition from some Conservative local authorities, while the present Conservative administration, which is keen to encourage the sale of council houses, encountered resistance from Labour-controlled district councils. It has often been to the advantage of a recalcitrant local authority to employ delaying tactics, in the hope that the next general election would bring a more sympathetic government to power before any decisive steps had been taken. Traditionally ministers and their civil servants have cajoled, exerted discreet pressure and uttered general threats, but they have usually held back from direct intervention in local affairs. More recently, however, we have seen legislation being enacted specifically to circumvent local authority opposition, such as the 'right to buy' provisions of the Tenants' Rights, Etc. (Scotland) Act, 1980, thereby intensifying local government anxieties about decreasing autonomy.

Three of the social services discussed in this book are primarily the responsibility of local government: education, the personal social services and housing. The last is subsidised separately by the exchequer through housing support grant, which is outlined in chapter 5. The others, however, are subject to the general system of local government finance, and it is useful briefly to describe the main features of the RSG system.

The chief purpose of RSG is to provide a varying amount of subsidy to local authorities depending on their needs and relative wealth. It is impossible to explain the RSG in detail but its main features are as follows. Each year the government announces what proportion (on average) of local expenditure it will meet from the exchequer: recently this has been over 60 per cent of the total. The entitlement of each authority is determined on the basis of two main 'elements': the needs element and the resources element. The needs element is calculated according to statistical criteria, such as proportions of groups such as children and the elderly in the population. The needs element now accounts for the bulk of RSG. The resources element is intended to compensate authorities with low rateable values per head. The more a local authority spends, and the higher the rate poundage which it levies, the greater is the amount of resources element received. A major reason for reducing the share of the resources element in RSG was that it was criticised for favouring 'spendthrift' authorities at the expense of others. (The total amount of RSG is limited in advance, so that the more one area receives the less is available to others.) The proportion of spending met by RSG varies widely, especially as between each of the district councils, with some authorities receiving over 90 per cent of the total, although unlike England and Wales all get at least some assistance from the exchequer.

Especially since the Conservative administration came to office in 1979, the government has been putting pressure on local authorities to reduce their spending. Not only has the amount of RSG been reduced in real terms (that is after allowing for inflation), but the government has endeavoured to induce local authorities to restrain rate increases. The Scottish Office obtained new powers to reduce RSG payable to councils which make what are seen as unreasonably high rate increases. This gives central government potentially immense power because it can effectively put a ceiling on local expenditure. A good deal of frustration has been caused to some councillors who feel that local authorities are becoming little more than agents of central government.

INTERMEDIATE GOVERNMENT

There are a large number of bodies which cannot be classified as either central or local government agencies. The term 'intermediate government' is sometimes applied to these, and they are very important for an understanding of the way government works in Scotland. Indeed, Scotland has a very large number of such bodies, which may be connected with the fact that there has been no separate government and parliament since 1707.

It is difficult to classify them or indeed to explain exactly why they exist at all, but some examples will illustrate their functions. There are, first of all, statutory bodies set up under an act of parliament to represent a group of people and to perform a function connected with them. The Joint Negotiating Committee for Teaching Staff in School Education brings together the representative of the teachers' organisations and the employers (in this case the education committee of the COSLA) to negotiate pay. The General Teaching Council is the regulating body of the teaching profession in Scotland and a majority of its members are elected by teachers. These bodies are, however, only partly independent of ministers. Thus, while the General Teaching Council controls entry to the teaching profession, it only advises the Secretary of State on matters concerned with teacher training and supply.

And, of course, the government with the consent of parliament can alter the powers of the council.

Then there are executive bodies of various kinds. The national health service is not directly run by the Scottish Home and Health Department in Edinburgh but by 15 health boards appointed by the Secretary of State. The boards are responsible for all aspects of the national health service except for common services such as ambulances which come under another statutory body, the Scottish Health Service Common Services Agency. An example from a different field is the five new town development corporations. All these executive bodies have a statutory basis.

There are also a large number of consultative and expert advisory bodies which may or may not be statutory. Examples include the Scottish Health Service Planning Council and, in the education field, the Central Committee on the Curriculum. Finally, there are so-called 'quangos' or quasi-non-government organisations. These are strictly speaking private bodies which nevertheless are partly or wholly financed by the government and carry out a variety of functions. Examples are the Scottish Consumer Council (which is an offshoot of the National Consumer Council) and the Scottish Special Housing Association.

Social policy is often made through or in consultation with intermediate government bodies, and this has given rise to complaints that they afford opportunities for political patronage with little democratic control. The Secretary of State for Scotland has some 5000 such appointments in his hands, although only about a dozen are full-time and most carry no salary. It is difficult at times to see to whom these bodies are accountable (other than to the Secretary of State himself). Yet proposals to 'democratise' them are often fiercely resisted by the relevant interests themselves. Thus doctors resist the placing of health services under local government, and teachers fought strongly for an independent General Teaching Council. There is, therefore, considerable support for, as well as criticism of, the present system.

THE POLICY PROCESS

Any account which was limited to describing the structure of government in Scotland would not do justice to the dynamics of policy formulation and execution. The most interesting thing about government is not a list of bodies and their functions but the question 'Who gets what, when, how'?, as the American political scientist Harold D. Lasswell put it.[5]

This broadens the perspective from governmental institutions to political parties, pressure groups and the people themselves. But it also narrows down the focus to the activities of the small elite of decision-makers in the civil service, professional bodies and trade unions, who often are as important as the elected politicians in wielding political power.

The concern of this book is the social services, and later chapters will deal with the different areas involved. Some general points can, however, be made at this stage. Scotland is not the only policy-making arena which affects the social services, and people in Scotland do not necessarily want to be different from those in the rest of Britain. Indeed, there is strong pressure to produce uniformity throughout the United Kingdom in such fields as health care, educational provision and social security benefits. Pressure groups and the civil service are also forces for assimilation. Many purely Scottish pressure groups (such as the teachers' organisations) watch closely what is happening in England to see whether their colleagues there are getting something which they are missing. Civil servants in Edinburgh are also happier if they can harmonise their practices with those of Whitehall.

But there is, of course, the other side of the coin: the desire for Scotland to go its own way and not be tied down by policy making in London, which may be appropriate only to English conditions. Thus there is often a distinctive Scottish dimension to policy. Most of it, however, is broadly consistent with a conception of social justice relating to the whole of Britain, and is certainly not diametrically opposed to what is going on in south of the border. To a large extent the Scottish differences reflect historic traditions and present-day problems which are peculiar to Scotland. Thus the teaching profession has developed its own training methods and qualifications, and its own examinations and courses. But the policies of comprehensive education and the raising of the school leaving age, for example, were accepted in Scotland as in England and Wales. In other words, there is much in common in the substance of educational policy thoughut Britain despite organisational differences.

This leads to a general conclusion about the policy process. Much policy in Britain has long been devolved to professions, interest groups and local authorities. But Britain is relatively small with a fairly consensual view of policy preferences, and it is also politically centralised through the concentration of power in the cabinet and the House of Commons. Our political parties are disciplined, and seek to implement their electoral mandates which voters throughout Britain have apparently endorsed. There cannot therefore be too much difference between parts of Britain if the party programme is to remain intact. So what is happening is in a sense a paradox: a drawing together of power at the centre, with at the same time a sharing of administrative authority between central government on the one hand, and different interests and territories on the other. Opinions vary, of course, about whether the centralisation is more effective than the sharing. The evidence shows that Scotland has had some kind of self-government in social policy since the union, but that it has usually willingly accepted the demands of centralisation and uniformity which have accompanied the welfare state.

*References*

1. Scottish Office, *Report of the Committee on Scottish Administration*, Cmd. 5563, HMSO, 1937.
2. M. Macdonald and A. Redpath, 'The Scottish Office 1954-1979' in H.M. Drucker and N. Drucker (eds.), *Scottish Government Yearbook 1979*, Paul Harris Publishing, 1978.

3. R. Parry, *The Territorial Dimension in United Kingdom Public Employment*. Studies in Public Policy No. 65, Centre for the Study of Public Policy, University of Strathclyde, 1980.
4. *Report of the Royal Commission on Local Government in Scotland 1966-69*, Cmnd. 4140, HMSO, 1969.
5. H.D. Lasswell, *Who Gets What, When, How*, McGraw-Hill, 1936.

## FURTHER READING

M. Keating and A. Midwinter, *The Government of Scotland*, Mainstream Publications, 1983.
An up to date discussion of central and local government and policy making in Scotland.

J.G. Kellas, *Modern Scotland*, Allen and Unwin, (2nd edition) 1980.
A history of political and social institutions in Scotland since 1870.

J.G. Kellas, *The Scottish Political System*, Cambridge University Press, 1975.
An account of the operation of central and local government in Scotland.

*The Scottish Government Yearbook*, Paul Harris Publishing, annual.
This useful collection of essays and survey of recent developments has been published for a number of years.

# 2
## Social Security

The term social security includes the whole range of cash benefits which are available to individuals and families: pensions, child benefit and many others as well as supplementary benefit. Sometimes benefits not provided directly by the state are also included: occupational pensions, sick pay schemes and so on from employers, in addition to various kinds of tax relief.[1] But limitations of space mean that this chapter is confined to state benefits. The focus is on broad policy issues in the social security field, and it does not deal with the details of benefits required by someone who is concerned with welfare rights (some guides to which are mentioned in the further reading at the end of the chapter).

Social security is not only the most expensive of the social services but it is the largest public expenditure programme of all, amounting to over a quarter of the total.[2] From the point of view of Scotland social security is unusual in that it is one of the few social services which are administered on the same basis throughout Britain — by the Department of Health and Social Security (DHSS) in London. Thus there is practically nothing different about social security provisions north of the border.

The chapter has three main parts. First, the development of the present system of benefits is briefly traced because an historical perspective is essential in order to understand its features, which often reflect decisions taken years ago. Second, the benefits which exist today are outlined. Third, the effectiveness of social security benefits in Britain is assessed.

DEVELOPMENT OF SOCIAL SECURITY IN BRITAIN

### Origins to the Second World War[3]

At the end of the nineteenth century the only source of a cash income from the state available to those in need was outdoor relief from the locally administered and financed poor law. The harsh terms on which poor relief was given meant that it was the last resort of a destitute minority of the population. The history of social security during the first half of the present century is to a large extent an account of how provision was made outside the poor law (and on a national rather than a local basis) on terms which were acceptable to the population as a whole.

There was also some provision through two voluntary channels: self-help and private charity. In the field of self-help there was an extensive network of friendly societies which provided benefits, particularly in times of sickness, in return for small weekly contributions. But the friendly societies were limited in their impact: they were largely confined to artisans — the skilled working class — because the unskilled could not afford contributions. Charities had grown in importance during the second half of the nineteenth century but they could only scratch the surface of need.

In the early 1900s there was a new awareness of the extent of poverty with the research of Charles Booth in London and Seebohm Rowntree in York. They demonstrated that poverty was a more serious problem than had been generally assumed, and that its chief causes were factors such as old age rather than the personal failings of the poor. At the same time there was widespread dissatisfaction with the poor law and a feeling that it should be reformed. Although some believed that its administration should be tightened up and that the principle of less eligibility should be enforced, the more general view was that the poor law should be further liberalised and made less deterrent. A Royal Commission on the Poor Laws and Relief of Distress (that is unemployment) was set up in 1905 and reported in 1909.[4] But in the meantime the first social security scheme in Britain in a modern sense was introduced by the Old Age Pensions Act, 1908. Modest though they seem now, old age pensions were of great significance because never before had there been a widely available cash income from the state outside the poor law.

It was felt to be undesirable that large numbers of old people should be obliged to resort to poor relief, and there had been a growing agitation for old age pensions. The Liberal government which came to office in 1905 agreed to introduce a scheme. Two of its features should be emphasised: first, pensions were financed from general taxation (rather than from special contributions); and, second, they were paid subject to a means test. Nevertheless, this was quite unlike the poor law: almost anyone aged 70 with an income below a specified level had a right to a pension.

The introduction of health and unemployment insurance by the National Insurance Act, 1911 was the most important measure in the social security field until after the second world war. The approach of the 1911 act is significant because it marked the adoption in Britain of contributory social insurance — or national insurance — as a method of financing social security. Contributory insurance is the basis of many benefits today. Yet at the time, although there was controversy about how the poor law should be reformed, most interested people expected this to be the focus of government action. In the event, however, nothing was done about the poor law for many years.

The creation of entirely new contributory schemes was politically attractive for a number of reasons. First, insurance contributions from employers and employees were a convenient way of raising revenue which did not seem to be just another tax. Second, poor law reform was unattractive because of the enormous task of reconstructing local government administration and finance which it involved. Third, many advocates of poor law reform had a highly paternalistic approach and believed that relief should be 'conditional': that anyone receiving assistance from the state should be required to behave in such a way that dependency would be ended as soon as possible. Contributory benefits, on the other hand, could be presented as a quasi-contractual return on contributions rather than a gift from the state demanding character reform. This approach of defining rights to benefit and of avoiding the personal investigation of claimants has been central to the national insurance system until the present time.

Some general points can be made about the 1911 legislation. The benefits were financed from special insurance contributions paid by workers and employers, together with a contribution from the exchequer and, also unlike pensions, they were not means tested. The benefits provided only for the insured person with no allowances for dependants. Beyond these main features, however, the two schemes, for sickness and unemployment, differed in many ways.

Part I of the 1911 act dealt with national health insurance which was the larger (and more controversial) of the schemes. It covered all manual workers and lower paid white collar workers — the bulk of the labour force. Two types of benefit were provided: a cash sickness benefit and medical benefit. The latter was basically the free services of a general practitioner and free drugs (and became part of the national health service in 1948). Sickness benefit was payable for up to six months when it was replaced by a smaller disablement benefit. There was also a lump sum maternity benefit.

Part II of the act covered unemployment insurance, the first state-run scheme of its kind in the world. It was small-scale and experimental, applying only to certain trades in which employment fluctuated, such as building and ironfounding. The scheme was administered through the recently established labour exchanges where the unemployed had to register in order to get benefit. This was payable for a strictly limited period of one week's benefit for every five contributions with not more than 15 weeks in any 12 months. The scheme was primarily intended to tide over the normally employed workman for short periods. It did little for the chronically unemployed who would soon run out of benefit even if they had paid enough contributions to qualify in the first place.

During a few years before the first world war, therefore, the beginnings of a system of social security benefits were established in Britain. The years between the wars, dominated by economic crises and mass unemployment, saw only modest improvements. In 1920 unemployment insurance was extended to practically the same categories of workers as were covered by health insurance. Shortly afterwards dependants' allowances were introduced as a cheaper way of making benefits more adequate at a time of inflation than increasing the main rates. But the post-war boom soon collapsed, unemployment greatly increased and the insurance scheme entered a decade of chaos. It was politically unacceptable to force large numbers of the long-term unemployed on to poor relief, so that insurance was adapted to cater for them. The rules were relaxed until an unemployed person could draw benefit almost without limit, and as a consequence outgoings exceeded income from contributions. The exchequer had to make up the difference, but the payments were regarded as loans so that the insurance fund built up a large debt.

The problem of unemployment insurance came to a head in the political crisis of 1931 when economies in public expenditure were demanded to balance the budget. The new National government both cut benefits (their real value had increased owing to falling prices) and limited entitlement to insurance benefit to six months so that, despite a high level of unemployment, the fund soon started repaying its debt. The long-term unemployed who ran out of insurance benefit could now obtain allowances only after a means test, and arrangements had to be made for carrying this out. Initially public assistance committees (which had assumed responsibility for poor relief when it was transferred to ordinary local authorities in 1930) operated the means test on behalf of the government. But the divorce between providing and spending money was unsatisfactory, and in 1934 a new national body, the Unemployment Assistance Board (UAB), was created to administer the allowances. This was an important innovation because for the first time responsibility for social assistance was given to a national body. The UAB, which set up a network of area offices, later became the National Assistance Board, the predecessor of the Supplementary Benefits Commission.

These events were significant for another reason because, though means testing has always been central to the poor law, only relatively small numbers of people had experienced it. (The personal means test for old age pensions was very different.) The means test was for the unemployed on a 'household' basis, the needs of everyone living in the same house being aggregated. An unemployed son could therefore be ineligible for assistance and obliged to rely on his parents. Sometimes unemployed children moved into lodgings to get some income of their own.

The other innovations during the inter-war period affected pensions. There were a number of criticisms of the existing scheme. First, the pension age of 70 was seen as being too high: many found it difficult to carry on working until then. Second, the means test was disliked. Third, there was no provision for widows. The government decided to apply the principle of contributory insurance to pensions in order to finance improvements, and it introduced the Widows', Orphans' and Old Age Contributory Pensions Act, 1925. For those who had been insured the pension age was reduced to 65 and the means test abolished, as well as widows' and orphans' pensions being introduced. The 1925 act did much to entrench the contributory approach to social security in Britain. Shortly after the outbreak of war the Old Age and Widows' Pensions Act, 1940 reduced the pension age for women from 65 to 60 (the origin of what may now seem a curious anomaly), and introduced supplementary pensions payable on a means-tested basis to pensioners and to widows of 60 and over. They were administered by the Assistance Board (previously the UAB), and removed substantial numbers from reliance on the poor law.

Thus by the second world war an extensive range of cash benefits had developed in Britain, mainly on the basis of contributory insurance. But they had severe limitations: for example, there were many separate schemes none covering precisely the same categories of people, they were administered by different organisations, and the level of some benefits was very inadequate. As well as gaps in provision for the non-employed, the problem of inadequate wages in relation to family requirements was ignored completely.

### The Beveridge Report

While the war was in progress the government started to consider reconstruction when peace came, and in 1941 an interdepartmental committee of civil servants under the chairmanship of Sir William Beveridge was appointed to undertake a 'survey of the existing national schemes of social insurance and allied services'.[5] Beveridge, who had long been concerned with social security, wanted far more radical reforms than had originally been envisaged and about which civil servants could not legitimately express views in public. They therefore became advisors and the report, published in November 1942, was signed by Beveridge alone. Though many changes have subsequently been made, social security benefits in Britain still owe much to the recommendations of the Beveridge report and, in order to evaluate their effectiveness, it is necessary to examine what he was seeking to achieve.

The theme which dominates the Beveridge report is the objective of guaranteeing to every citizen an income at subsistence level or, in other words, sufficient resources to keep people out of poverty (or what he called 'want'). In proposing rates of benefit Beveridge relied on pre-war poverty studies such as those of Rowntree, who acted as an adviser. Beveridge believed that the role of the state in social security should be limited to providing a subsistence income. He recognised that many people would wish to have a higher income when they were not working but believed that this should be obtained through voluntary insurance.

Beveridge identified two causes of poverty: the interruption or loss of earning power (for example during sickness, unemployment or old age), and the failure of wages to relate to the needs of families of different sizes. He believed that the abolition of poverty required a 'double redistribution of income'[6]: from those currently at work to those not at work, chiefly through social insurance; and from individuals and small families to larger ones through family (or 'children's') allowances.

The main part of the report was concerned with interruption or loss of earning power. A range of benefits already existed for those not at work — old people, widows, the sick, the unemployed and so on — for the most part on a contributory basis. Beveridge wholeheartedly approved of social insurance: he believed that people preferred benefits in return for contributions and without a means test. (There is no technical reason why non-contributory benefits should be means tested but in practice they usually have been: family allowances (now child benefit) have been the major exception.) Social insurance should continue to be the main method of providing incomes for those not at work, and it would be necessary to improve the existing schemes in three directions: they should be extended to cover persons (chiefly white collar workers) and risks then excluded, and benefit rates should be raised to a subsistence level.

Social insurance was, however, to be only one of three methods of providing social security: the others were to be voluntary insurance and national assistance. The role of voluntary insurance in providing an income in excess of the subsistence level has already been mentioned but, as Beveridge's specific ideas have not had a great impact, this aspect of his proposals may be left aside. Social insurance would on its own not be capable of providing everyone with an income even at the subsistence level, and to supplement it (or to act as a 'safety net') there should be a non-contributory national assistance scheme of means-tested allowances to those in need. National assistance would cover all categories of need including those still met by cash payments from the poor law.

Assistance was envisaged as having only a very limited permanent role in meeting the few needs not covered by insurance benefits. (Beveridge proposed that increased retirement pensions should only be phased in over 20 years so that in the interim assistance would cater for large numbers of old people. But higher pensions were not delayed.) There were in essence three kinds of need for which assistance would be required. First, there would be those who had not fulfilled the contribution conditions for insurance benefit, for example because they had never worked. (The unemployed who run out of benefit after a year are in a rather similar position, but this limitation was not proposed in the report.) Second, there would be those in circumstances (or 'contingencies') which were thought not sufficiently widespread to warrant an insurance benefit: in practice lone parents (other than widows) have been by far the largest group in this position, but Beveridge did not foresee the rapid growth in their numbers. Third, there would be those who, although entitled to an insurance benefit, had exceptionally large needs. Insurance benefits were to be set at a level sufficient to provide a subsistence income for those with average needs, but they would be inadequate in cases such as a high rent or illness requiring a special diet. Only in this third category of need would assistance be paid in addition to insurance benefits.

Beveridge did not regard inadequate wages in relation to family needs as falling within his terms of reference, and instead he dealt with family allowances as one of three 'assumptions' which were essential to the success of his plan for social security (the others were a national health service and the maintenance of full employment). There had been a campaign for family allowances throughout the inter-war years, led by Eleanor Rathbone and the Family Endowment Society, which had made little progress.[7] As wages are unrelated to family needs a combination of low income and number of children can be a cause of poverty. But Beveridge was concerned with family allowances not only as a method of preventing poverty. He was also concerned about the potential overlap between the level of wages and benefits (especially during unemployment) from the point of view of work incentives. Without family allowances, paid whether the head of the household was working or not, either benefits for larger families would have to be set below the subsistence level or in some cases they would be higher than wages.

Beveridge proposed family allowances, on a non-means-tested basis and financed by the exchequer, at an average of eight shillings a week (though they might in practice be varied according to age). Eight shillings was his estimate of the subsistence cost of keeping a child at the assumed post-war price level (taking into account benefits in kind such as subsidised school meals and milk to the value of a shilling). Family allowances were to be paid in respect of second and subsequent children, exclusion of the first child being justified on two grounds. First, Beveridge believed that 'very few men's wages are insufficient to cover at least two adults and one child'.[8] Second, he said that it was desirable that the cost of maintaining children should be shared between the family and the state. In reality Beveridge was also constrained by the level of expenditure to which the Treasury was willing to agree.[9] Exclusion of the first child approximately halved the cost of any given level of allowance, as about half of all dependent children are first or only children. Whereas a subsistence level allowance would prevent additional children pushing a family into poverty, the alternative of a smaller one payable in respect of every child could not do this.

The bulk of the recommendations of the Beveridge report were accepted by the government and implemented in a number of uncontroversial acts of parliament. The Family Allowances Act, 1945 was introduced by the Coalition government before the end of the war, while the rest were passed by the post-war Labour government: the National Insurance Act, 1946 which reformed contributory benefits, the National Insurance (Industrial Injuries) Act, 1946 which replaced workmen's compensation, and the National Assistance Act, 1948 which abolished the poor law and set up the National Assistance Board. Family allowances were first paid in 1946 while the other measures came into force in 1948. Nevertheless, there were divergences from the recommendations of the Beveridge report, chiefly affecting the rates of benefit, which were crucial. Limited as these changes may seem, they undermined the whole approach of the Beveridge plan and greatly diminished the effectiveness of the post-war social security system in eliminating poverty.

In the case of benefits for those not at work (national insurance and national assistance) the divergences altered the proposed relationship between the levels of the two types of payment. It will be recalled that national insurance benefits were intended to provide a subsistence income in all normal cases. Those receiving insurance benefits would only require to have them supplemented by assistance where genuinely exceptional needs existed. Thus non-means-tested social insurance would generally be adequate to prevent poverty. But because many more people are entitled to insurance benefits than to means-tested assistance, the cost of providing a given level of payment through assistance is much less. Therefore in setting the initial payment levels (whose relativities have been more or less maintained since 1948) the government decided to depress insurance benefits, which was done by fudging the adjustment for inflation required on Beveridge's provisional figures. National assistance rates could have been similarly depressed which, while being hard on those in need, would have maintained the intended relationship between the two benefits. In the event, however, the government set national assistance at a level approximating to Beveridge's subsistence scale. In consequence a comparatively large minority of those entitled to national insurance benefits, practically all those without income from a source such as an occupational pension, have been entitled to have them supplemented by assistance.

What happened can be clarified by focusing on the treatment of rent. Beveridge recommended that a notional amount (he suggested ten shillings a week) should be included in insurance benefits for rent, so that only those few with housing costs in excess of this figure would, on grounds of exceptionally high rent, require assistance. In practice, however, no part of insurance benefits was attributed to rent while the scale rates for individuals were similar to those under national assistance. Therefore housing costs were, until the introduction of housing benefit, an important cause of entitlement to assistance amongst insurance beneficiaries.

The much greater reliance on assistance than Beveridge intended — stemming partly from the limitation of entitlement to unemployment benefit and the growth in the numbers of single parents, but most importantly from the distortion of relative payment levels outlined above — had important consequences. Apart from an excessive reliance on what was in Beveridge's eyes a less desirable form of social security, the problems centre on the incomplete take-up of means-tested benefits. In so far as the Beveridge plan envisaged a role for assistance there would, in any event, have been a problem of low take-up but it has in practice been very much exacerbated. It is the major reason why, in the case of those not at work, the post-war system of benefits has failed in its overriding objective of preventing poverty. These disadvantages must, however, be balanced against the provision of higher benefits (albeit with the disadvantages of means testing) for a given expenditure through the concentration of resources on those with demon-strated financial need.

There was also a divergence from Beveridge's recommendation in the level at which family allowances were set. On grounds of cost the government set allowances at only five shillings a week (with vague and unfulfilled promises of increased services in kind) so that when they began to be paid after the war they fell far below the subsistence needs of a child. Not only were allowances initially inadequate to guarantee that family size would not be a cause of poverty but the reluctance of successive governments to uprate them to take account of inflation meant that they became increasingly ineffective.

The Beveridge report represented a major step forward in social security provisions and some of its proposals were radical, such as the extension of benefits to the whole population and the limitation of the role of means testing. But in others, like the emphasis on subsistence level benefits financed by regressive flat-rate contributions, it was conservative. The way in which the recommendations were implemented, however, has meant that the new benefits have been far from completely successful in achieving Beveridge's primary aim of abolishing poverty. Beveridge himself recognised this in the 1950s and became disillusioned with the treatment given to his plan. The last section of this chapter will examine the effectiveness of the social security system today, but first the various benefits which now exist are outlined.

THE BENEFITS SYSTEM

Benefits which are designed to provide the main or only income during loss or interruption of earnings fall into three categories: contributory (national insurance) benefits, supplementary benefit, and a number of non-contributory, non-means-tested benefits chiefly for the disabled. (There is also a separate industrial injuries scheme which provides more generous benefits for those injured at work or suffering from industrial diseases.) After these have been described, family income support measures, housing benefit and the remission of various charges will be examined. The different benefits are listed in Figures 2.1, 2.2 and 2.3.

*Contributory (National Insurance) Benefits*

Contributory benefits have changed little, except for uprating, since they were introduced in 1948. They are financed from the national insurance fund into which are paid contributions by employees and employers plus a modest amount (now reduced to about one-seventh of the total) from the exchequer. They are payable without a means test to people suffering specified contingencies who have fulfilled the relevant contribution conditions (which vary between benefits). With the exception of unemployment benefit they are payable for as long as need lasts. A statutory sick pay scheme was introduced in 1983 under which employers became responsible for making at least a minimum allowance (which they can off-set against liability for national insurance contributions) in place of sickness benefit for the first eight weeks of incapacity. Since 1973 there has been a distinction between 'short-term' benefits (for sickness, unemployment and maternity), and 'long-term' benefits (for invalidity, widowhood and retirement) which are paid at a higher rate. Flat rate contributions (to which a graduated element had been added in 1961) were replaced by a wholly earnings-related system in 1975. This takes the form of a percentage of earnings up to an upper limit paid by both employers and employees.

There is very little discretion in the administration of contributory benefits. When someone suffers a contingency for which a benefit exists,

FIGURE 2.1    Contributory (National Insurance) Benefits

| | |
|---|---|
| Unemployment benefit | Payable after three days and continuing for up to a year. |
| Sickness benefit | Payable after eight weeks (following statutory sick pay) until replaced by invalidity pension after six months' incapacity. |
| Invalidity benefit | Invalidity pension replacing sickness benefit and payable for as long as incapacity for work continues. |
| | Invalidity allowance, varying with age at which incapacity began, provided this was more than five years before retirement age; payable as long as incapacity continues. |
| | Earnings-related addition to invalidity pension based on earnings from 1978. |
| Maternity allowance | Payable for 18 weeks, starting 11 weeks before the baby is due, if the mother has worked and paid full contributions. |
| Retirement pension | Basic pension paid on retirement at or after age 60 for women, 65 for men (plus addition if over 80 and increments for deferred retirement). |
| | Graduated pension based on earnings-related contributions paid between 1961 and 1975. |
| | Earnings-related pension based on earnings from 1978 (if not contracted out into occupational scheme). |
| Widows' benefits | Widow's allowance payable for first 26 weeks of widowhood. |
| | Widowed mother's allowance payable when widow's allowance ceases, for as long as the widow has a dependent son or daughter under 19. |
| | Widow's pension payable either when widow's allowance ceases (if widow was over 40 on husband's death and is not entitled to widowed mother's allowance), or when widowed mother's allowance ceases (if then over 40); reduced if widow is under 50 when husband dies or widowed mother's allowance ceases. |
| | Earnings-related addition to widowed mother's allowance or widow's pension based on husband's earnings from 1978. |
| Child's special allowance | Payable to a divorced woman on her former husband's death, for a child towards whose maintenance he was contributing or liable to contribute. |
| Death grant | Lump sum payable on death. |

provided that the appropriate contributions have been paid, he or she is entitled to benefit regardless of other resources (such as savings or an occupational pension). Whether in a particular case someone is entitled to a benefit may occasionally be a complex question, but this is decided on the basis of legal entitlement and not whether the person is in need. If the conditions are not fulfilled, no matter how great the need may be, no benefit is payable. Nor do contributory benefits take account of individual variations in need except of course family size. As will be seen these attributes of the national insurance system are in contrast to how supplementary benefit operates.

The Beveridge plan did not include earnings-related benefits, but in the 1950s there was a growth of occupational pensions and there were demands that higher incomes in retirement should be extended to the rest of the workforce through a state scheme. A rather limited 'graduated' pension scheme was introduced in 1961 for those not entitled to an occupational pension (though another motive was that additional earnings-related contributions were a source of extra revenue for the national insurance fund). This scheme was seen as very inadequate but it continued for some years

FIGURE 2.2   Non-Contributory (Non-Means-Tested) Benefits

| | |
|---|---|
| Child Benefit | Payable for each child under 16 (or under 19 but still at school) whether the parents are in work or not. An extra 'one-parent benefit' is paid for the first child in a one-parent family. Child benefit is paid to whoever has responsibility for the child (not necessarily the parents). |
| Non-contributory invalidity pension | Payable to people of working age, incapable of work for at least 28 weeks, who do not qualify for contributory invalidity benefit (married women can claim only if they are also unable to do normal housework). At lower rate than contributory benefit. |
| Attendance allowance | Payable to severely disabled people needing attention or supervision. |
| Non-contributory retirement pension | Payable, at lower rate than the basic retirement pension, to those over 80 who would not otherwise get this amount of pension. |
| Invalid care allowance | Benefit for a person of working age, other than a married woman, caring for a severely disabled person who is getting attendance allowance. |
| Mobility allowance | Allowance for physically disabled persons aged five or over and under 65 who are unable or virtually unable to walk. On reaching 65 those already getting the allowance can continue to receive it until they are 75. |
| Guardian's allowance | Payable to a person providing a home for a child whose parents are both dead (or sometimes on the death of only one parent where, for example, the parents are divorced). |
| Maternity grant | Lump sum payable before the birth of a child. |

FIGURE 2.3   Means-Tested Benefits

| | |
|---|---|
| Supplementary benefit | Supplementary pension payable to persons of pensionable age not in full-time work (at 'long-term' rates). |
| | Supplementary allowance payable to persons under pensionable age not in full-time work (at 'ordinary' rates for one year and thereafter — except for unemployed — at 'long-term' rates). |
| Family income supplement | Payable to families with children where either the husband or wife is in full-time work. |
| Housing benefit | Rate rebates payable to tenants and owner occupiers. |
| | Rent rebates payable to local authority, new town and SSHA tenants. |
| | Rent allowances payable to private tenants. |
| | (Full rent and rates of those receiving supplementary benefit are automatically met.) |
| Ancillary benefits | Free dental treatment<br>Free glasses<br>Free prescriptions<br>Free milk and vitamins<br>Free school meals |
| | Available to those receiving supplementary benefit or family income supplement through the 'passport'. |

during which there was a good deal of controversy — particularly about the proper role of state and occupational pensions —and two abortive attempts at reform which came to nothing owing to changes of government in 1970 and 1974. (Between 1966 and 1982, when they were abolished as an economy measure, there were also earnings-related supplements during the first six months of sickness, unemployment and widowhood.)

Since 1978 every employee has had to contribute towards an additional earnings-related pension. About half the workforce are 'contracted-out' from the new state scheme because they are members of an approved occupational scheme which provides benefits which are at least as good. The state scheme is based on employees' best 20 years of earnings. It is being phased in over this period so that people will not retire with full additional pensions until the end of the century. Similar additions are payable with widows' benefits and invalidity pension. Though existing retired people are not helped, as time goes on a growing proportion of the elderly will enjoy increasingly more adequate incomes from an occupational or state additional pension. This will have important implications for the number of old people living in poverty.

*Supplementary Benefit*

Supplementary benefit (frequently though incorrectly called 'social security') is the British version of what in international terminology is referred to as social assistance. It replaced national assistance in 1966; the name was altered when there were some modest administrative changes. Between 1966 and 1980 the scheme was under the control of the Supplementary Benefits Commission (the successor to the National Assistance Board), the chief function of which was to guide the exercise of, and to take responsibility for, discretion in individual cases. Since 1980, when discretion in the administration of supplementary benefit was much reduced, the scheme has been under the direct control of the DHSS.

The functions of supplementary benefit are essentially the same as those already outlined for national assistance: to meet the needs of those who are not entitled to a contributory benefit and to provide an addition to such a benefit when it is inadequate. The largest category of recipients are old people who claim supplementary benefit to top up retirement pensions, and the second largest, which has grown rapidly, the unemployed who have exhausted their entitlement to insurance benefit. Supplementary benefit, in contrast to contributory benefits, is means tested but is not subject to contribution conditions, nor is it limited to specific contingencies (though claimants must have a legitimate reason for not working — in practice the main difference is that it is available to lone parents who are not widows). In principle anyone aged 16 or over who is not in full-time work or at school and whose resources are less than his or her needs can obtain supplementary benefit. Married (and cohabiting) couples and their dependent children are counted as a single 'assessment unit' on behalf of which only one claim can be made.

Supplementary benefit is much more closely adjusted to individual circumstances than contributory benefits so that there is a significant element of discretion in its administration.

Three types of requirements may be included in the calculation of supplementary benefit: normal requirements, housing requirements and additional requirements. The normal requirements of an assessment unit are calculated on the basis of 'scale rates' which lay down different weekly amounts for householders, non-householders, dependent adults and children of different ages. This is the main (in some cases the only) element in supplementary benefit. Supplementary pensions are calculated according to higher 'long-term' rates, and supplementary allowances, paid to those under pension age, according to lower 'ordinary' rates. But after a year recipients of supplementary allowances, except for the unemployed, move on to long-term rates.

Since the introduction of housing benefit in 1983, which is described below, housing requirements have become much less significant and now relate mainly to the mortgage interest payments, feu duty and maintenance costs of owner occupiers. The rent of tenants and all rates are covered by housing benefit. Generally the calculation of normal and housing requirements is clear cut and rarely involves the exercise of discretion. The same is not true of additional requirements.

Provision for individual variations in need is central to a social assistance scheme like supplementary benefit because it is the last resort of those who do not have adequate resources from elsewhere. Allowances and grants in respect of additional requirements (before 1980 called exceptional circumstances additions and exceptional needs payments) were in the days of national assistance made by individual officers largely on a rule of thumb basis, but over the years extensive codes of guidance were built up. These additional payments caused an administrative burden, and friction between claimants and staff, disproportionate to the relatively small expenditure upon them. A particular cause of difficulty was demands for clothing grants: weekly payments are supposed to cover the need but some claimants found them inadequate to do so. Since 1980, following a review of the supplementary benefits scheme, entitlement to additional payments has been closely defined by regulations approved by parliament, with less discretion in individual cases. The change undoubtedly has both advantages and disadvantages from the point of view of claimants. While legally defined rights may be a gain, the restriction of discretion to assist hard cases is a loss. At the time of writing the new arrangements are suffering from problems of implementation, particularly the unfamiliarity of staff with the regulations, and it remains to be seen how they will work out in the long term.

## Non-Contributory Benefits

The third main category of social security provision for those not at work is a number of non-contributory, non-means-tested benefits. Benefits of this kind were not envisaged in the Beveridge report, and they are of comparatively recent origin, all being introduced in the 1970s. The non-contributory old person's pension was introduced in 1970 and is payable to anyone aged over 80 who is not entitled to a contributory pension. Its main purpose was to deal with the temporary problem of those who were not insured before 1948 and were not able to pay contributions for ten years thereafter. The non-contributory invalidity pension (NCIP), the housewives' non-contributory invalidity pension (HNCIP) and the invalid care allowance (ICA) followed in 1975.

The NCIP and HNCIP were designed to provide a non-means-tested income for those who, because of disablement, had not been employed and did not qualify for a contributory benefit. The NCIP is payable to those who have been incapable of work for six months, and the difference between it and the HNCIP is that married women are subject to the additional condition that they must be 'incapable of performing normal household duties'. The rationale for this rule, which has aroused much opposition, is that married women can normally expect to be maintained by their husbands. The ICA is payable to someone looking after a disabled person who is entitled to an attendance allowance, and is designed to help, for example, an unmarried daughter who stays at home to care for elderly parents. All these benefits have a serious limitation: their rate is only about 60 per cent of contributory benefits. For people with a private income they are a useful addition, but in the majority of cases they are simply offset against entitlement to supplementary benefit so that the same payment is received under two heads rather than one. Thus many of those who are eligible do not bother to claim the benefits, and most of those who do so lose an equivalent amount of supplementary benefit, so that their net cost to the exchequer is small.

Two non-contributory benefits are designed to provide an additional income to meet the special needs of the disabled. The attendance allowance was introduced in 1970 for severely disabled people in need of frequent attention or continual supervision during either the day or night (when the lower rate is payable) or both (when the higher rate is payable). It is not taken into account in calculating other means-tested benefits. Mobility allowance was phased in from 1976 and can be claimed by people between five and 65 who are unable to walk or virtually unable to do so. Maternity grant was originally a national insurance benefit, but contribution conditions were abolished in 1982.

### Child Benefit and Family Income Supplement

There are two schemes which provide an additional income related to number of children during employment. Child benefit, which is the successor to family allowances, is also paid when earnings are interrupted but this is not the case with family income supplement.

Before the introduction of child benefit there were two main systems of income support for families with children: family allowances and child tax allowances. Family allowances were replaced by child benefit in 1977 and tax allowances were phased out over the following three years. Family allowances had continued in their original form but with only occasional upratings. The reason for their neglect was that they were perceived by politicians as unpopular and unnecessary in an affluent society. The work on poverty by Brian Abel-Smith and Peter Townsend published in the mid-1960s challenged the view that family allowances were no longer required, and the Child Poverty Action Group was formed to campaign for their improvement. Substantial increases were implemented in 1968 which approximately halved the number of working families living below the poverty line. But in order to limit the cost to the exchequer the increases were effectively restricted to those who paid little or no income tax through the use of 'clawback', which made offsetting reductions in child tax allowances.

The chief justification for introducing child benefit was that the poorest families gained little or nothing from tax allowances while highest paid gained most. The value of child benefit is the same for any family of a given size so that those affected least by the abolition of tax allowances had the largest net gain. There was controversy when Frank Field, then director of the Child Poverty Action Group, published confidential cabinet papers he had been given which suggested that the government might not go ahead with child benefit. It believed that, at a time of pay restraint, the reduction in (usually men's) take-home pay with the abolition of tax allowances in favour of child benefits (usually paid to mothers) would be unpopular, and the leaks seem to have been instrumental in persuading the government to go ahead with the new scheme.[10]

Apart from the distributional effects benefiting lower income families, there are two main differences between family allowances and child benefit. First, child benefit is not itself taxable (after the abolition of child tax allowances, adding it to husbands' incomes for tax purposes as was done with family allowances would mean that the more children they had the lower would be their take-home pay). Second, it is payable in respect of all children including first or only children. A special addition is payable for the first child of lone parents. Child benefit is not means tested and it is paid regardless of whether the parent or parents are working or are in receipt of any other benefit. But it is taken into account in assessing means-tested benefits (except family income supplement). Anyone under the age of 16 automatically qualifies for child benefit as do those under 19 who are in full-time school (or other non-advanced) education. It is normally payable to the mother.

Family income supplement (FIS) is a means-tested allowance payable to parents of dependent children. It is complementary to supplementary benefit because, whereas the latter is not normally payable to persons in full-time work, FIS can only be claimed where at least one parent is in full-time work. Therefore a family with a low income may be entitled to either FIS or supplementary benefit but is never eligible for both. Compared with family allowances and child benefit, FIS covers only small numbers of recipients and has only a modest cost to the exchequer. The government justified the introduction of FIS in 1970, instead of increasing family allowances, on grounds of cost. There was little scope for limiting the cost of the latter through clawback as tax thresholds were already very low. FIS certainly concentrates resources on those in greatest need and provides the poorest with a scale of help inconceivable with a non-means-tested scheme. If suffers, however, like most means-tested benefits from low take-up. The scheme was introduced with impressive speed and is simple (reflected in low administrative costs for a means-tested benefit).

FIS does not attempt to take into account the varying needs of households beyond level of income and number of children. It is normally assessed purely on the basis of a postal application form. A 'prescribed amount' is laid down for different numbers of children, and FIS makes up half the difference between this and actual income if lower. The choice of a 50 per cent 'taper' was a compromise between conflicting objectives: to make up as much of the shortfall in income as possible, but to minimise the 'poverty trap' effect caused by additional earnings reducing benefit. Also to minimise the poverty trap (and for administrative convenience) once awarded FIS is normally payable for a year at the same rate even if income changes.

*Housing Benefit*

There are many forms of assistance with housing costs available to people in different tenures (which are discussed in chapter 5) but here the concern is with means-tested payments of relevance mainly to tenants. A national scheme of rent rebates was introduced in 1972, together with a parallel scheme of rent allowances for private tenants (the only important difference being that the latter receive a cash payment rather than a reduced rent). Rate rebates, which are available to owner occupiers as well as tenants, had been introduced in 1966 following evidence of hardship suffered by lower income households. In 1974 the means test for rate rebates was put on a similar basis to that for rent rebates and allowances, and in the case of tenants the two benefits are normally dealt with together. The one category of person who is not eligible to apply for a rent or rate rebate or rent allowance is someone in receipt of supplementary benefit.

In 1983 rent rebates and allowances, rate rebates, and housing payments to those receiving supplementary benefit were subsumed under a new housing benefit scheme. The change was, however, chiefly of significance to supplementary benefit claimants, because the rebate and allowance schemes have continued much as before as part of housing benefit.

Until 1983 housing costs were met as part of supplementary benefit payments but, since the introduction of housing benefit, rent and rates have not been counted as a requirement. This means that total requirements were reduced by an amount equal to housing costs, and a limited number of claimants (who were previously entitled to less supplementary benefit than their rent and rates) were floated off supplementary benefit altogether. They can now claim rebates in the same way as anyone else. The bulk of claimants, however, were still entitled to supplementary benefit. In these 'certificated' cases the DHSS informs the housing authority, which automatically awards housing benefit in the form of 100 per cent rent rebates (or allowances) and rate rebates. There are arrangements for special 'housing benefit supplements' paid through housing authorities to people floated off supplementary benefit (on to rebates) who would otherwise be worse off under the new arrangement. This could happen because of the different means tests for supplementary benefit and housing benefit.

At central government level responsibility for housing rebates has been transferred from the Scottish Development Department to the DHSS, thus recognising them as primarily income support measures. The main rationale for the introduction of housing benefit was the 'better-off' problem: it was known that some of those receiving supplementary benefit purely in respect of housing costs would have gained more by claiming rebates instead. Such people no longer have an entitlement to supplementary benefit. But the problem of those claiming rebates who would be better off on supplementary benefit remains, and a new difficulty is likely to be identifying those who are eligible for housing benefit supplements, at least when the initial application is made to the local authority rather than to the DHSS.

The rebate schemes operate on the basis of a 'minimum' rent (or rates) equal to 40 per cent of the total, and a 'needs allowance' for households of different sizes. When actual income after disregards is exactly equal to the needs allowance the minimum rent is payable and the remaining 60 per cent is rebated. When income is higher or lower than the needs allowance 'tapers' operate whereby a percentage of the excess (or shortfall) in income is added to (or subtracted from) the minimum rent. For example, in the case of rent rebates and allowances 21 per cent in income in excess of the needs allowance is added to the minimum rent (or in other words subtracted from the rebate or allowance).

Three main criticisms have been levelled at housing benefit. First, there is likely to be a continuing problem of low take-up. In the case of council tenants the take-up of rent and rate rebates is comparable to that for supplementary benefit, but it is much lower in the case of private tenants. Second, despite the introduction of housing benefit, there is no overall system of subsidies giving assistance to people in different tenures on a coherent and fair basis. Third, the government's insistence on introducing the scheme on a 'nil-cost' basis meant that there were losers as well as gainers from the change.

### Remission of NHS and Other Charges

The use of charges in the social services was much reduced in the post-war reforms, but there has been a tendency for them to grow again. In particular, in 1948 virtually all national health service provisions were entirely free but charges were soon introduced for prescriptions, glasses, dental treatment and so on. At the same time, in order to safeguard lower income groups, exemptions from charges for those receiving national assistance (supplementary benefit) were introduced, as well as for others with incomes at about the same level on a means-tested basis. With the introduction of FIS these exemptions were extended and the 'passport' procedure was introduced. Under the passport anyone who is receiving either supplementary benefit or family income supplement can obtain exemption from various charges on the basis of a simple application without a separate means test. Others can obtain most of the exemptions with a separate application and means test. While take-up of exemptions through the passport is reasonably good by the standards of other means-tested benefits, in the case of separate applications it is extremely low. As the government has since 1979 followed a policy of increasing charges in the social services, exemption from them has been of growing significance to poorer people.

The main NHS charges from which remission can be obtained are those for prescriptions, dental treatment and glasses. (About half of prescriptions are in any case free to categories such as children under 16, pensioners and expectant mothers.) In the case of charges for dental treatment and glasses, those with incomes some way above the supplementary benefit can obtain partial exemption. Expectant mothers and children under school age can obtain free milk and vitamins. Until 1980 there was a national income scale for free school meals under which eligibility extended well above the supplementary benefit level. As an economy measure this was abolished (and local authorities were allowed discretion over what to charge for meals). They are now only obliged to provide free meals (and indeed any meals at all) to children whose parents are receiving supplementary benefit or FIS, though many local authorities have continued with exemptions for other families.

Table 2.1 provides an indication of the relative cost of different benefits. If expenditure on supplementary benefit for old people is added to that on pensions, provision for the elderly accounts for more than half the total. About half the expenditure on supplementary benefit goes to the unemployed, and all benefits to this group account for approaching one-fifth of the cost of social security. The modest share of contributory unemployment benefit reflects the fact that many of the unemployed have exhausted their entitlement to it.

EFFECTIVENESS OF THE BENEFITS SYSTEM

The final section of the chapter is concerned with evaluating the effectiveness of social security benefits in Britain. Evaluation requires the selection of appropriate criteria, and the main one used here is the objective, which was central to the Beveridge report, of preventing poverty. The extent to which benefits during loss or interruption of earnings maintain normal income levels will also be examined.

TABLE 2.1

Proportion of Expenditure on Different Benefits 1980/81

|  | % |
| --- | --- |
| Retirement pensions | 48.4 |
| Invalidity benefit | 5.3 |
| Sickness benefit | 2.9 |
| Unemployment benefit | 5.9 |
| Widows' benefits and guardian's allowance | 2.9 |
| Maternity benefit | 0.8 |
| 'Christmas bonus' for pensioners and others | 0.5 |
| Death grant | 0.1 |
| Industrial injuries benefits | 1.7 |
| Total contributory benefits | 68.5 |
|  |  |
| Supplementary benefit | 13.2 |
| Old persons' pensions | 0.2 |
| Non-contributory invalidity pension | 0.5 |
| Attendance and invalid care allowance | 1.1 |
| Mobility allowance | 0.6 |
| Child benefit | 13.8 |
| Family income supplement | 0.2 |
| War pensions | 1.9 |
| Total non-contributory benefits | 31.5 |

Sources: *First Report of the Social Security Advisory Committee 1981*, HMSO, 1982; and *The Government's Expenditure Plans 1982-83 to 1984-85*, Cmnd, 8494, HMSO, 1982.

*Defining Poverty*

Ever since 1948, given the objectives of the Beveridge report, the poverty line has implicitly been represented by national assistance (now supplementary benefit). This was at first largely unrecognised, but since the 1960s it has been very widely accepted — by political parties, civil servants, pressure groups, academics and so on — that the supplementary benefit level is the appropriate definition of poverty in Britain. It is often referred to as the 'official' poverty line, and it is worth briefly outlining how this came about.

The systematic investigation of poverty was pioneered by Seebohm Rowntree who undertook his first study of York at the turn of the century. His approach to defining poverty, which was followed by many others up to the second world war, was to assemble scientific and medical evidence about the quantities of food and other 'necessities' required to maintain a tolerable minimum standard of living (described in his first study as 'merely physical efficiency'). Poverty defined in this way is often called 'absolute' poverty because, in principle, it should be valid for all time (except for advances in scientific knowledge such as the discovery of vitamins). Poverty lines of this sort depend for their legitimacy — and a poverty line which does not enjoy legitimacy has little practical value — on the scientific knowledge of those responsible for their definition.

But in the 1960s the absolute approach to the definition of poverty came under attack. The essence of the criticism was that a poverty line is basically a social and political rather than a scientific construction. Notions of poverty are in reality always related to standards of living prevalent in a society, and vary over time and from place to place. An absolute approach, which claims to be based on objective scientific knowledge, cannot accommodate this reality except by fudging (which, for instance, Rowntree did in his second and third studies of York in 1936 and 1950, arbitrarily raising his poverty line). A distinction between 'necessities' and 'luxuries', on which an absolute definition must rely, may make sense in poorer societies, where the bulk of most people's expenditure is devoted to basic food, shelter and clothing, but it has little meaning in more affluent ones. One only has to list some common consumer durables — vacuum cleaner, fridge, freezer, radio, television, telephone — to see that what is a luxury is a matter of opinion, and changing opinion, rather than scientific fact.

Criticism of the absolute approach was crystallised by Brian Abel-Smith and Peter Townsend in *The Poor and the Poorest*, published in 1965.[11] Abel-Smith and Townsend did important empirical work on the measurement of poverty, and their method of using the Family Expenditure Survey (FES) was adopted by the government. They are often credited with having 're-discovered' poverty and in a sense this is true in that they revealed a more widespread problem than had been thought to exist. But it may be truer to say that they redefined poverty. They rejected an absolute approach in favour of a 'relative' definition. (The poverty line is relative to general standards of living at a particular time and place, and is a national standard; it must not be confused with Runciman's concept of relative deprivation which is concerned with an individual's perception of his own circumstances.[12]) Relative poverty is centred on the notion of participation in the normal life of society; people are poor if their resources are so low as to exclude them from the ordinary activities of their relatives, friends and workmates.

A difficulty for Abel-Smith and Townsend was that no way had been devised of directly quantifying a measure of relative poverty (and indeed even after Townsend's subsequent work this problem has not been satisfactorily solved). They therefore decided to adopt the national assistance (as it then was) standard as a poverty line (though this had already been done less explicitly by others). The justification was not that they personally believed that the national assistance scales were necessarily right, but that they had legitimacy: 'Whatever may be said about the adequacy of the National Assistance Board level of living as a just or publicly approved measure of "poverty", it has at least the advantage of being in a sense the "official" operational definition of the minimum level of living at any particular time'.[13] But the national assistance or supplementary benefit level does not only have the advantage of legitimacy as a measure of poverty; it also leads to an evaluation of the benefits system. The Beveridge plan was designed to provide the minimum income for all, and therefore, if significant numbers of people in fact have incomes which fall below that level, there must have been shortcomings in the proposals themselves or in their implementation. Some of these shortcomings have already been mentioned but, before the effectiveness of the current benefits system is examined, evidence on the extent of poverty will be briefly reviewed.

*The Extent of Poverty*

Evidence on the extent and incidence of poverty in Britain can only be dealt with in bare outline, but a number of studies of the topic are available.[14] It should be made clear first of all that there are technical and conceptual difficulties in using the supplementary benefit standard, so that estimates are highly sensitive to the assumptions made. Two examples may be mentioned. One of the most important is the treatment of those actually receiving supplementary benefit. In principle their incomes should by definition never fall below the poverty line, and estimates made by the DHSS assume that this is the case. Independent estimates based on FES data, however, show that a significant proportion of those in poverty are in receipt of supplementary benefit, owing either to miscalculation of entitlement or recent changes in circumstances. This is a major cause of discrepancies between official figures and non-official ones which tend to be substantially higher. DHSS estimates also use the concept of 'normal income' which ignores periods of sickness and unemployment of less than 13 weeks, so reducing the apparent number with incomes below the poverty line. Other difficulties are inherent in the use of data from a sample survey. FES is a continuous survey of a cross-section of households in Britain carried out by the Office of Population Censuses and Surveys. Its primary purpose is to collect information about expenditure patterns so that the correct weighting can be given to different items in constructing the retail price index. The number of low income households covered by FES is relatively small so that all statistics on numbers in poverty are subject to significant sampling error which is substantial in the case of smaller groups such as one-parent families. For the same reason it is not possible to obtain detailed information about differences between Scotland and the rest of Britain from FES.

Some statistics on the extent and incidence of poverty in Britain derived from the 1979 FES are contained in Table 2.2. This must be seen as a minimum estimate of numbers below the supplementary benefit level, and independent researchers using different assumptions have argued for figures more than twice as high. The statistics can be looked at from two points of view: the relative importance of different causes of poverty and the 'risk' of poverty experienced by people in different circumstances.

It will be seen that there are significant differences in the relative importance of various causes depending on whether families or individuals are

TABLE 2.2

Poverty in Britain 1979

Families and persons with 'normal incomes'* below supplementary benefit level

| | Families (000s) | Propor-tion of Poor Families | 'Risk' of Poverty† | Persons (000s) | Propor-tion of Poor Persons | 'Risk' of Poverty† |
|---|---|---|---|---|---|---|
| | | % | % | | % | % |
| Total | 1,420 | 100 | 6 | 2,130 | 100 | 4 |
| Total *over* Pension Age | 860 | 61 | 13 | 1,130 | 53 | 13 |
| Married Couples | 240 | 17 | 11 | 510 | 24 | 11 |
| Single Persons | 620 | 44 | 15 | 620 | 29 | 15 |
| Total *under* Pension Age | 550 | 39 | 3 | 1,000 | 47 | 2 |
| By Family Type: | | | | | | |
| Married Couples with Children | 110 | 8 | 2 | 450 | 21 | 2 |
| Single Persons with Children | [40] | [3] | [5] | 110 | 5 | 5 |
| Married Couples without Children | [40] | [3] | [1] | 90 | 4 | 1 |
| Single Persons without Children | 350 | 25 | 5 | 350 | 16 | 5 |
| Of which Large Families (3 or more children) | [30] | [2] | [2] | 170 | 8 | 2 |
| By Employment Status: | | | | | | |
| Normally in Full-time Work (or Self-employed) | 190 | 13 | 1 | 480 | 23 | 1 |
| Sick or Disabled for more than 3 months | [40] | [3] | [5] | 60 | 3 | 4 |
| Unemployed for more than 3 months | 100 | 7 | 16 | 150 | 7 | 12 |
| Others | 230 | 16 | 16 | 310 | 15 | 12 |

Estimates of persons living in private households derived from the 1979 Family Expenditure Survey, rounded to nearest 10,000. Figures in square brackets are subject to very considerable proportionate error.

* Income from work where the head of household has been sick or unemployed for less than three months.

† Proportion of families or persons with specified characteristics with incomes below the supplementary benefit level.

(Source: Department of Health and Social Security, *Social Security Statistics 1982*, HMSO, 1982.)

counted. The reason for this is that some categories, for example old people, tend to live as individuals or small families, and therefore bulk larger amongst the count of families than of individuals. The opposite is true of families with children. Those who are not working for whatever reason and are primarily dependent on benefits account for about 90 per cent of families in poverty and 80 per cent of individuals. By far the largest category are the elderly who constitute about half of all the poor. Despite the growth of unemployment (which has risen substantially further since these data were collected) it is not one of the largest causes of poverty. A combination of low wages and number of children where the head of household is in full-time work accounts for some 10 per cent of poor families and 20 per cent of individuals (though many more have incomes only slightly above the supplementary benefit level). Furthermore, the number in poverty would be much greater without second incomes provided by working wives.

Turning to the risk of poverty amongst families and individuals in different circumstances, it can be seen that two groups, the elderly (especially single people) and the unemployed, have the highest proportion with income below the supplementary benefit level. There is a very low risk of poverty where the head of household is in full-time work though, as there are many people in this position, they constitute a significant proportion of those with low incomes.

Statistics of poverty in Scotland are not regularly published by the DHSS, and in any case they could only be very approximate owing to the limitations of FES. Such evidence as there is suggests that the extent of poverty in Scotland as a whole is not substantially different from the average for Britain (or at any rate that it is only slightly higher). Factors such as the proportion of the elderly in the population, the level of earnings and the unemployment rate confirm that this is likely to be the case. Variations within Scotland (as between the regions of England) are, however, very substantial. Although FES cannot provide information at this level, it is well known that the Glasgow area and central Clydeside generally have above average levels of poverty.

In examining why the benefit system fails to prevent poverty as the Beveridge report intended, it is necessary to look separately at the non-working and the working poor.

*The Non-Working Poor*

The reasons for the ineffectiveness of social security benefits in preventing poverty amongst those not at work — the elderly, the unemployed, one-parent families and so on — were touched on in discussion of the implementation of Beveridge's proposals. They are in essence the extensive reliance on means-tested national assistance (supplementary benefit), and the consequent problems of low take-up. The causes of this problem are examined below. There is no doubt that non-take-up of supplementary benefit — by about a quarter of those who are eligible to claim it — is the chief cause of poverty within the non-working population.

When the new benefits system was being introduced after the second world war, politicians and civil servants were aware of the divergence from the Beveridge plan but they did not foresee the problem of low take-up. The intense dislike of means testing as it had been applied to the unemployed in the

1930s was believed to be a thing of the past; it was thought that all the objectionable features had been ended by the Determination of Needs Act, 1941 which introduced a personal assessment of needs.[15] When, however, the assumptions of the post-war planners proved unduly optimistic and the extent of low take-up became apparent, it never seemed possible or a sufficient priority to spend the (admittedly large) resources required to return to the Beveridge plan of providing the national minimum primarily through non-means-tested benefits.

*The Working Poor*

Both the pre-war advocates of family allowances and Beveridge recognised that, as wages take no account of the cost of bringing up children, some households where the head is in full-time work would be in poverty. The persistence of this problem reflects the inadequacy of family income support through family allowances and child tax allowances and, more recently, child benefit, as well as the low take-up of FIS. Taking first the non-means-tested benefits, it is interesting to look at the value of family allowances plus child tax allowances and of child benefit which replaced them. Owing to the irregularity with which family allowances were uprated, the real level of support fluctuated from year to year though a trend is apparent. The value of child benefit in the early 1980s is not grossly different (after allowing for inflation) from that of family allowances and tax allowances combined immediately after the second world war. (Poor families have enjoyed some gain as they did not benefit from tax allowances.) But a more significant criterion of the effectiveness of income support measures is their proportional contribution to family budgets; as living standards rise so also does the cost of children. Over the same period the value of family income support as a proportion of average earnings has been very roughly halved. This reflects a tendency over many years for the tax and benefits system increasingly to favour single people and childless couples at the expense of families with children. It now seems to be accepted that child benefit should be regularly uprated to keep pace with inflation, though it will have to be increased in real terms if inroads are to be made into poverty amongst those in full-time work.

The main problem with family income supplement has been low take-up. When FIS was introduced there was an extensive publicity campaign involving newspaper and television advertisements. Estimates of the number of eligible families, and therefore of the take-up of FIS, have been subject to large sampling errors owing to the limitations of FES. A recent estimate using data from a special survey of low income families suggests, however, that take-up is less than 50 per cent, substantially lower than had been thought.[16] If non-take-up could somehow be reduced, FIS could do much to eliminate low incomes among families with wage earners in them. But this is likely to be difficult to achieve.

*Problems of Means Testing*

The advantage of means-tested benefits (and services) in concentrating public expenditure on those in greatest need is obvious enough, but against this have to be set a number of major drawbacks. Argument about selectivity and universalism is one of the major debates in social policy and it cannot be dealt with here. But two aspects, low take-up and the 'poverty trap', which are of particular importance to the social security system are briefly examined.

It has been seen that low take-up is a major reason why social security benefits fail to raise the incomes of a substantial number of people to the poverty line. There has in fact not been a great deal of research on the reasons for low take-up so there is a shortage of hard information. Nevertheless, some causative factors can be outlined. First, there is the stigma of claiming means-tested benefits — in a society which places a high value upon economic success, some people regard it as shameful to declare their inability to manage without outside help. To say that means-tested benefits are a right, while true, is not a complete answer because an entitlement which is conditional on need is widely seen as being qualitatively different from an absolute one. The association of means-testing with the poor law is often used as an explanation but as time goes on this becomes increasingly implausible, and there is little doubt that stigma is not merely an historical hangover. Second, there is lack of knowledge about means-tested benefits. As they tend to be received by relatively small numbers of people there may be ignorance about the existence of some benefits (though this clearly does not apply, for example, to supplementary benefit). A shortage of information seems more generally to apply to eligibility levels; there appears to be a widespread tendency to underestimate the amount of income someone may have from other sources and still make a successful claim. Third, there are problems involved in the actual claiming process such as filling in detailed forms and getting verification of earnings (though neither applies to supplementary benefit). Where problems arise with supplementary benefit, such as over irregular maintenance payments to lone mothers, claimants are likely to have to spend hours waiting in unattractive local offices.

Whatever the precise causes of low take-up, it is a substantial and intractable problem. In the case of supplementary benefit (and some other major schemes such as rent rebates) take-up rates of around 75 per cent are achieved. Take-up of some other benefits, notably FIS, is much lower. Overall rates for particular benefits hide the fact, however, that there is a relationship between the amount of entitlement and take-up. Taking supplementary benefit as an example, while only a minority of those eligible to a small sum in addition to a national insurance benefit claim it, those who would otherwise be virtually destitute almost always overcome any feelings of stigma, lack of information or problems in claiming. In a sense, therefore, low take-up is less serious than it might at first appear, though even the loss of a modest amount of money is significant to people with incomes below the poverty line. There is no doubt that the simplification of claiming procedures and advertising campaigns could increase take-up to some extent, but experience has shown that there are no easy answers. Low take-up is an inherent disadvantage of means testing.

The term 'poverty trap' is widely used but often not understood. It has a specific meaning and refers to those, chiefly families with children, who are working for relatively low wages. If they get an increase in pay this is offset by income tax, national insurace contributions and the loss of means-tested benefits, notably housing rebates, FIS and 'passport' benefits (such as free school meals). The result is that a family can be worse off in terms of total resources following a pay increase, though more usually it is a matter of their being only slightly better off. Over a wide range of earnings a family with children (assuming means-tested benefits have been claimed in the first place) will have an almost constant overall income. The term 'poverty plateau' which has also been used is apt.

The poverty trap became severe during the early 1970s owing to a combination of factors: the tax threshold had dropped very low; national insurance contributions had been put on an earnings-related basis, and new means-tested benefits were introduced (for example FIS and the national rent rebate scheme). More recently the abolition (on a national basis) of the separate and more generous means test for free school meals has sharpened the poverty trap because in some areas this benefit is now lost at the same point at FIS. The severity of the poverty trap is reduced because eligibility for FIS lasts for a year, so that when it has to be reapplied for the income limits will have been raised.

The poverty trap is the inevitable result of the extensive use of means-tested benefits (and of low tax thresholds). There is a dilemma that either a large proportion of income shortfall below a desirable level can be made up, when the poverty trap will be severe (if 100 per cent of the shortfall is made up the whole of an income increase up to that level is offset), or benefits will be relatively inadequate. The way out (though a costly one) is of course non-means-tested benefits. The poverty trap can be seen as undesirable both from the point of view of incentives to move to a better paid job or to work longer hours (very like the arguments about the effects of tax rates paid by higher income groups), and from that of feelings of fairness.

The poverty trap should be distinguished from what has been called the 'unemployment trap'. This is a problem of those who are out of work as well as those working for low wages. Where someone has children and only a modest earning potential, a job may bring little or no increase in income compared with unemployment. In recent years the government has been much exercised by the effects of the unemployment trap on work incentives, and its remedy has been to hold down the rate of benefits available to the unemployed (for example denying them the long-term rate of supplementary benefit). Others have argued for increasing child benefit which raises incomes in work but not during unemployment (because it is offset against benefits).

*Income Maintenance*

Finally, attention is turned to the effectiveness of social security benefits in replacing previous income from employment. Although replacement ratios obviously vary between households, a general indication can be obtained by comparing benefits with average earnings. At the same time, given the use of supplementary benefit entitlement as the 'official' poverty line, an indication is provided of changes in that standard.

As the levels of contributory and supplementary benefits (excluding housing costs) have remained close since 1948 the latter can be used for purposes of illustration. In 1973 a distinction was made between 'long-term' benefits (retirement pension, invalidity pension and widows' benefits as well as long-term supplementary benefit rates) and short-term benefits (sickness benefit, unemployment benefit, maternity allowance and ordinary supplementary benefit rates). Until 1980 long-term benefits were uprated in line with earnings or inflation, whichever was higher, whereas short-term benefits were uprated in line with inflation. (Now all benefits are adjusted for inflation.) During the late 1970s long-term benefits moved substantially ahead of short-term ones, and in 1982 the value of the latter was more than a quarter higher than that of the former. It is difficult to accept that a difference in entitlement of several pounds a week is justified in terms of the greater needs of long-term claimants. One result of this is that DHSS statistics on poverty are drawn up on the basis of widely varying standards for different categories of household.

Between 1948 and 1982 short-term benefits approximately doubled in real value while long-term benefits increased by about two and a half times. Thus in absolute terms those on benefit, especially the elderly and others getting long-term rates, have enjoyed a very substantially increased standard of living. But on a relative view of poverty and standards of living there must also be concern with how the value of benefits has changed compared with incomes in general. In relative terms (for example in comparison with average earnings) the increase in the value of benefits has been much less dramatic.

Although the criteria used in uprating benefits were not made explicit until the 1970s, it is clear that the policy from 1948 was to keep them broadly in line with average gross earnings. But owing to increases in income tax and national insurance contributions they have risen in relation to net earnings. In the case of short-term benefits the change has been small but it has been more substantial with long-term ones. For a single householder national assistance and long-term supplementary benefit rates (excluding housing costs) rose from about a quarter of average net earnings in 1948 to about a third in 1982, and for a couple from nearly two-fifths to about half. In households containing dependent children replacement ratios are higher. This is also the case when child benefit is added to income during employment because it is less than supplementary benefit child additions.[17]

Whatever view is taken of the adequacy of benefits, and of the poverty line implicit in them, prospects for the future are uncertain. At the time of writing the government was committed to increasing benefits in line with inflation, thus maintaining their value in absolute terms. But assuming that real earnings increase, as they have done for most of the post-war period, unless corresponding increases are made to benefits the living standards of recipients and the poverty line will fall in a relative sense.

The elderly are in a different position from most other groups of those not at work in that, as has been explained, people retiring in the future will be entitled to an additional earnings-related pension, either from their work or the state scheme. Thus, as more of the newly-retired will have contributed long enough to qualify for a substantial additional pension, their incomes will rise well above the poverty line. Eventually old people, now the largest group receiving supplementary benefit, should have little need for assistance. By the same token there should be much less poverty amongst the elderly. The chief problem with pensions is likely to be whether people of working age, who must bear the cost of providing for the elderly through reduced consumption in the expectation of themselves enjoying similar benefits, will be prepared to continue paying rising contributions.

The development of social security in Britain has been marked by short periods of innovation and reform: the establishment of the system before the first world war, the Beveridge report and the post-war measures, and most recently the introduction of new benefits for the disabled, improved earnings-related pensions and child benefit in the 1970s. At best there now seems to be what might be referred to, euphemistically, as a period of consolidation. Unless economic conditions improve it is likely to be lengthy. In the case of the elderly, however, improved pensions will lift the great majority well above the poverty line and dependence on supplementary benefit. It is impossible to be similarly optimistic about other groups. There is little hope of non-means-tested benefits being increased so as to reduce the use of supplementary benefit, and the best that can be expected is some improvement in take-up rates through advertising and simplification of claiming procedures. The chances of substantial increases in child benefit, so as to reduce the number of the working poor, are perhaps slightly better but not good. If poverty is seen as an essentially relative condition it can only be reduced through redistribution of incomes leading to greater equality. The extent of redistribution and the increase in equality required to close what has been called the 'poverty gap'[18] and to prevent poverty — the central objective of the Beveridge Report over 40 years ago — would be comparatively modest, and would in no sense usher in an egalitarian society. But the will does not seem to exist to achieve even this modest aim.

*References*

1. See for example: P. Townsend, *Poverty in the United Kingdom*, Penguin Books, 1979.
2. *The Government's Expenditure Plans 1982-83 to 1984-85*, Cmnd. 8494, HMSO, 1982.
3. On this topic see for example: B.B. Gilbert, *The Evolution of National Insurance in Britain*, Michael Joseph, 1966; B.B. Gilbert, *British Social Policy 1914-1939*, Batsford, 1970; and P. Thane, *Foundations of the Welfare State*, Longman, 1982.

4. *Report of the Royal Commission on the Poor Laws and Relief of Distress*, Cd. 4499, HMSO, 1909; and *Royal Commission on the Poor Laws and Relief of Distress: Report on Scotland*, Cd. 4922, HMSO, 1909.
5. *Social Insurance and Allied Services: Report by Sir William Beveridge*, Cmd. 6404, HMSO, 1942.
6. *Ibid.*, p. 7.
7. J. Macnicol, *The Movement for Family Allowances*, Heinemann, 1980.
8. *Social Insurance and Allied Services*, p. 155.
9. J. Harris, *William Beveridge: a Biography*, Oxford University Press, 1979.
10. F. Field, *Poverty and Politics*, Heinemann, 1982.
11. B. Abel-Smith and P. Townsend, *The Poor and the Poorest*, Occasional Papers on Social Administration No. 17, Bell, 1965.
12. W.G. Runciman, *Relative Deprivation and Social Justice*, Routledge and Kegan Paul, 1966.
13. Abel-Smith and Townsend, *The Poor and the Poorest*, p. 17.
14. See for example: W. Beckerman and S. Clark, *Poverty and Social Security in Britain since 1961*, Oxford University Press, 1982; R. Berthoud and J.C. Cooper, *Poverty and the Development of Anti-Poverty Policy in the United Kingdom*, Heinemann, 1981; G.C. Fiegehen, P.S. Lansley and A.D. Smith, *Poverty and Progress in Britain 1953-73*, Cambridge University Press, 1977; R. Layard, D. Piachaud and M. Stewart, *The Causes of Poverty*, Royal Commission on the Distribution of Income and Wealth: Background Paper No. 5, HMSO, 1978; Townsend, *Poverty in the United Kingdom*; and Royal Commission on the Distribution of Income and Wealth, *Report No. 6: Lower Incomes*, Cmnd. 7175, HMSO, 1977.
15. A. Deacon, 'An End to the Means Test? Social Security and the Attlee Government', *Journal of Social Policy*, Vol. 11, Part 3, 1982.
16. I. Knight, *Family Finances*, Office of Population Censuses and Surveys: Survey Division, Occasional Paper No. 26, 1981.
17. Data from: Department of Health and Social Security, *Social Security Statistics 1981*, HMSO, 1981.
18. Beckerman and Clark, *Poverty and Social Security in Britain since 1961*.

## FURTHER READING

*Poverty and Social Security*

R. Berthoud and J.C. Brown, *Poverty and the Development of Anti-Poverty Policy in the United Kingdom*, Heinemann, 1981.
A wide-ranging review of the causes of poverty, with a chapter on the social security system, by the Policy Studies Institute.

G.C. Fiegehen, P.S. Lansley and A.D. Smith, *Poverty and Progress in Britain 1953-73*, Cambridge University Press, 1977.
A study of the problems of measuring poverty and of changes in its extent over time.

R. Layard, D. Piachaud and M. Stewart, *The Causes of Poverty*, Royal Commission on the Distribution of Income and Wealth: Background Paper No. 5, HMSO, 1978.
An analysis of the factors causing low income based on data from the General Household Survey.

P. Townsend, *Poverty in the United Kingdom*, Penguin Books, 1979.
As well as a discussion of the concept of poverty this major work includes the findings of a special household survey.

Social Security Advisory Committee, *Annual Reports, 1981-*, HMSO, 1982-.
The reports of the recently-constituted advisory committee contain useful discussion of current policy issues and statistics.

*Welfare Rights*

R. Lister, *Welfare Benefits*, Sweet and Maxwell, 1981.
A detailed account of the social security benefits system by the director of the Child Poverty Action Group.

T. Lynes, *The Penguin Guide to Supplementary Benefits*, Penguin Books, (4th ed.) 1981. Excellent in its field.

Child Poverty Action Group, *National Welfare Benefits Handbook* and *Rights Guide to Non-Means-tested Social Security Benefits*, CPAG, annual. These guides, which deal with means-tested and non-means-tested benefits respectively, have the advantage of regular updating.

# 3

## *Health Services*

This chapter is primarily concerned with the national health service (NHS) in Scotland, except as it relates to the care of the mentally ill and handicapped which is dealt with in Chapter 4. The NHS is used by most people in Britain, and its cost amounts to some ten per cent of public expenditure. The great bulk of the finance comes from general taxation, while NHS contributions, which are collected as part of the national insurance system, make up little more than ten per cent of the total, and charges to patients even less than this. About four-fifths of total expenditure is on hospitals (together with community health services), while family practitioner services (GPs, dentists, opticians and pharmacists) account for the remainder. The NHS in Scotland is separately administered and is the responsibility of the Secretary of State through the Scottish Home and Health Department.

HISTORICAL BACKGROUND

There are important differences in NHS organisation from England and Wales, and many of these can be linked to the historical development of health care provisions in Scotland. Four kinds of factor may be seen as accounting for the rather separate character of health services in Scotland: professional, educational, clinical and governmental. The first two factors are interconnected. In Britain medical education on an organised basis largely began in the universities of Edinburgh and Glasgow, and separate Scottish specialty colleges (the Royal College of Physicians of Edinburgh, the College of Surgeons of Edinburgh, and the Royal College of Physicians and Surgeons of Glasgow) were established in the eighteenth century. The qualifications offered by these organisations were not accepted as a basis for professional practice in the lucrative London market until the mid-nineteenth century, when the Medical Act, 1858 established national standards of training and accreditation. Thereafter the proportion of medical students trained in Scottish universities continued to increase. By 1964-65 the Scottish medical schools produced 22 per cent of all medical graduates in the United Kingdom. The figure for 1979-80 was still over 15 per cent, the fall reflecting the growth of medical school places elsewhere.[1]

As for clinical factors, the numbers of Scottish doctors far exceeded the needs of Scotland, and they exercised a major influence in government service, the armed forces and the colonies, as well as on the development of medical science. Specialists were responsible chiefly for medical care provided in major hospitals, while that in smaller hospitals was provided by local general practitioners. The medical profession in Scotland was also familiar with existing forms of salaried practice (for example with trade union lodges, civic associations and welfare associations). The National Insurance Act, 1911, which provided insured persons with limited medical care by general practitioners (though not the services of specialists) was therefore more easily accepted in Scotland then elsewhere. The national health insurance scheme, however, suffered from the same limitations in Scotland as in the rest of Britain, and the factors which brought it to an end in 1948 were much the same.[2]

There were various governmental factors making for a Scottish dimension in health care. Long before the idea of a national health service was seriously considered, the problem of the remoter parts of Scotland resulted in the creation of the Highlands and Islands Medical Service.[3] The proposal made before the first world war that there should be funded medical services, supported by full-time salaried nurses and a government financed hospital, was entirely unconventional. In the context of the area and its health needs this arrangement seemed an obvious development, but the fact that a committee of enquiry had little difficutly in persuading both the profession and the Treasury is more remarkable. The service was created by the Highlands and Islands Medical Act, 1919. The second world war brought a further governmental factor: the Emergency Medical Service of 1940-45 under which the state effectively took over many hospitals and created a new administrative organisation. The service added substantially to the resources available for health care in Scotland on a long-term basis.[4]

TRIPARTITE ADMINISTRATION 1948-74

The national health service came into operation in 1948. The National Health Service (Scotland) Act, 1947 had set up a 'tripartite' structure of hospitals, general medical services (now known as family practitioner services), and local authority services. This structure utilised much of the existing administrative machinery. As far as the general medical services were concerned, the national health insurance system had already introduced many general practitioners to the idea of payment by the state. The NHS obliged virtually all of them to accept it. They continued, however, to be paid as independent contractors (as were pharmacists, dentists and opticians). Their affairs were regulated in each of 25 areas by local executive councils. The larger local authorities (cities, large burghs and counties) remained part of the system through their provision of what are now called community health services. These consisted of district nurses, health visitors, and maternity and child welfare services, under the control of local medical officers of health (who were also responsible for the school health service).[5]

The new element in the service was the inclusion of the hospital sector, though the administrative arrangements were based on those of the Emergency Medical Service. This involved both voluntary hospitals and local authority hospitals (transferred from the poor law after 1930). The hospital sector could not easily be encompassed within local authority administration, and, more importantly, this was opposed by the medical profession. Instead, five major centres — Aberdeen, Dundee, Edinburgh, Glasgow and Inverness (except for the last also centres of medical education) — became the bases for regional hospital boards. The Northern board based on Inverness required extensive assistance from Glasgow and the Western board; and the highlands and islands received some support services from other boards while retaining their separate arrangements.

The Scottish arrangements differed from those south of the border in a number of important respects. First, the Scottish act did not create distinctions between teaching and non-teaching hospitals. To reinforce this equality of status among hospitals the Scottish legislation took some £300,000 of the voluntary hospitals' endowments and created a fund available for use in each hospital board area. A medical education committee was created in each region, representing the university medical school and the hospital board, to consider how best use could be made of hospitals for teaching purposes. In this way the teaching and clinical functions of the health service became formally inter-related.

Health centres, much discussed before 1947 as places where primary care by general practitioners and local authority community services could be brought together, were to be provided by the central department (rather than, as in England and Wales, by the local authority). This had dual advantages. It encouraged the government to overcome the difficulties likely to arise in arrangements requiring joint general practitioner and local authority services. It also enabled health centres to be developed in under-doctored areas which existed both in sparsely populated rural communities and in the large housing estates constructed on the edge of cities like Glasgow. For many years these were the only kinds of area where health centres were provided and even then on a very selective basis.[6]

Lastly, there was the problem of providing services requiring organisation on a scale larger than that of the regional hospital board. These included staff training, blood transfusion services and ambulances. Also the central department wished to retain direct authority to determine which major capital projects should be approved and how the various regions should be treated for purposes of capital development. This became more important with the development of new population centres.

The tripartite system of administration proved less of a burden in Scotland than in England. Problems of co-ordination were in any case not a paramount consideration for some ten years after the service came into operation. The early years were more concerned with questions of service development than of administrative organisation.

Expenditure on the NHS boomed during the second half of the 1960s, growing at some 3.6 per cent per year, and continued to grow at an average of about three per cent per year to the mid-1970s. In 1962 a ten year hospital building programme was announced for Scotland, under which some 37 per cent of the 63,158 beds in service during 1961 would be closed. These resources were concerned with diseases no longer considered serious problems or with kinds of care where hospital treatment was no longer thought appropriate. The remaining 63 per cent of beds were to be progressively replaced or up-graded, concentrating on services like maternity care, care of the chronically sick and mental deficiency, where expenditure had been very low. For the first time in a century the creation of major new hospitals was envisaged. At some stage in the plan every major teaching hospital in Scotland would be affected.[7]

Between 1962 and 1966, eleven new or substantially modernised hospitals were either opened or nearing completion. In 1966 the plan was revised because it had become clear that progress in the building of hospitals had to be matched by the development of community health and social services, and by greater resources in the primary care sector. In addition, technical advances in medical care made a time scale of hospital development requiring ten years from drawing board to opening too long to foresee clinical requirements accurately. (The parallel development of renal transplant surgery and renal dialysis treatment is a classic illustration of the difficulty in making health service decisions.) Finally, the 1960s had prompted a realisation that the demise of cottage or small community hospitals in favour of large district general hospitals might not be cost-effective nor in the best interest of patients (although the concentration of major specialty services in large centres was still considered essential).

The revised 1966 plan therefore attempted to deal with hospital development and planning in the wider context of health service resources as a whole. Its aim was to develop the 'hospital complex': a district general hospital at the centre of population, serviced by smaller and more specialised units elsewhere in the region and by local health centres. The revision of the general practitioners' contract of service in 1966 created greater incentives for them to work in groups and in larger premises. The General Practice Finance Corporation provided assistance with practice expenses and costs. Fears that to work in health centres would be tantamount to accepting direct employment by the state diminished as familiarity with the service grew.[8]

As a result the period 1966-70 saw the preparation of plans for the creation, improvement and redevelopment of 15 district general and specialist hospitals, as well as the inauguration of a major health centre building programme which coincided with inner-city redevelopment schemes. From about 1967 onwards, developments in the organisation of health care were recommended which emphasised the need to unify provision for particular client groups (such as the elderly, expectant mothers and young children) by linking the hospital based teams of clinicians with primary care and community services. These proposals came from working parties representative of the professions and NHS administrators. The working party reports also emphasised the strain being imposed upon professional workers and managers in the service by the tripartite system of administration. Three groups of people in each area were taking decisions independently about priorities and resource allocation. Any concept of planning for hospitals was therefore of limited value if plans for primary care and local authority services did not dovetail with them. All of these factors pointed to the need to unify management of the service before making major changes to the system of service provision.[9]

The opportunity to make such a change came in two forms. First, the government decided to examine the structure and functions of local government throughout Britain. Second, the Social Work (Scotland) Act, 1968 grouped many of the community care resources of local authorities, such as home helps, within unified social work departments. The latter change in particular made necessary consideration of the future role of local authority health services. Proposals were published in a green paper in 1967 for changes in the structure of the health service in Scotland, following preliminary negotiations with the professions and local authorities.[10] Final agreement on the form of reorganisation was completed within a year. The change of government in 1970 made virtually no difference to Scottish arrangements, but action was delayed for two reasons: to ensure that administrative reorganisation took place at the same time throughout Britain, and the need to await final decisions on the parallel reorganisation of local government areas. A white paper outlining the new arrangements was published in 1971,[11] which was followed by the National Health Service (Scotland) Act, 1972 implementing them.

The objectives of reform were to provide unified administration of services in each area; to complement this with unified professional teams; to achieve more effective consultation with professions in the taking of decisions; and to avoid problems of liaison with local authorities responsible for services such as social work and education by establishing (as nearly as possible) co-terminous boundaries between the new health boards and regional councils. Within this structure it was hoped that more flexible deployment of professional personnel might be possible and better teamwork achieved. Less obvious benefits might also be a movement of health service resources away from hospital care (by the early 1970s becoming very expensive) and the provision of opportunities for the public as users of the service to express opinions about their treatment.

FROM REORGANISATION TO THE ROYAL COMMISSION

The reorganised structure came into operation in 1974 (Figure 3.1). The Secretary of State for Scotland became responsible for the provision of all health services with the elimination of local authorities from NHS administration. General practitioners and others providing primary care

FIGURE 3.1    National Health Service Organisation in Scotland

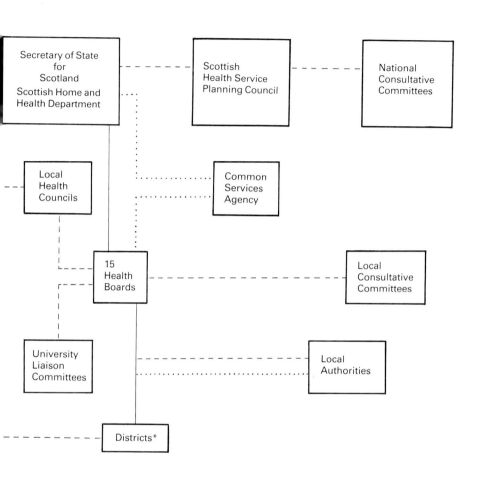

* where applicable

Responsibility _____

Consultation/Advice _ _ _ _ _ _ _ _ _ _ _ _ _ _

Services ...........................................

FIGURE 3.2—National Health Service, Scotland Health Board Boundaries

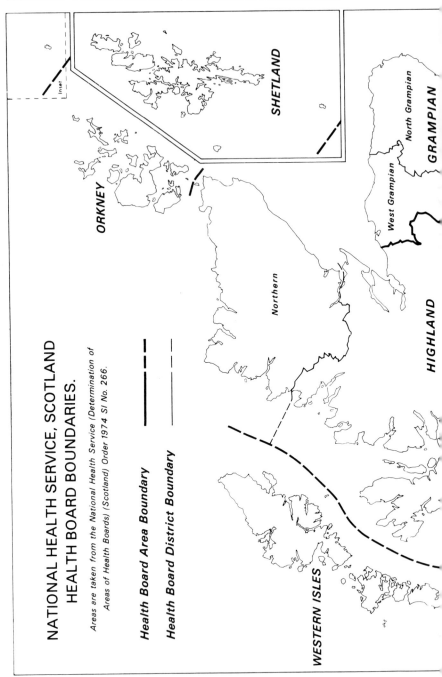

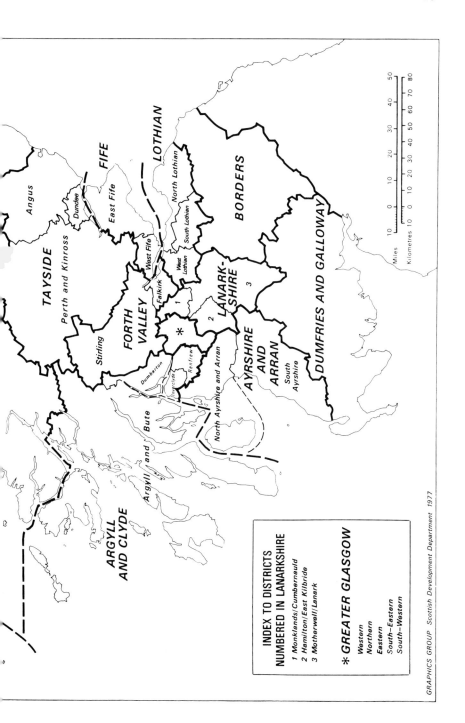

INDEX TO DISTRICTS
NUMBERED IN LANARKSHIRE

1 Monklands/Cumbernauld
2 Hamilton/East Kilbride
3 Motherwell/Lanark

\* GREATER GLASGOW

Western
Northern
Eastern
South—Eastern
South—Western

GRAPHICS GROUP  Scottish Development Department  1977

(such as dentists and opticians) continued normally to work as contractors rather than on a salaried basis (though separate family practitioner committees as in England and Wales were not set up). The government promised further progress with the health centre programme and improvements to other practice accommodation and faciltes.

## Health Boards

The agencies through which the Secretary of State provides a unified health service are 15 health boards. The regional tier of administration was removed and boards have a direct link with the Scottish Home and Health Department (SHHD). They have extensive autonomy (at least on paper) in deploying the resources made available to them. Eleven boards were originally divided into districts for administrative purposes but, following recent proposals for the simplification of NHS administration, four of them have abandoned districts. At the time of writing seven boards retain districts. (Figure 3.2 shows the original district boundaries of 1974.)[12]

The resources available to boards differ enormously: in 1980-81, for example, Greater Glasgow at one extreme had a revenue expenditure of over

TABLE 3.1

Health Board Resources 1980-81

| Health Board | Population (000s) | Revenue Expenditure (£000s) | Capital Expenditure (£000s) | Average Equivalent Full-time Staff | Average Available Staffed Beds |
|---|---|---|---|---|---|
| Argyll and Clyde | 452.4 | 88,001 | 8,137 | 8,483 | 4,499 |
| Ayrshire and Arran | 374.1 | 58,788 | 4,678 | 5,226 | 2,828 |
| Borders | 100.5 | 18,053 | 1,488 | 1,578 | 911 |
| Dumfries and Galloway | 144.2 | 30,751 | 807 | 3,098 | 1,588 |
| Fife | 340.2 | 57,030 | 3,011 | 5,285 | 2,916 |
| Forth Valley | 273.0 | 54,839 | 2,153 | 5,374 | 3,609 |
| Grampian | 483.0 | 105,986 | 4,147 | 10,027 | 5,388 |
| Greater Glasgow | 1,001.8 | 311,020 | 13,690 | 31,967 | 14,078 |
| Highland | 192.0 | 45,003 | 5,758 | 4,154 | 2,424 |
| Lanarkshire | 570.1 | 102,097 | 2,469 | 9,383 | 5,540 |
| Lothian | 746.1 | 188,054 | 6,892 | 17,909 | 8,381 |
| Orkney | 18.9 | 3,391 | 40 | 264 | 131 |
| Shetland | 25.9 | 4,086 | 378 | 297 | 160 |
| Tayside | 396.8 | 114,211 | 5,507 | 11,528 | 5,464 |
| Western Isles | 30.6 | 5,881 | 306 | 475 | 198 |
| TOTAL | 5,159.5 | 1,187,198 | 59,463 | 115,048 | 58,115 |

Sources: Scottish Home and Health Department, *Scottish Health Service Costs 1980-81*, SHHD, 1981; and The Registrar General for Scotland, *Annual Estimates of the Population of Scotland 1981*, HMSO, 1982

£300 million, more then 30,000 staff and 14,000 hospital beds; while at the other Orkney spent little more than one per cent as much to fund 264 staff and 131 beds (Table 3.1). There is extensive inter-dependence between boards and Greater Glasgow, for instance, is a specialty centre for certain services throughout Scotland and for others within Strathclyde region. This creates problems in determining an appropriate allocation of resources between boards because the needs of the local population cannot be the only criterion. Health board areas are, however, co-terminous with those of regional councils (except that Strathclyde contains four boards), so that collaboration with other services, especially the personal social services provided by social work departments, should be facilitated. In 1980-81 some £1 million of the NHS budget was put aside for 'support finance' projects with local authorities.

Board members are appointed by the Secretary of State, about one-third after consultation with local authorities in each area, and frequently chairmen are active in local government as well as health service affairs. The remaining members are appointed after consultation with any university in the area which has a medical school, the professional advisory committees and, in the words of the 1972 act, 'such other persons and organisations as appear to the Secretary of State to be concerned' (which for the most part means voluntary bodies). The membership of boards varies according to the population of the area and is at present between 14 and 22. Boards include at least two doctors, a nurse, two other employees, a university nominee and two or three trade unionists. Members are, however, appointed for their 'managerial' competence rather than as representatives of particular interests.

*The Common Services Agency*

There remain needs which can still be met only on a Scotland-wide basis, and these are the responsibility of the Common Services Agency, which has a management board appointed by the Secretary of State representing both the SHHD and each health board. It is responsible for the ambulance and blood transfusion services, and for health education; and provides the expertise required for the execution of major capital works programmes. The latter is an arrangement designed as much to ensure that the central department keeps a tight hold on major capital allocations as to provide design teams for the smaller boards. The agency is also responsible for non-clinical recruitment services, post-entry training and placement of administrative staff.

Boards which could provide most of these services for themselves tend to resent the existence of the agency. But the Royal Commission on the National Health Service thought that its role in providing boards with comparable expertise and its ability to centralise supply services made it valuable in increasing efficiency. Its greatest weakness has been its inability to make any real impact on administrative training, mainly because of its detachment from individual boards and their consequent lack of commitment to it. It is, however, useful to the SHHD to the extent that it prevents the department having to take on additional functions.[13]

*The Scottish Health Service Planning Council*

The council is the point at which the SHHD, health boards, the professions and universities come together. At the time of writing, it consists of representatives of each of the 15 health boards, each university with a medical school, the Common Services Agency and four civil servants from the SHHD. A representative of local health councils in Scotland has been added, a significant change since the inception of the system.[14]

The council's statutory remit is to identify health service needs and to develop programmes designed to meet them, taking account also of political priorities and available resources. It does this through five programme planning groups, each covering a major area of health care (for example, mental disorder, care of the elderly and child health). Each group establishes plans and priorities within its own sector, often calling upon the services of additional persons for specialist knowledge. Each also contributes to the working group on health priorities established to develop longer-term plans for allocation of health resources, an issue which is discussed later.

The council has no staff of its own beyond a small secretariat. Apart from the specialist knowledge of its planning group members, it relies upon the planning unit staff of the central department, emphasising again the close ties between the SHHD and the council. In the last resort, of course, the department is not bound by the opinion of the council. But it is persuasive because it represents a collective view from all of those whom central government needs to consult before committing resources. Where the council (and the SHHD) are weaker is in meeting the additional remit, to oversee the implementation, review the progress, and analyse the effects of health service planning.

*The Professional Advisory Committees*

One group not formally represented on the planning council are the health care professions themselves. They have a dual relationship with the service. On the one hand, they bargain centrally with the government about terms and conditions of service. On the other, they deal with the service as professionals, providing advice at both health board and central level through formally constituted advisory committees. There are seven recognised groups of professions and other staff, each with a central and area advisory committee: doctors, dentists, pharmacists, nursing and midwifery staff, para-medicals, scientific staff and optical staff. The chairmen of these committees at the central level attend the discussions of the planning council as expert assessors. Additionally, they are asked to offer expert advice to the council and its groups looking at specialised topics.

Similarly, at health board level the professional groups are extensively involved in the planning and provision of services. But here the principal role of the area committees is to deal with professional officers of the board about the problems of patient care. By convention the chairmen of advisory committees (or at least the medical committee) are also allowed to attend health board meetings. This arrangement was designed to make those who take decisions about patient care and therefore commit scarce resources openly accountable.

The National Medical Consultative Committee (NMCC) representing doctors provides a not untypical illustration of the way in which these bodies operate. It has a membership of about 20, drawn from representatives of each branch of medical care (primary, hospital and community medicine). This basis is augmented by ensuring representation for the specialty colleges, the Scottish Council of the BMA and the universities with medical schools. Electoral groups have been formed, and this system of election is supplemented by selection by a medical panel for the remaining places, so as to ensure a balance of representation. In the course of a year the NMCC may offer through its working groups advice on matters as diverse as practice accommodation and heart transplant surgery. The working groups absorb the time of many other doctors who are not full members of the NMCC but who are called upon for their expertise in relation to specific problems.

This extensive demand on the time of professionals, both at central and health board level, became a major cause of criticism of the new structure, which the royal commission was asked to review. There is no agreement about how well the advisory structure in general has worked in meeting its original objectives, but certain trends are clear. One is that it has helped certain non-medical groups to establish their professional status in the eyes of the public. This in turn has raised questions about why staff should be so much more fortunate than consumers of the service in influencing policy and management; and why some groups of staff have been favoured more than others.[15]

*Local Health Councils*

To provide consumers with an opportunity to make known their views of the service, the 1972 act instituted local health councils in every board area (or district where these exist). The members of the council are appointed in roughly the same way as health boards themselves. In the period since their inception councils have had mixed fortunes, some proving dynamic and forceful, and others finding it difficult even to persuade health boards to provide essential information or to consider representations seriously.

The royal commission took the view that local health councils were only one of the ways in which consumers might influence the service. Others included greater use of patients' committees in general practice working directly with doctors, together with an efficient system of suggestions and complaints in hospitals (including clinical complaints). But, so long as local health councils remained, they ought to be provided with adequate funds to undertake or commission research on aspects of patient care of concern to the local community. Ministers were less convinced of the need to retain such bodies and have done so only under political pressure. The one event certain to bring councils to life is the threat of a hospital closure, when they often find themselves working in collaboration with the local medical professional and other providers of service.[16]

### The Health Service Commissioner

The centralisation of medical care in hospitals in the post-war period has meant that everyone is now likely to have at least one hospital stay in a lifetime as well as outpatient attendances. Inevitably this results in complaints about both clinical and non-clinical matters. In order to deal with these problems a new official, the Health Service Commissioner (or 'Ombudsman') was introduced in 1974. He is able to receive complaints either from patients or their representatives, after an initial complaint to the health board in question has failed to resolve the matter. The system does not include the primary care professionals (such as general practitioners) who have a separate system of tribunals.

Local health councils have not played a significant part in assisting patients to prepare their complaints, and difficulties seem to have arisen from lack of public awareness of the commissioner. Not only is there no separate Scottish commissioner but there are only two investigators, based in Edinburgh, for northern England and the whole of Scotland. Once again it is the attitude of health boards that contributes to the success or failure of the commissioner. Most boards have shown no desire to publish their own complaints ratings (although this information is easily available for regional health authorities in England). Since 1981 the commissioner has been able to investigate not merely administrative complaints but also the clinical aspects of care. In the light of previous experience this seems a somewhat ambitious undertaking. There is little doubt that it was prompted in large part by the view of the royal commission in favour of developing quality control standards in patient management, for the benefit of both the public and the exchequer.[17]

### The Royal Commission on the National Health Service

Following the administrative reorganisation of the early 1970s demand grew for a review of management structure. This arose for several reasons: what were seen as poor and deteriorating industrial relations within the newly-constituted health service authorities; the apparently spiralling costs of health service provision; the difficulties created by multiple tiers of authority (not a problem in Scotland); and the new Labour government's dislike of the creation of their predecessors. The government set up a royal commission to investigate these problems in 1976 and its report was published in 1979. The report provides a useful basis upon which to describe health service developments and provision in the subsequent period.

While not exempting from criticism the Scottish arrangements established by the 1972 act, the commission's report noted that:

> Although some of the comments we have made about the DHSS apply to the health departments in Scotland, Wales and Northern Ireland, they operate in a very different context. In general relations between them and the health authorities, professions and trade unions are more direct and informal.[18]

Many of its criticisms were therefore not directly relevant to either the SHHD or the health boards. Nevertheless, the central department issued a consultative paper in 1979 indicating that, in order to respond to the general approach of the report, it would endeavour to persuade boards to abolish the district level of administration. In future only large boards such as Greater Glasgow might need to retain districts, but even here more responsibility should be given to those who manage individual hospitals and community care teams.

The royal commission came to the conclusion that resources in the NHS were being misapplied in two ways. First, they were not distributed on a territorially equitable basis, especially in England but also in Scotland. The result was that both between and within health boards there are inequalities of provision. Second, the deployment of resources between different types of care was not satisfactory. The trend has been for hospitals to be favoured at the expense of the rest of the service, so that the primary and community sectors have been denied resources. This problem is particularly severe in urban areas where practice accommodation for doctors and dentists is getting harder to find outwith health centres. The royal commission also pointed out that there were few means by which additional resources could be found for the NHS. But by concentrating on the prevention of ill health, through, for example, the discouragement of smoking and excessive drinking and the diagnosis of disease at an early stage, more resources could be made available for developments in the service.

In Scotland thought was already being given to such issues under the impetus of two pressures. One was preparation for devolution under the abortive Scotland Act, 1978 and the consequent need to identify Scottish expenditure on the health service as part of the block grant. The other was the imposition by central government of the system of cash limits, under which expenditure by health boards is restricted to annually predetermined levels. In certain respects the NHS in Scotland is in the enviable position of having the ability over time to meet the recommendations of the royal commission. Compared with England and Wales, it has relatively extensive resources per head and there is less need to use private facilities to clear waiting lists; it is staffed (especially at senior levels) largely by doctors born in the United Kingdom or Eire; and it has a bed capacity far exceeding the British average and few under-doctored areas. But problems remain: one is the cost of maintaining this extensive network of services, and another the imposition by central government of norms of service which will be financed centrally. These problems and their implications for strategy have occupied the thinking of those concerned with health services in the past few years.

## Patterns of Health and Disease

When the NHS came into existence in 1948 it was assumed that the long-term objective would be the reduction of ill-health. In practice this has not happened. What has occurred is a revelation of how much ill-health exists and a changing pattern of disease. The measurement of 'good health' in a population is virtually impossible. But it is possible to measure (clinically and statistically) the trends in disease and their prevalence. Evidence demonstrates clearly that the diseases prevalent when the NHS was conceived are now far less common: tuberculosis, the major infectious diseases and diseases related to malnutrition (Table 3.2). Other measures of morbidity, however, suggest that disease *per se* has not decreased. We have merely exchanged one type of illness for another. Most measures of morbidity and mortality show that the Scots are less healthy than residents of the United Kingdom as a whole, and

TABLE 3.2

Major Causes of Death in Scotland

|  | Standardised Mortality Ratio[1] | | Total Deaths (1979) | |
|---|---|---|---|---|
|  | Males | Females | Males | Females |
| Tuberculosis (respiratory) | 139 | 105 | 50 | 14 |
| Malignant neoplasm (cancer) |  |  |  |  |
| stomach | 101 | 104 | 631 | 494 |
| lung, bronchus, trachea | 120 | 123 | 3,105 | 1,010 |
| cervix, uteri | — | 106 | — | 224 |
| Diabetes | 139 | 132 | 268 | 379 |
| Chronic rheumatic heart |  |  |  |  |
| disease | 133 | 117 | 127 | 286 |
| Ischaemic heart disease | 119 | 121 | 10,488 | 7,959 |
| Cerebrovascular disease | 138 | 128 | 3,696 | 5,940 |
| Peptic ulcer | 114 | 92 | 239 | 191 |
| Cirrhosis of the liver | 202 | 164 | 255 | 176 |
| All causes[2] | 115 | 112 | 32,844 | 32,863 |

Notes [1]The Standardised Mortality Ratio shows the number of deaths in Scotland as a percentage of what would be expected if the UK mortality pattern applied to Scotland. Where the ratio is greater than 100 mortality from that cause is higher than for the UK generally.
[2]Including causes other than those shown in this table.

Source: Scottish Health Service Common Services Agency, *Scottish Health Statistics 1980*, 1982

are more addicted to alcohol and tobacco. Equally, the United Kingdom is a less healthy place than many other nations of comparable economic, social and medical development. Health problems today stem largely from social, economic and demographic factors: the greater length of life and the increasing prevalence of degenerative diseases such as heart disease, cancer, renal failure and cerebro-vascular disorders.

At the same time the appropriate forms of treatment have altered. Where once hospitalisation was regarded as the best form of health care, it is now realised that many of the common diseases require greater reliance upon primary care and health education, if possible to prevent their occurrence and if necessary to diagnose them. By the hospital stage it is frequently too late for effective treatment. Similarly, attempts are being made to discover the influence of lifestyle and environmental factors upon health: living conditions, smoking, drinking, drug abuse and so on.

*Resources*

High levels of spending on health care, even by contrast to other parts of the United Kingdom, can be justified in Scotland by reference to the main determinants of that expenditure: population density and sparsity; incidence of illness; degree of inner city deprivation; and the existing facilities to be maintained, practitioners to be paid, and teaching responsibilities of universities. Even by Treasury estimation Scotland is entitled on these sorts of criteria to a larger proportional share of health service expenditure than any other part of Britain. But the existing resources are frequently in the wrong place and of the wrong type. Where there are hospitals there may need to be community and nursing homes for old people; and where there are under-doctored areas there may need to be more health centres rather than new hospitals.

Attempts to assess these difficulties and to reapportion resources were undertaken in 1975/76 and the results for Scotland were published in 1977 in *Scottish Health Authorities Revenue Equalisation* (SHARE). A formula was developed for re-distributing resources between health board areas in accordance with the main determinants of expenditure on health services, especially population movements. It is anticipated that over a ten year period from 1978-79 to 1988-89 there will be a reallocation of more than three per cent of the total NHS budget between areas. The formula has scope for periodic updating to take account of population flows and cross-boundary service arrangements.[19]

On the face of it the report makes excellent sense: reapportioning resources from over-provided areas like Tayside to under-provided areas like Ayrshire and Arran. It also encourages reliance on cheaper forms of care. Arguments arise over the weight to be given to the various factors in deciding relevant health service expenditure and to the accuracy and importance of population measures. Sizeable changes have had to be made to take account of the 1981 Census figures which have demonstrated rather larger shifts in population than anticipated in the SHARE report. Equally, the programme is affected by the ability of services provided by local authorities to make their contribution towards shifting the burden of care for client groups like the elderly and handicapped away from hospitals and into the community. This does not vitiate resource allocation projections: indeed some 0.8 per cent of the total was reallocated on the formula between 1977-78 and 1979-80. But the existence of overall public expenditure restraints, the need to demonstrate that short-term costs involved in long-term reallocations are value for money, and the difficulties encountered in carrying the professions along with the plan have undoubtedly slowed its full implementation.

*Priorities for the Future*

Any long-term plan must embody both lessons from past attempts to plan services and current political thinking. It must also accord with health trends and the preferred strategies for dealing with health problems. This involves, first, a programme of priorities expressed mainly in terms of the needs of client groups; second, a serious attempt to state publicly the need to move from acute services towards preventive measures, involving greater attention to the social and environmental factors in ill-health; and, third, a greater willingness to estimate the staffing implications of proposals. Only since 1980 have general practitioners been required to undertake vocational training. Only recently has a parliamentary select committee called for greater treatment of patients by the consultants at the head of medical teams. More dramatically, the move towards prevention places greater value on para-medical professions (such as radiographers) thus upsetting the traditional hierarchy of health service staff.[20]

There is also a need to decide upon appropriate levels of provision for residents in different health board areas, requiring in turn the involvement of boards themselves in decision making. Finally, it is essential to maintain consultation with those involved in the health care field. As a result the Health Service Planning Council has worked almost since its inception in 1974 towards the creation of a long-term programme meeting these needs. Immediately after reorganisation the SHHD issued a temporary scheme outlining priorities for the use of resources until about 1980. Thereafter the Planning Council working party on health priorities was expected to provide comprehensive guidance to boards. Their report, published in 1980 under the title *Scottish Health Authorities: Priorities for the Eighties* (SHAPE) is based upon the work of the council's programme planning groups and re-commendations from professional advisory bodies, and is guided by the resource allocation framework.

The SHAPE programme envisages three categories of priority for expenditure in the next ten years or so. *Category A* consists of the development of preventive services, services for the multiply deprived, services for the handicapped, community nursing services, and care of the elderly (including the elderly with mental disability and mental illness). Expenditure on these client groups and areas of service should grow faster than on the NHS generally. The services involved will clearly be of benefit to groups other than those specified. *Category B* expenditure, which consists of the primary medical, dental and ophthalmic services, together with community dentistry and maternity services will also be encouraged. Expenditure should keep in line with the overall level of NHS spending. Because the primary care (or family practitioner) services are not paid for until they have been provided, it is difficult to determine what level of additional expenditure is going to be involved. To this extent attempts to increase charges as a means of offsetting increases in primary care costs are understandable. The drug bill is the fastest growing single item of health service expenditure, and is incurred in large measure through general practitioners and others in the primary care sector. *Category C* services which are only to be expanded where resources can be saved from the uses described above or through other economies in each health board area, are therefore likely to suffer real decline. These include child health and other acute hospital services, and the general pharmaceutical service.[21]

Recommendations for capital expenditure to accompany these developments are more circumspect, beginning with the assertion that there is little central information on much of the building programme for which health boards do not have to seek specific central approval. However, in general the proposals for Category A services only involve substantial capital outlay to improve or expand residential and hospital accommodation for the elderly and for day centres. Services for the multiply deprived would be provided by community health centres and clinics, many of which already exist or are planned. Even in Category C expansion of child health, should it ever become financially possible, would take the form of additional outpatient resources, paid for by closure of paediatric units. Similarly, other acute services would be financed only at the cost of reduced accident and emergency services, or through the adaptation of traditional patterns of care in favour of cheaper options. Expansion in Category C is limited to the few high technology areas where no alternative to surgery is available, such as pacemaker services and joint replacement surgery (which in any case primarily benefit older age groups).

CONCLUSIONS

It is fair to say that many of the factors which made the NHS in Scotland distinctive in 1948 are no longer so important. The effect of medical technology, the increasing dependence upon drugs for treatment of disease and so on reduce distinctions created by traditional patterns of care. At the same time attempts have been made to reduce disparities between parts of Britain. Greater emphasis upon the costs of the NHS, the consequent establishment of cost norms and the concentration upon specific services have worked in the same direction. Most recently the application to the medical faculties of Scottish universities of the general reduction in support for higher education has diminished the ability of medical schools to make their traditional contribution to clinical service within the NHS. Finally, the fact that expenditure on health is part of an overall Scottish cash limit enables the SHHD to level out provision in line with norms agreed with Whitehall for the whole United Kingdom. In the same way recommendations, such as those of the royal commission to all specialty colleges to develop measures of 'quality control' in the provision of services, make essential the application of the same standards throughout the United Kingdom.[22]

At the level of implementing policy, however, differences between Scotland and the south continue to exist. Inter-corporate relations and support financing of projects involving both health boards and local authorities are proving difficult to get started. Similarly, the expanded health education programme is culturally distinctive and, some would say, more aggressive in character. Even where one might suppose that common policies already exist throughout Britain this turns out not to be the case on closer inspection. Examples vary from the extent of knowledge about and interest in services for the handicapped to decisions about NHS management structure.

The position of the NHS in Scotland as far as resources are concerned is on the whole a relatively favourable one: in 1982-83, for instance, some £280 was expended per head of population compared with £223 upon each person in England.[23] Nevertheless, the service throughout Britain faces much the same dilemma: ever increasing demands upon it at a time of constraints on public expenditure unprecedented since the second world war. The efficient use of available resources and their proper allocation are therefore even more important than in the past.

*References*

1. D.N. Hamilton, *The Healers: A History of Medicine in Scotland*, Canongate Press, 1981.
2. F. Honigsbaum, *The Division in British Medicine*, Kogan Page, 1979; and B.B. Gilbert, *The Evolution of National Insurance in Britain*, Michael Joseph, 1966.
3. Scottish Home and Health Department, *General Medical Services in the Highlands and Islands* (Birsay Report), Cmnd. 3257, HMSO, 1967.
4. H. Eckstein, *The English Health Service*, Harvard University Press, 1958; and *Report of the Committee on the Scottish Health Services*, Cmd. 5204, HMSO, 1936.
5. Scottish Home and Health Department, *Administrative Reorganisation of the Scottish Health Services*, HMSO, 1968.
6. Honigsbaum, *The Division in British Medicine*; and I.M.L. Robertson, *Accessibility to Social Facilities in a Peripheral Housing Estate: Drumchapel, Glasgow*, Discussion Paper No. 4, Centre for Urban and Regional Research, University of Glasgow, 1981.
7. Department of Health for Scotland, *A Hospital Plan for Scotland*, Cmnd. 1602, HMSO, 1962.
8. Scottish Home and Health Department, *Review of the Hospital Plan for Scotland*, Cmnd. 2877, HMSO, 1966; and British Medical Association, *A Charter for the Family Doctor Service*, BMA, 1965.
9. Scottish Home and Health Department, *Administrative Practices of the Hospital Boards in Scotland*, HMSO, 1965; and Scottish Home and Health Department, *Organisation of Medical Work in the Hospital Service in Scotland*, HMSO, 1967.

10. Royal Commission on Local Government in Scotland, *Minutes of Written Evidence, Vol. 7*, HMSO, 1967; and SHHD, *Administrative Reorganisation of the Scottish Health Services*.
11. Scottish Home and Health Department, *Reorganisation of the Scottish Health Services*, Cmnd. 4734, HMSO, 1971.
12. Scottish Home and Health Department, *Structure and Management of the NHS in Scotland*, HMSO, 1979.
13. *Report of the Royal Commission on the National Health Service*, Cmnd. 7615, HMSO, 1979.
14. Scottish Home and Health Department, *Scottish Health Service Planning Council: Report for 1980*, HMSO, 1981.
15. Royal Commission on the National Health Service, *Research Paper No. 1: The Working of the National Health Service*, HMSO, 1978.
16. D. Bochel and M. McLaren, 'The Establishment and Development of Local Health Councils', *Scottish Health Service Studies*, No. 41, HMSO, 1979.
17. Health Service Commissioner, *Annual Report, 1980-81*, HC368/1980-81, HMSO, 1981.
18. *Report of the Royal Commission on the National Health Service*, p. 305.
19. HM Treasury, *Needs Assessment Study: Report*, HM Treasury, 1979; and Scottish Home and Health Department, *Scottish Health Authorities: Revenue Equalisation* ('SHARE'), HMSO, 1977.
20. House of Commons, Social Services Committee, *Medical Education*, HC 31/1980-81, HMSO, 1981.
21. Scottish Home and Health Department, *Scottish Health Authorities: Priorities for the Eighties* ('SHAPE'), HMSO, 1980.
22. House of Commons, Public Accounts Committee, *Financial Control and Accountability in the National Health Service*, HC 255/1980-81, HMSO, 1981
23. House of Commons, *Supply Estimates 1982-83*, HC 214-X and XV/1981-82, HMSO, 1982.

## FURTHER READING

R. Berthoud and J.C. Brown, *Poverty and the Development of Anti-Poverty Programmes in the UK*, Heinemann, 1981.
Chapter 7 provides a useful review of the relationship between health and poverty.

D. N. Hamilton. *The Healers*, Canongate Press, 1981.
The most authoritative source on the history of specifically Scottish aspects of health services.

Scottish Home and Health Department, *Scottish Health Authorities: Priorities for the Eighties*, HMSO, 1980.
The SHAPE programme contains proposals for the development of the NHS in Scotland and sets out priorities for expenditure.

P. Townsend and N. Davidson (eds.), *Inequalities in Health*, Penguin, 1982.
A reprint of the report of the DHSS Working Group on Inequalities in Health (the Black Report) which provides a valuable analysis of disparities in health and health care provisions between social classes.

B. Watkin, *The National Health Service: The First Phase*, Allen and Unwin, 1978.
A general review of the development, structure and administration of the NHS.

*Report of the Royal Commission on the National Health Service*, Cmnd. 7615, HMSO, 1978.
A major stock-taking of the working of the NHS with recommendations for change.

# 4

## *Mental Health Services*

This chapter considers the development, present pattern and possible future of provisions for a number of groups in the population whose needs cannot be adequately met within the limits of any one sector of the social services. Specifically, we shall be looking at the care and management of mental illness, of alcohol abuse and of mental handicap. Each of these makes major though different demands on both health and personal social services, while in the case of mental handicap the education services also have a very important role. In different ways and in varying degrees, voluntary as well as statutory bodies are also involved in the overall pattern of provision for each of these client groups. In all of them we can identify both significant shifts of emphasis in the recent past in the way in which the respective problems are conceptualised, and major areas of uncertainty at the present time as to the best means of striking a balance between the relevant services and ensuring that there is effective co-ordination between them.

SERVICES FOR THE MENTALLY ILL

In Scotland, as in England and Wales, a central feature of the debate about the care of the mentally ill has been uncertainty as to the future role of specialist mental hospitals. Although the average size of these institutions was smaller than south of the border, and although they have in general been less remote from the populations that they served, they embodied an essentially similar tradition and a set of assumptions about the nature of mental illness.

Most mental hospitals came into existence in the latter part of the nineteenth or early in the twentieth century, often under the auspices of the poor law, as 'lunatic asylums' — institutions for the custodial care of the incurably insane. Their medical staffs were with a few notable exceptions not of the highest quality, and their attendants untrained with functions a good deal closer to those of prison warders than of hospital nurses. Some asylums no doubt offered greater comfort than others and some greater kindness; but the range of variation must necessarily have been limited, as the knowledge and skills necessary for the effective treatment of mental illness did not exist. Contemporary attitudes were both reflected in and influenced by the legal framework within which mental illness was managed.[1]

Both the role and the image of the mental hospital began to alter in the

1930s, though at first only slowly, as a result of the discovery of physical methods of treating some mental illnesses. In the post-war period, administrative, clinical and attitudinal changes interacted so as to bring about quite rapidly a re-drawing of the whole pattern of psychiatric care. With the inauguration of the national health service, specialist psychiatric hospitals were removed from the control of local authorities, vested in the Secretary of State, and administered together with general hospitals through a common system of regional hospital boards. This may have helped a little to remove some of the stigma attaching to these institutions, but it was of less importance than the impact of the rapid advances in the 1950s in the development of drug treatments for psychiatric disturbances. These gave added impetus to a greater liberalism towards mental illness and the mentally ill that was becoming apparent in public attitudes, and to a more enlightened and better informed approach on the part of general medical practitioners. As a result of such changes, the hospitals came to emphasise more and more a therapeutic rather than a merely custodial role. Admission rates rose, there was increasing emphasis on voluntary admissions rather than the use of compulsory powers, and the average length of stay in hospital dropped sharply. Some though not all psychiatric hospitals began to develop an active interest in social and industrial rehabilitation to balance the generally predominant emphasis on drug treatment. Outside the hospital wards there was a steady growth of out-patient services, though little in the way of other community provisions on either side of the border.[2]

The Mental Health (Scotland) Act, 1960 provided the legal basis of mental health services for over twenty years. But in 1983 new legislation was passed. The 1960 act had the same general purpose as an English act passed in the previous year: that is to ensure that legal formalities did not stand in the way of the most effective utilisation of recently developed medical knowledge. It was designed to keep to a minimum the use of compulsory powers for the admission of patients to, and their detention in, psychiatric wards and hospitals. So far as possible, patients should be free to enter and leave such establishments with no more formality than is associated with the use of general medical and surgical facilities; and, indeed, these conditions now apply to more than 90 per cent of psychiatric patients. There are, however, some patients who, for their own health or safety or for the protection of others, need hospital treatment but are unable or unwilling to seek it voluntarily. When in such cases compulsory measures are required, the Scottish act incorporates a legal safeguard for which the corresponding English legislation makes no provision; the approval of a sheriff is normally required to an application for compulsory admission. The application (as in England) must be made by a mental health officer or the patient's nearest relative and supported by recommendations from two doctors, one of whom should generally be the patient's family doctor and the other a psychiatrist. The welfare of psychiatric patients who are unable to look after their own interests is the concern of the Mental Welfare Commission for Scotland. This has independent powers to discharge any patient if it considers that detention is no longer necessary, to advise and assist any psychiatric patient, whether voluntary or compulsory, and to investigate complaints of improper detention, ill-treatment or inadequate care.

But, whereas in England and Wales the Mental Health Act, 1959 was followed by a ministerial decision to reduce drastically the scale of in-patient provision involving the closure of many mental hospitals and a major shift of emphasis to psychiatric units in general hospitals, the official view taken in Scotland was much more cautious and non-committal. In the event, the rundown of in-patient provision in England has proved to be a good deal slower than was originally forecast, no hospital has actually been closed and the build-up of community services has been slow and patchy. In Scotland the move from a hospital-oriented to a community-oriented system of care has been almost imperceptible.

*Trends in the Use of Psychiatric Services*

Between 1960 and 1980 the number of consultant posts in psychiatry in Scotland increased from 80 to 100. The total nursing staff increased from approximately 7000 to 10,000, but the proportion of qualified (registered) nurses among them fell from about one-third to one-quarter; that is to say, the actual number of the latter remained fairly constant at around 2400.[3]

The number of patients admitted each year either to a mental hospital or to a psychiatric unit attached to a general hospital rose steadily until the early 1970s; since 1972 it has remained fairly constant at around 25,000, corresponding to a frequency of about 4.8 per 1000 of the Scottish population. The majority of these are patients who have been admitted on a previous occasion; the number of *new* admissions to in-patient care has fluctuated between 10,000 and 11,000, more than two per 1000 of the population. The number of discharges has in most years been fairly close to the number of admissions, so that the resident population has not fallen dramatically — from around 19,000 in the late 1960s and early 1970s to rather over 17,000 at the end of the 1970s. A census of Scottish psychiatric hospitals and units on any given day would account for one in every 300 of the population. This may be compared with the position in England and Wales at the same time, where the corresponding proportion was almost exactly half that in Scotland. Clearly, the degree of dependence on hospital in-patient provision has remained markedly higher north than south of the border.[4]

There was also a considerable rate of expansion of psychiatric out-patient provisions in hospital and peripheral clinics. Between 1964 and 1980 the number of new out-patients went up from 17,500 to more than 31,000: an increase of 77 per cent. This was very much greater than the overall growth of out-patient services during that time, which was only one-third. If we examine these trends side-by-side with the data on hospital admissions and discharges, it is evident that the out-patient services have been bringing psychiatric assessment and treatment to a wider range of the emotionally disturbed rather than providing an alternative service for those who would otherwise have been admitted to a psychiatric ward.

These figures remind us that measures derived from hospital treatment statistics cannot provide anything resembling an accurate estimate of the frequency of psychiatric disturbance in the community. We know from general population surveys that although there are some persons who seek no professional help with the treatment of symptoms as serious as those with which psychiatrists are regularly confronted, the majority do in fact consult their general practitioners. In most instances the latter are the only treatment agency involved. The extensive availability of psychotropic drugs has made this possible, though it may be argued that a higher proportion of patients might benefit from more specialised investigation; the proportion actually receiving it, although still very much a minority, seems to have been on the increase.

*New Legislation*

The Mental Health Amendment (Scotland) Act, 1983 does not aim to alter the basic principles of the 1960 act, but makes changes in the rules governing compulsory admission and detention of mentally ill (and mentally handicapped) patients and in the functions of the Mental Welfare Commission.

One interesting feature of the amendment Act is the requirement for local authorities to appoint social workers with appropriate training to function as mental health officers; their role will be, in cases where compulsory admission is under consideration, 'to interview the patient and satisfy himself that detention in hospital is in all the circumstances the most appropriate way of providing the care and medical treatment the patient needs'.[5]

The Act does not touch upon questions of the organisation and delivery of services. It is partly a tidying-up operation, designed to take account of the implications of other recent legislation, partly an attempt to reduce inessential differences between Scottish and English legislation, and in large measure a response to a growing concern with possible dangers to civil liberties, a concern which has been reflected in recent decisions of the European Court of Human Rights.

*Future Trends*

However desirable the objectives of the recent legislative changes, in reducing the risk of avoidable compulsion and in giving better protection to patients' civil liberties, it cannot be emphasised too strongly that they will do little or nothing to achieve a better balance of hospital and community services for the mentally ill or to improve the quantity and quality of supportive services available to the mentally disturbed and their families. The problems of comprehensive care arise from the fact that although modern drug treatment can indeed bring about impressive improvements in the condition of a high proportion of patients in a short space of time, the underlying condition is frequently not eradicated but remains liable to give rise to further breakdown, perhaps within months of discharge from hospital. We may note, by way of illustration, the high proportion of re-admissions among all those admitted to psychiatric wards. There is a good deal of research evidence to show that social and personal crises can in many cases serve both to precipitate and to reactivate psychiatric disturbance; at the same time, both vulnerability to stress and the capacity to resist it are shaped in part by personal relationships and earlier life experiences.[6] In short, it can be argued that an excessive concentration on a view of mental illness that is narrowly conceived in conventional medical terms has led to an under-estimate of the part played by social and psychological factors, and that this in its turn has been responsible for a badly balanced approach to the planning of services for treatment and prevention.

This imbalance in our understanding and interpretation of psychiatric disturbance, which has only recently begun to be corrected, is matched by a disproportion in the distribution of resources between hospital-based and community-based services. This has not developed as a result of a calculated if erroneous national plan. In fact, there is not and never has been a national policy for the care of the mentally ill. Hospital and personal social services for the mentally ill have each been left to develop within the respective frameworks of the NHS and the local authority system, with no planned integration between them nationally, regionally or (with some isolated exceptions) locally. Within these different service sectors, separately administered and separately financed, the extent and standard of provision for the mentally ill and their families have depended on the relative degrees of priority they have been able to achieve in the struggle for resources. In common with other branches of medicine dealing with long-term and recurrent conditions, psychiatry could not easily compete with the claims of high cost, high technology medicine during the years of expanding NHS resources. This is not to say that the available provisions were reduced, only that their rate of growth was relatively modest; as we have seen, both medical and nursing staffs expanded during the 1960s and 1970s. While many benefits could undoubtedly have been achieved had there been further shifts in resource allocation in favour of psychiatric hospitals, at least an established service of long standing has been maintained and indeed enhanced.

The problem on the local authority side has been that, unlike the NHS, there was no established base on which to build. In the rapid expansion of local authority social work services after the Social Work (Scotland) Act, 1968 (see chapter 6), priority was given to statutory responsibilities, to the management of social crises, and to work in the child care field. There was virtually no tradition of community provision for the mentally ill, and it would have required extraordinary dedication and persistence for staff and finance to be channelled to meet the needs of this client group. Given the established view of mental illness as essentially a medical problem, it was easy for those with competing priorities to argue that local government could not afford to pay to meet what were seen as NHS responsibilities. It is not altogether surprising therefore that in 1980 there were in the whole of Scotland only some 140 persons living in hostels or group homes provided by local authorities, with none at all in Strathclyde region; another 40 were living in similar accommodation run by voluntary bodies. No day centres for the mentally ill were provided by or with the support of Scottish local authorities until 1981, when two such centres were opened offering a total of 55 places.[7]

There is, therefore, something of a paradox. By the standards now prevailing in England — which are not themselves exceptionally advanced — the resident population of Scottish mental hospitals is far larger than it needs to be; yet it is clear that community services are so under-developed that it would be difficult to justify either a large-scale emphasis on rehabilitation and discharge programmes for long-stay patients or a significant move to direct new cases away from in-patient care. There is a striking lack of integrated thinking, directed at the design of comprehensive caring services, as well as the more obvious lack of integrated action to provide such services. The small amount of finance now specifically available to support social work developments that reduce the burden on health services has not so far made a perceptible impact.

A gleam of hope may perhaps be seen in the new 1983 Amendment Act for mental health. It is intended that, from a date to be prescribed by the Secretary of State, compulsory admissions to psychiatric units must be preceded by a family interview by a social worker; and that the regional and islands authorities shall designate named social workers for this task, who must have received appropriate specialist training. The importance of this proposal may lie less in the effect it has on the use of compulsory powers than in its implications for social work specialisation. The creation of a small body of community-based social workers with a major interest in mental health may perhaps lead to some pressure within the local authorities to respond more effectively — in some areas to respond at all — to the needs of this neglected client group. Welcome though such a trend would be, however, it would need powerful support and reinforcement, not least from central government, if Scottish services for the mentally ill are to move decisively forward.

All things considered, the prospect of a continuing division of responsibility, of growing pressure on the NHS and even more on local authority resources, and a widespread lack of imaginative enthusiasm do not augur well for the future.

ALCOHOL-RELATED PROBLEMS

We turn now to problems associated with the use, or abuse, of alcohol, because in many respects their treatment raises similar issues to mental illness. Each year more than 5000 people are admitted to psychiatric hospitals or psychiatric units in general hospitals in Scotland for the treatment of alcoholism, amounting to more than one-fifth of all admissions.[8] Over the past 15 years the overall number of admissions falling into this diagnostic category has approximately doubled. This increase is one, but only one, reflection of the growing burden of alcohol-related problems in Britain generally and in Scotland in particular. These admissions are of course only a fraction of all the people whose lives are adversely affected by alcoholic abuse, but it is virtually impossible to say what is the total size of the group. 'Alcoholism', 'alcohol-related problems' and 'problem drinking' are all imprecise terms. They would not provide a basis for accurate measurement even if we were in a position to survey complete populations and could rely upon receiving accurate information in answer to our questions. A certain amount is in fact known about levels of expenditure on alcohol. The data are not precise, because it is clear that there is a significant tendency, for example in the Family Expenditure Survey, for spending on alcohol (and on tobacco) to be under-estimated. But even more important is the fact that, although we have reasonable working assumptions about what constitutes a 'safe' level of drinking, it would not take us very far to define as an alcoholic everyone who exceeded that level.

Although the vast majority of people in our society consume alcoholic drinks from time to time, only a small proportion develop alcohol dependency. By alcohol dependency we mean a state in which there is a sense of compulsion to drink; a feeling that alcohol is a necessity for which the person craves. The withdrawal of alcohol leads to painful physical and mental symptoms, which can be dissipated only by a return to alcohol, and — perhaps for a considerable period of time though not indefinitely — the body becomes able to tolerate increasing levels of alcohol without obvious social or physical breakdown. Commonly the development of alcohol dependency is spread over a number of years. It is principally with the problems of those with alcohol dependency that the NHS and personal social services have become increasingly concerned over the past 20 years. Welcome though this attention is, we should remember that the period which leads up to a full-scale alcohol dependency, during which drinking becomes increasingly heavy and compulsive, can produce very serious personal and social problems, and remember also that it offers scope for helpful intervention.[9]

The harmful consequences of excessive drinking and alcohol dependency are hard to estimate with any degree of precision, for they are wide-ranging in their nature, and their human costs are borne by the drinkers themselves and by members of their immediate families as well as by the wider society. Perhaps most obvious and most easily enumerated are the consequences in terms of ill-health and reduced life expectancy. Follow-up studies of patients admitted to psychiatric wards with a diagnosis of alcoholism indicate high comparative mortality rates, not only for cirrhosis of the liver, which is universally agreed to be alcohol-related, but also for violence, suicide, accidents and cancers. Peptic ulcer is disproportionately common among heavy drinkers, and some forms of damage to the brain and nervous system are particularly associated with prolonged excessive alcohol consumption.

This section of the chapter began with a reference to those alcoholics who are admitted to psychiatric hospitals or psychiatric units in general hospitals. Although severe mental disturbance is far from rare, many more excessive drinkers experience deterioration of personality which, although it may not be met with psychiatric help, is nevertheless of a degree sufficient to cause profound disturbance in their family, employment and wider social relationships. How seriously and how rapidly the personal and social life of the excessive drinker disintegrates depends upon the interaction of many factors in his or her environment. Without attempting to quantify all such effects, we may confidently say that alcohol dependency contributes massively to marital tension, unhappiness and breakdown; to violence towards women and children; to extreme pressure on family budgets and a consequent build-up of unmanageable debts; and to incompetence at work, absence from work and loss of employment. There is a rich vein of alcohol that runs through a very large proportion of social problems, not least in the industrial areas of Scotland. In a class of its own is the effect of alcoholic excess on road traffic accidents; various studies suggest that between one-third and one-half of serious accidents are associated with high levels of blood alcohol, and 20 per cent of all road deaths are caused by drunken drivers.[10]

*Causation and Treatment*

Because of the difficulty of measuring accurately the frequency of heavy drinking or of alcohol dependency, international comparisons are hazardous. All the indications available, however, suggest that alcohol related problems are significantly more common in Scotland than in England. If we consider such varied measures as the number of deaths from cirrhosis of the liver, the number of hospital admissions associated with alcoholism and the number of convictions for drunkenness, we are likely to conclude that Scotland is about twice as heavily afflicted with alcohol dependency; and this would suggest that Scotland should be included among the more seriously affected European countries. Why this should be the case is not immediately obvious; the pattern of causes underlying alcoholic excess is complex, and does not lead to a simple generalisation which neatly explains national differences.

In respect of all forms of behaviour that are damaging to the individual and are seen as harmful to society, we find a widespread public preference for straightforward, preferably single-factor, explanations. Alcoholism is no exception, and tends to be 'explained' in terms of moral weakness or personality disturbance or social pressures, according to the prejudices of the person who is giving expression to his opinions. In fact, a dispassionate examination of the large body of research evidence indicates that genetic factors, personality make-up and socio-cultural influences may all be implicated, and that the relative contribution of each of these can vary. As far as modern Scotland is concerned, to explain the prevalence of heavy drinking at least in part by reference to a tradition of heavy drinking is by no means a circular explanation, even though it leaves open the question of how the tradition became established. Patterns of drinking tend to be self-perpetuating over the generations. The young person growing up is presented, not with a 'tradition' in some abstract sense, but with a set of assumptions woven into the everyday behaviour of adult relatives and neighbours, including assumptions about the appropriateness and social acceptability of certain styles and levels of alcohol consumption. Research suggests that in many sub-cultures, including perhaps those that prevail in several sectors of Scottish society, heavy drinking is a means by which an image of hard masculinity is created and presented and, at a deeper level, a way in which the need for personal power can be satisfied in phantasy terms.[11]

For a variety of reasons, a view of the person with severe drinking problems as someone in need of help and treatment rather than moral condemnation and exhortation has been slow to develop. It is of course arguable that there was little to be gained from promoting such a view until such time as useful, practical help could in fact be made available on acceptable terms to those who needed it. However, during the past ten or 15 years there has been an increasingly open recognition of the scale and severity of alcohol-related problems, and a marked increase in provision in the health services, the social work departments and the voluntary sector, as well as a significant investment in health education directed at the prevention and early recognition of alcohol-related problems.

Although it has in recent years become unfashionable to speak of alcoholism as a 'disease' and of people with alcohol dependency as 'sick', it remains the case that a large part of the responsibility for meeting the needs of those alcoholics who seek help rests with the health services. We cannot say with any confidence how far general practitioners are involved in this work, but it seems unlikely that their contribution (other than as referring agents) is a major one. Most medical or medically-related treatment of alcoholics is the responsibility of psychiatrists. In addition to the in-patient admissions referred to earlier, psychiatrists run a number of out-patient clinics, including some that are not geographically linked with a hospital. While a minority of in-patients suffer from severe psychiatric disorders associated with brain damage caused by prolonged excessive drinking and may require traditional long-term hospital care, most of them and virtually all out-patients are less permanently damaged; their need is to gain control of their drinking habits and often to obtain help with a variety of associated personal problems. The treatments available are varied, and include group therapy and the use of drugs to aid withdrawal from alcohol. Clinical psychologists as well as psychiatrists are on the staff of most alcohol treatment units and have developed the use of behaviour modification techniques by which the patient learns new ways of dealing with his or her inner needs and tensions.[12]

There has been a marked growth of interest in recent years in 'detoxification' — a process involving a rapid, enforced withdrawal from alcohol with the use of drugs to counter the painful and dangerous symptoms associated with such withdrawal. These procedures require carefully controlled conditions and the use of well-trained nursing staffs. So far, detoxification has tended to be associated with the management of deteriorated, often homeless alcoholics, who might otherwise find themselves occupying police and prison cells. Section 5 of the Criminal Procedure (Scotland) Act, 1980 empowers a police officer who arrests an offender and has reason to believe that he (or she) is drunk to take him to a 'designated place' for detoxification instead of placing him in custody. The first such purpose-built centre in Scotland will be constructed shortly, and it will be important to assess its effectiveness.

Voluntary bodies also play an important part in helping those with drinking problems. Indeed, it could be said that Alcoholics Anonymous (AA) played a unique pioneering role in offering the alcoholic access to help in a non-medical setting, as well as raising general public awareness of the significance of drinking problems and of the fact that these can often be treated. The activities of AA, which emphasise group support, have steadily expanded and it is now concerned also with the families of alcoholics. Another major development on the voluntary front has been the growth of local councils on alcoholism. There are now 24 of these bodies in Scotland, offering both individual and group counselling to clients with alcohol related problems of varying degrees of severity. More than 300 counsellors provide this service. They come from a wide variety of backgrounds, including some who have themselves in the past been dependent on alcohol. Trained under a national scheme organised by the Scottish Council on Alcoholism, these voluntary workers now see about 4000 new clients each year.[13]

Although alcohol enters directly or indirectly into a high proportion of all the problems dealt with by social workers, the latter have on the whole been reluctant to open up this difficult and sensitive topic. Recently some social work departments have identified alcoholism as an area in which they should be actively involved.[14] Strathclyde region is running a number of advice and resettlement centres for alcoholics, and is concerned to improve the competence of social workers in this aspect of practice.

The proliferation of services raises questions about a rational division of responsibility. Which clients find their way to which facilities seems to be very much a matter of chance. To make best use of the resources available, we need to have a clearer understanding of the ways in which people with alcohol dependency of varying degrees, and with associated personal problems of varying type and severity, are brought into contact with different treatment agencies. We also need to have firmer knowledge of the extent to which alternative approaches to treatment are more or less effective with different types of clients. Reported 'success' rates vary between 20 per cent and 60 per cent, but it is by no means certain that in comparing outcomes in different agencies we are really comparing like with like. That services should have developed in an unco-ordinated fashion is vastly preferable to their not developing at all. The next step forward, however, seems to call for a greater shared awareness of what each can accomplish most effectively, with an associated strengthening of mutual referral systems based on agreed criteria.

SERVICES FOR THE MENTALLY HANDICAPPED

There are some parallels between the way in which ideas about the care and management of mentally handicapped people have evolved and the development of services for the mentally ill. Central to professional thinking about both these broad client groups has been a shift away from the traditional emphasis on large custodial institutions. There are, however, important differences between mental illness and mental handicap, in spite of the fact that they are covered by the same legislation as far as compulsory hospital admission is concerned.

When we speak of mental handicap we are concerned first and foremost with intellectual retardation. Mental deficiency, mental defect and mental subnormality are all terms that have been used in the past (in legislation as well as in professional writing) to refer to the same broad range of problems. The causes of mental handicap are still imperfectly understood; or, to be more precise, a wide variety of conditions may give rise to or be associated with mental handicap. Research has thrown light on the causes of some of these conditions, but by no means all. In general, we are dealing with conditions that are present from birth, whether resulting from damage to the foetus, from birth injury, from the operation of rare recessive genes or from the interaction of genetic processes that give rise to the 'tail-end' of the normal distribution of intelligence. In exceptional cases infection or brain injury after birth may also be responsible for mental handicap. Whatever the causal background, however, the problem is not one of illness which can be relieved or cured by treatment in the medical sense.[15] The practical question is how best to maximise whatever potential the mentally handicapped person may have and to ensure that he or she is enabled to live the fullest and most satisfying life possible.

This has not always been the objective of social policy. Special institutions for mental defectives, like those for the insane, were initially an outgrowth of the poor law. The Mental Deficiency Act, 1913, which extended the scope of compulsory certification, was intended in part to protect society from the mental defective, who was assumed to contribute altogether disproportionately to the sum-total of pauperism, vice and crime, and in part to protect the defective from ill-treatment and exploitation at the hands of the unscrupulous. By extending provision for certification to the large class of high grade defectives, it encouraged the growth of large and over-crowded asylums. By setting up social inefficiency as the criterion by which mental defectives became 'subject to be dealt with', the act gave almost unlimited currency to an essentially custodial conception of care. It is only in the past 25 years that we have seen the emergence of a decisive shift away from traditional patterns. This change to some extent reflects more tolerant and understanding public attitudes, but it has been powerfully reinforced by the findings of research. This research has been the work of educational and clinical psychologists, and it has shown how changes in the pattern of care and training can produce significant improvements in competence. It will be some time, however, before service provision is sufficiently reoriented to take full account of modern knowledge.

### Recent Research and its Implications

What we have learned from research is that mentally handicapped children tend to make better progress in both intellectual and social development if they are brought up by their parents rather than in institutions, and that if residential care is unavoidable the emphasis should be on small, family-like homes rather than institutions of traditional scale. There is evidence that residential establishments of the former type can be planned to meet the needs of identifiable communities, and can be more readily integrated into them than those which draw their inmates from a large area and are geographically remote.[16]

Few would go so far as to argue for the abolition of all residential care for the mentally handicapped. The most severe cases generally have serious physical disabilities and need constant attention; the resulting burden is one that many parents feel they are unable to accept, and there are no compelling reasons why their wishes should not be respected. Even in the case of those who are 'seriously' rather than 'profoundly' handicapped — for example, most children suffering from Down's syndrome — parental attitudes may include large elements of shame, guilt and anxiety, and while it is right that such parents should receive careful advice and sensitive help in reaching a decision, their right to opt for a residential placement should not be denied. What is important is that the latter choice should offer the prospect not merely of good physical care — though even that has been shown to be lacking in some institutions (not in Scotland) where major scandals have erupted — but also of education and training. One very significant development in recent years has been a sharply increased interest in more effective methods of training mentally handicapped children. Among the well-founded practical approaches that have emerged are procedures by which professionals train parents, who in turn can then train their own children.[17]

Although a great deal of the discussion and research into mental handicap has focused on problems of childhood, it is vital not to lose sight of the dramatic changes that have taken place in the life expectancy of the mentally handicapped. Because modern medicine can cope with the infectious and other diseases which used to kill large numbers of mentally handicapped children, the majority now survive to middle age and beyond. Expectations about the level of functioning of the mentally handicapped adult have also changed, and there is a good deal of experience to show that under suitable conditions a high proportion can be trained to carry out a variety of industrial tasks. However, in a period of generally contracting employment opportunities marginal groups such as the mentally handicapped and the mentally ill are likely to be doubly disadvantaged. But even under better economic circumstances one would still expect to find a continuing need for some kind of support in a high proportion of cases; and very frequently the death or increasing infirmity of an elderly parent precipitates a crisis in the life of a mentally handicapped person. Admission to institutional care for the first time in middle age is common, and in the opinion of many observers should be unnecessary. Hostels offering a high degree of independence and some forms of group tenancy arranged by housing associations have attractive possibilities as community-based alternatives.

*Recent Trends in Scotland*

If the type and quality of service provision in Britain have so far fallen short of the requirements that modern knowledge has shown to be appropriate to the needs of the mentally handicapped and their families, the discrepancy in Scotland between the actual and the ideal has been and remains particularly striking. The Scottish Society for the Mentally Handicapped, like its English equivalent, has performed a valuable task in bringing together the families of the mentally handicapped to exert pressure for reform on central and local government, and has also moved into direct service provision. Excellent work is also done by smaller, specialised bodies such as the Down's Children Association, which bring parents together for mutual aid and support, and help to diffuse relevant knowledge. In spite of these forces for change, however, the general pattern of services has been slow to alter. Dependence on hospital provision remains high, and the build-up of community services has been slow. Although both the staffing position and the characteristic pattern of usage of the hospitals have improved, many of them are both larger in scale and more remote from the populations they serve than is desirable.

Since the early 1970s, hospital nursing staffs, including trained as well as student and auxiliary nurses, have increased by about 50 per cent. There has been no growth in the number of medical consultants, but more clinical psychologists are now involved in this area of hospital work. Over this period the number of hospital in-patients fell by about ten per cent, from 7400 to 6700, in spite of an increasing admission rate from 1000 to 1700 per year.[18] This apparent contradiction points, of course, to a reduced average length of stay. The number of discharges has doubled in a decade, and the average length of time spent in hospital by those discharged has been halved. The increased admission rate conceals two opposite trends: the number of first admissions has tended to fall, while the number of re-admissions has risen steeply. More patients than in the past, it would seem, now alternate between hospital care and life in the community; what quality of life they and their families experience, and what factors are associated with re-admissions, are questions that research has not so far addressed.

The central problem is the failure of the local authority sector to allocate adequate resources to this area of work or to plan provisions in partnership with the NHS. The failure has been less extreme than in the case of mental illness; in mental handicap there is a longer tradition of involvement and perhaps also a sense that the dimensions of the problem are more clearly understood. There was a genuine spurt in developments in the early 1970s, but with a slow-down since about 1976 under the impact of financial restraints. An official committee, reporting in 1979 on services for the mentally handicapped in Scotland, referred to a shortfall of about 2000 places in local authority or voluntary residential homes and of nearly 3000 places in adult training centres. The same report identified needs, as yet very imperfectly met, for social work support for families, in terms of practical help of many kinds, at the emotional level, and in the form of short-term respite care. The report's conclusion, that 'the steps so far taken by all statutory agencies in Scotland to achieve this desirable end [that is an increasing emphasis on care in the community] have been inadequate and almost without exception have had little effect on the transfer of patients from hospital to community care'[19], cannot easily be brushed aside. Economic constraints have been and remain a major obstacle. While these must be overcome before there can be significant progress, it will be at least equally important to create the means by which disparate services can rise above the barriers which at present inhibit joint planning, joint financing and joint implementation of provisions: barriers which are in part administrative and institutional, but are also embedded in attitudes and values.

During the past 25 years our understanding of the problems of the various client groups considered in this chapter, of some of the causes of those problems, and of the ways in which the various social services can treat or alleviate them, has grown very substantially. There is still, of course, plenty of scope for further research, to throw additional light on the factors involved in the varieties of mental illness, in mental handicap and in alcohol dependency; but we cannot claim that the development of appropriate services is being seriously held up by a lack of relevant knowledge. The sad truth is that we still have a long way to go before we can say that full use is being made of the knowledge that we already possess. In many respects the gap between achievement and potential is even more marked in Scotland than in England. In the short term the prospects are not encouraging. The financial difficulties under which all the social services now labour will make it even harder to promote causes which have never been politically attractive or accorded very high priority by the professional groups concerned. But there is experience to show that even in generally unfavourable circumstances local innovations and limited experiments are possible; an essential requirement is a readiness to work hard at the task of overcoming organisational difficulties. Successful local developments can be publicised, so as to encourage others and to provide norms for the expansion of services when circumstances are more propitious. In the meantime, the enthusiasm and ingenuity of the few people to whom these causes are important must be the main source of hope for the mental health services.

*References*

1. K. Jones, *Mental Health and Social Policy 1845-1959*, Routledge and Kegan Paul, 1960.
2. G.F. Rehin and F.M. Martin, *Patterns of Performance in Community Care*, Oxford University Press, 1968, chapter 1.
3. Scottish Health Service Common Services Agency, *Scottish Health Statistics 1980*, HMSO, 1982.
4. Department of Health and Social Security, *Health and Personal Social Services Statistics for England 1982*, HMSO, 1982.
5. Scottish Home and Health Department and Social Work Services Group, *Review of the Mental Health (Scotland) Act, 1960*, SHHD and SWSG, 1982.
6. G. Brown and T. Harris, *Social Origins of Depression*, Tavistock Publications, 1978; and G. Brown, J.L.T. Birley and J.K. Wing, 'Influence of Family Life on the Course of Schizophrenic Disorders', *British Journal of Psychiatry*, No. 121, 1972.
7. Social Work Services Group, *Residential Accommodation for the Elderly and Certain other Adults, Scotland, 1980 (SWSG Statistical Bulletin)*, SWSG, 1981; and SWSG, *Home Care Services: Day Care Establishments (SWSG Statistical Bulletin)*, SWSG, 1982.
8. Scottish Health Service Common Services Agency, *Scottish Health Statistics 1980*.
9. Royal College of Psychiatrists, *Alcohol and Alcoholism*, Tavistock Publications, 1979.
10. S. Hollerman and A. Burdrace, *The Costs of Alcohol Misuse*, Department of Health and Social Security, 1981.
11. D.C. McClelland, W.N. Davis, R. Kalin and E. Warner, *The Drinking Man*, Free Press, 1972.
12. Royal College of Psychiatrists, *Alcohol and Alcoholism*.
13. R.I.F. Brown and P.J. O'Donnell, 'Barefoot Counsellors on Alcoholism: The Scottish Experiment', unpublished paper presented at 26th International Institute on Prevention and Treatment of Alcoholism, 1980.
14. Strathclyde Social Work Committee, *Addiction: Collusion or Cover Up?* (Report of an Officer/Member Group), Strathclyde Regional Council, 1978.
15. A.M. Clarke and A.D.B. Clarke (eds.) *Mental Deficiency: the Changing Outlook*, Methuen, (3rd edition) 1974.
16. J.K. Wing and R. Olsen (eds.) *Community Care for the Mentally Disabled*, Oxford University Press, 1979, chapters 6 and 7.
17. *Ibid.*
18. Scottish Health Service Common Services Agency, *Scottish Health Statistics 1980*.
19. Scottish Home and Health Department and Scottish Education Department, *A Better Life for the Mentally Handicapped in Scotland*, HMSO, 1979.

## FURTHER READING

A. Clare, *Psychiatry in Dissent*, Tavistock Publications, (2nd edition) 1980.
An admirable discussion of present-day psychiatry and its problems which is both scholarly and readable.

D. Goldberg and P. Huxley, *Mental Illness in the Community*, Tavistock Publications, 1980.
An account of the findings of research into the processes that bring people into contact with psychiatric services.

L. Hunt, *Alcohol Related Problems*, Heinemann, 1982.
A clearly presented review of alcohol problems and their management which is broadly based but with a fairly strong social work orientation.

J. Wing and R. Olsen (eds.), *Community Care for the Mentally Disabled*, Oxford University Press, 1979.
A series of essays reviewing modern ideas on provisions for those with long-term problems of mental illness and mental handicap.

# 5

## *Housing*

Housing is not always counted as a social service and it certainly has important differences from, for example, health or education. Four of these differences may be highlighted: first, housing is far from being free at the point of use and consumer charges are very important; second, direct public sector provision in the form of council housing comes nowhere near possessing a monopoly; third, a great deal of housing is bought and sold in the market rather than allocated administratively; and, fourth, professional staff whose work is the basis of most social services play only a relatively minor role in the housing field. Nevertheless, housing in Britain has developed characteristics which justify its inclusion in a list of social services.

Most obviously there is the growth in council housing which is allocated primarily according to need rather than ability to pay. But the modification of the market has gone far beyond the provision of council housing. The great bulk of housing is subsidised in one way or another while the rent acts provide a legal framework within which private landlords let houses and limit the rents which they are permitted to charge. Legislation lays down minimum standards relating to such things as sanitation and the state of repair of dwellings. In short, housing is pervaded by financial subsidies and official regulation, and it is a major concern of social policy.

There is no single, authoritative summary of the objectives of housing policy but a concise statement was included in the green paper on Scottish housing in 1977: 'The Government's fundamental housing aim is still to enable every family to have a decent home at a price it can afford'.[1] Scarcely anyone could disagree with objectives expressed in such general terms, though opinions differ about what precisely is meant by 'a decent home' and 'a price it can afford'. Nevertheless, attention is focused on the issues with which housing policy must be concerned. First, if every family is to have a separate home the quantity of houses in relation to the size and structure of the population is important. Second, account must be taken of the quality of the housing stock. Third, subsidies may be required to ensure that adequate housing can be afforded. These issues of the quantity, quality and finance of housing are basic to this chapter.

There are 56 housing authorities in Scotland — 53 district and three islands authorities (see Figure 1.2) — each with a wide range of responsibilities in the housing field which go well beyond the provision of council houses.

Each authority has to deal with a unique combination of circumstances relating, for example, to the age and condition of the stock, the extent of any shortages and the tenure mix.

Housing policies in Scotland have tended broadly to follow those south of the border, reflecting the priorities of the government of the day. But differences of policy or at least administration arise from the existence of a separate Scottish legal system, from variations in building methods (for example, flats are much more common in Scotland) and from the fact that local authorities have worked with the Scottish Office since the nineteenth century. Today the Scottish Development Department is responsible for practically all housing matters in Scotland. Separate procedures have tended to be more common where there is a local authority responsibility, for example with council housing or improvement, than in the case of, say, owner occupation. Another factor in this last field is that the purchase of houses in Scotland is dominated by building societies which operate throughout Britain.

A final point which should be made by way of introduction is that the word 'house' will be generally used as a synonym for dwelling. Houses include flats, maisonettes, bungalows and so on unless the context makes clear that the more specific meaning is intended.


HISTORICAL BACKGROUND

There has been public involvement in housing since the second half of the nineteenth century though for many years the concern did not extend beyond attempting to ensure that minimum standards were achieved. The city of Glasgow, for example, was a pioneer of slum clearance in Britain. In 1917 the Royal Commission on the Housing of the Industrial Population of Scotland reported.[2] The commission had been appointed before the outbreak of the first world war, but new problems arose during the war from the cessation of building and the movement of workers to munitions factories, with consequent increased pressure on housing in areas such as Clydeside. It was shown that working class housing in Scotland was deplorable, that standards were lower than south of the border, and that a substantial building programme was urgently required. Not only were houses often insanitary, badly built and falling into disrepair: they were far too small for the families which had to live in them. Overcrowding was widespread and acute: nearly a quarter of the population was living at a density of more than three persons a room and approaching half at a density of more than two persons per room. (Today only a small proportion of the population lives at a density of more than one and a half persons per room.) The commission believed that it would not be realistic to expect private landlords to build the new houses which were quickly required and recommended that local authorities should be given the responsibility of providing them. Exchequer subsidies would be needed to make up the difference between the costs of building the houses and income from rents.

In 1914 the great bulk of houses, about 90 per cent of the total, were rented from private landlords. Owner occupation was on a small scale and the number of council houses was minuscule. Since the first world war the tenure pattern has been transformed by the growth of owner occupation and council housing. There has been proportionately greater provision of council housing in Scotland compared with England and Wales but a slower development of owner occupation. As a result of economic conditions and lower incomes there was less building for owner occupation, particularly during the 1930s when Scotland did not share in the private housing boom south of the border. Neither was there such a plentiful supply of decent pre-1914 housing in Scotland to be purchased by owner occupiers. Consequently council housing was much in demand and most local authorities built on a large scale. Another factor is that a relatively greater proportion of housing needs in Scotland have arisen from slum clearance and the abatement of overcrowding than from population growth which also increased the role of council housing. Council rents have tended to be lower in Scotland; one reason is that the low rents of privately rented housing, reflecting its poor quality, set a norm which limited what councils could realistically charge.

The development of council housing has been marked by a number of distinct phases during which new building had different purposes, and these are reflected in the public sector stock as it now exists.[3] In the 1920s council houses were built mainly to overcome shortages (for 'general needs') rather than directly to replace unsatisfactory housing, and they tended to be occupied by upper working (and lower middle) class families. The poorest and worst housed were supposed to be assisted through a process of 'filtering up' whereby the whole population would move a few rungs up the housing ladder. Accommodation was usually built as semi-detached houses or, more often, four-in-a-block 'cottage flats'. Estates built at this time tended to develop stable communities and, despite their age, are usually still some of the most pleasant and popular council housing.

Then in the 1930s the function of council building was changed from meeting general needs to rehousing people from slums and overcrowded accommodation. Tenements became the characteristic building form. The original inhabitants were relatively poor, often with larger families and suffering high unemployment. Housing schemes built during the 1930s tended to gain a poor reputation and to have a rapid turnover of tenants. Today they are frequently amongst the most deprived and difficult-to-let part of the public sector. The problems of council housing, including some built much more recently, are examined later in the chapter.

As well as council housing, public sector rented accommodation is provided by the Scottish Special Housing Association (SSHA), other housing associations and the new towns. The SSHA, which was set up in 1937, is not a housing association in the ordinary sense but a central government agency which supplements the housebuilding of local authorities. Its initial function was to build houses in areas of high unemployment, devising new construction methods in which unskilled labour could be employed.[4] In 1982 the SSHA owned about 90,000 houses throughout Scotland. (Other types of housing associations are outlined below.)

There are five new towns in Scotland, each under the control of a development corporation, which altogether provide about 50,000 houses. The first two, East Kilbride and Glenrothes, were designated in 1947 and 1948, Cumbernauld in 1956, Livingston in 1962 and Irvine in 1966. The chief purpose of the Scottish new towns, especially those in the west, was to house overspill population from Glasgow as well as attracting new industry to the region. East Kilbride, which is the largest new town, has also been the most successful in building up industry.

SCOTTISH HOUSING IN THE EIGHTIES[5]

*The Housing Stock: Quantity*

During the period since the first world war the population of Scotland and the number of households and dwellings have all increased (Table 5.1) but at differing rates. Between 1921 and 1981 the population grew by five and a half per cent, the number of households by 65 per cent and the number of dwellings by 90 per cent. The housing stock is now over two million dwellings. This means that there is far less sharing of houses and overcrowding than in the past. The number of households has grown much more rapidly than the population, reflecting a decline in average household size. There is now a substantial crude surplus of dwellings over households though for a number of reasons this statistic should be treated with caution. First, it is an average of many local situations in some of which shortages remain. Local shortages and surpluses reflect the fact that the location of housing is fixed and that it has an extremely long life of up to 100 years or longer. But the population of different

TABLE 5.1

Population, Households and Dwellings in Scotland 1921-1981

|  | Population (000s) | Average House- hold size | Households (000s) | Dwellings (000s) |
|---|---|---|---|---|
| 1921 | 4,883 | 4.4 | 1,099 | 1,058 |
| 1951 | 5,096 | 3.5 | 1,436 | 1,375 |
| 1961 | 5,179 | 3.3 | 1,570 | 1,627 |
| 1971 | 5,229 | 3.1 | 1,686 | 1,809 |
| 1981 | 5,150 | 2.8 | 1,815 | 2,012 |

Sources: *Scottish Housing: A Consultative Document*, Cmnd. 6852; and *Scottish Housing Statistics*.

areas is marked by relative growth and decline related, for example, to local employment opportunities. Second, a certain number of houses are always vacant because, for instance, they are changing hands, have recently been completed or are second homes.

Overcrowding has been much reduced but, with 14 per cent of households living at density of more than one person per room in 1981, Scotland was not so well placed as England and Wales with only three per cent. An alternative and more discriminating measure of overcrowding is the bedroom standard used by the Office of Population Censuses and Surveys. It determines the number of bedrooms required by each household according to age, sex and marital status with no more than two persons being required to share. In the late 1970s nine per cent of households in Scotland were one or more bedrooms below the standard, double the proportion in England and Wales. The chief reason for the greater amount of overcrowding in Scotland is the smaller size of houses rather than larger households which on average are only slightly bigger than south of the border.

As well as a shortage of larger houses there are not enough small ones. There has been a rapid increase in the number of one and two person households in Scotland which now account for over half the total. Reasons for this trend include a tendency for young people to leave the parental home sooner, a greater rate of marriage break-up and, above all, an ageing population. Some small households are happy to occupy larger accommodation but many, particularly the elderly, would prefer to move to a more easily managed and economical home.

Although there is no longer a general shortage of houses in Scotland, the rate of building is still important. New houses are required to meet needs arising from population movements and the growth of the number of households, as well as to replace dwellings which have come to the end of their useful life or have to be demolished for other reasons. There has been a sharp fall in the number of houses completed from over 40,000 in 1971 (itself less than previously) to less than 17,000 in 1982 (Table 5.2). It will be seen that the balance between the public and private sectors has substantially changed. Whereas the public sector predominated until a few years ago, in 1978, for the first time since the 1920s, new owner-occupied houses were in a majority in Scotland. While fewer new houses are needed than when there were acute shortages and a high rate of slum clearance, a continuation of the low level of output reached at the beginning of the 1980s would be a cause for concern.

*The Housing Stock: Quality*

The quality as well as the quantity of Scottish housing has greatly improved. The housing stock is rather newer than that in the rest of Britain, reflecting the relatively greater rate of building since the second world war. In 1981 over half the houses in Scotland had been built during this period. But nearly a third were built before the first world war and, though some are

TABLE 5.2

Housing Completions in Scotland 1971-1981

| | Public Sector | % | Private Sector | % | TOTAL |
|---|---|---|---|---|---|
| 1971 | 29,169 | (72) | 11,614 | (28) | 40,783 |
| 1972 | 20,157 | (63) | 11,835 | (37) | 31,992 |
| 1973 | 17,818 | (59) | 12,215 | (41) | 30,033 |
| 1974 | 17,097 | (60) | 11,239 | (40) | 28,336 |
| 1975 | 23,952 | (70) | 10,371 | (30) | 34,323 |
| 1976 | 22,823 | (62) | 13,704 | (38) | 36,527 |
| 1977 | 15,188 | (56) | 12,132 | (44) | 27,320 |
| 1978 | 11,316 | (44) | 14,443 | (56) | 25,759 |
| 1979 | 8,607 | (36) | 15,055 | (64) | 23,662 |
| 1980 | 8,357 | (41) | 12,142 | (59) | 20,499 |
| 1981 | 8,966 | (45) | 11,039 | (55) | 20,005 |
| 1982 (provisional) | 4,859 | (29) | 11,710 | (71) | 16,569 |

Source: Department of the Environment, Scottish Development Department and Welsh Office, *Housing and Construction Statistics 1971-1981*, HMSO, 1982; and Scottish Development Department.

excellent houses, it is amongst these that problems of lack of amenities and disrepair are concentrated.

The availability of basic amenities — an inside WC, a hot water supply and a bath — not only reflects new building (and the clearance of the worst houses) but also the improvement of the existing stock. An extensive system of improvement grants has existed since 1949, and more recently policies have been developed for the rehabilitation of areas of older housing which are discussed below. Taking the use of fixed bath or shower as an example, in 1951 about half Scottish households did not enjoy this amenity, dropping to 13 per cent in 1971 and to less than three per cent in 1981 (which was lower than the figure for England and Wales). Within Scotland the islands areas stand out, over ten per cent of households in Orkney lacking a bath.

Another and more severe measure of the quality of housing is the number of dwellings which fall below the statutory tolerable standard. Sub-tolerable houses are the worst of the stock and local authorities have a duty to deal with them either by improvement or clearance. The tolerable standard is broadly equivalent to unfitness for human habitation in England and Wales but, by placing greater emphasis on lack of amenities (a tolerable house must have a hot water supply and an inside WC though it need not have a bath) as well as state of repair, it is designed to achieve more precision in identifying unsatisfactory housing. In 1982 there were estimated to be nearly 100,000 sub-tolerable houses in Scotland or about five per cent of the total stock. The figures are obtained from local authorities and are fairly approximate, but there has been a clear trend for the size of the problem to fall. Continued progress will depend on new building and improvement counteracting the inevitable deterioration in the state of repair of older houses. The tolerable standard does not, however, take into account the significant number of council houses which, while possessing basic internal amenities, suffer from problems such as dampness or poor environment, and are clearly not a satisfactory part of the housing stock.

The distribution of sub-tolerable houses is very uneven. At one extreme less than one per cent of the housing stock falls below the tolerable standard in Eastwood, Cumbernauld and Kilsyth, and Bearsden and Milngavie districts. Old industrial centres in the Clydeside conurbation such as Clydebank and Motherwell have below average proportions as a result of large-scale clearance and rebuilding programmes. But in Glasgow some nine per cent of houses fall below the tolerable standard which, while a great improvement, still amount to over a quarter of the Scottish total. It may seem surprising that the districts with the highest proportions of sub-tolerable houses are some of those in the highlands and islands: for example the Western Isles 23 per cent, Skye and Lochalsh 20 per cent, and Argyll and Bute 17 per cent. The problem of rural cottages which lack modern amenities is very different from that of nineteenth century tenements but it is none the less real.

For a very long time there has been a strong tradition of living in flats in Scotland and approaching half of all dwellings are flats, about two and a half times the proportion south of the border. Flats can provide fine homes but, other things being equal, many people prefer a house with a garden, and the predominance of flats in Scotland is on balance a disadvantage.

*The Housing Stock: Tenure*

The basis on which people obtain accommodation, either by buying or renting it, pervades practically every aspect of housing policy. The different tenures are characterised by varying terms of access and qualities of accommodation, and they tend to be used by different groups in the population. The main tenure categories are owner occupation, public sector (public authority plus housing association) renting and private sector renting (Table 5.3). The largest sector in Scotland is public authority renting which is dominated by council houses, with a relatively small contribution from the SSHA (four and a half per cent of the total stock) and new towns (two and a half per cent). Although other housing associations are usually regarded as being in the public sector, for the purposes of tenure statistics they are counted as part of the 'private rented and other' category (and make up about one and half per cent of the total stock). Comparing Scotland with England and Wales, public sector renting and owner occupation change places as the largest and second largest tenures. In recent years the public sector proportion has been fairly stable as a result of reduced building programmes and sales, while owner occupation has continued to grow and private renting to decline.

There are, however, wide variations in the relative size of the public and owner-occupied sectors in different areas. At one extreme a number of districts have over 80 per cent of their housing stock in the public sector: Cumbernauld and Kilsyth, East Kilbride (both including new towns), Monklands and Motherwell. At the other extreme the smallest proportions of public sector housing are found in some suburban and rural areas: for example, Eastwood 11 per cent, Bearsden and Milngavie 15 per cent, and Skye and Lochalsh 16 per cent.

TABLE 5.3

Housing Tenure (1981)

|  | Scotland % | England and Wales % |
| --- | --- | --- |
| Owner Occupied | 37 | 58 |
| Public Authority Rented | 54 | 29 |
| Private Rented and Other | 10 | 13 |

Source: Department of the Environment, Scottish Development Department and Welsh Office, *Housing and Construction Statistics 1971-1981*, HMSO, 1982.

The quality of housing provided by the different tenures varies widely. Privately rented houses are generally the oldest and least well-equipped. Council and other public authority rented housing, whatever the environmental shortcomings of some estates and blocks of flats, has virtually all been built since 1919 and is almost fully provided with basic amenities. Owner-occupied housing displays the greatest contrasts; the sector includes the best accommodation and some of the worst.

In terms of the socio-economic status of households there is a gradient from owner occupation through the public sector to private renting but there is a great deal of overlap between tenures. Previously the poorest households tended to be concentrated in the privately rented sector but with its decline they have been moving increasingly into council housing. But in comparison with England and Wales the larger public sector in Scotland means that a greater proportion of all income groups make use of it than south of the border. Private tenants are also a mixed group: on one hand many are elderly households which have lived in their homes for many years whilst, on the other hand, this tenure also includes young families and single persons such as students occupying rooms in shared dwellings usually for fairly short periods.

## Housing Associations

As in the rest of Britain the contribution of the housing associations, often called the voluntary housing movement, is still modest in numerical terms, providing in 1981 about 30,000 dwellings in Scotland, but it has grown rapidly since the Housing Act, 1974. Housing associations vary greatly in size and type but most of them are relatively small with less than 1000 houses. They are non-profit making bodies and are sometimes referred to as the 'third arm' of housing provision in the sense that they are seen as a counterweight to the growing dominance of owner occupation and the council sector. The Housing Corporation, which was set up in 1964, is a government financed agency which promotes and supervises housing associations. Its powers over associations in receipt of exchequer subsidies, which must be registered with it, were greatly strengthened in 1974 and it is the channel through which these grants are paid. It has increasingly been the policy of the corporation to give priority to projects directed at those with particular housing needs.

Many housing associations cater for groups such as single people, the elderly, the disabled and single parent families. They often specialise in one bedroomed accommodation, in some cases with communal facilities as in sheltered housing for old people. Other associations are primarily concerned with the rehabilitation of older housing. Housing associations have been particularly important in carrying out rehabilitation of old, usually sub-tolerable, tenemental property in Glasgow, where they are 'community-based': only a small area is covered and all residents are eligible to be members.

POLICIES FOR OLDER HOUSING

Policies for housing which fails to meet the tolerable standard are of two main kinds: first, those which involve its clearance and the rehousing of residents (generally called slum clearance) and, second, those for its improvement and rehabilitation which in recent years have been of increasing importance. Improvement is also of relevance to older housing which is above the tolerable standard.

*Slum Clearance*

The demolition of slums was started in the nineteenth century on a small scale, but the first really extensive clearance programme did not begin until the 1930s and was soon cut short by the outbreak of the second world war. Immediately after the war the overwhelming need was for extra houses to compensate for the cessation of building for five years and the increased number of households. It was not until the mid-1950s that slum clearance was restarted on a significant scale and the level of activity built up to a peak around 1970. Over 20,000 houses were demolished in Scotland in 1971, but the number has fallen drastically and only about 5000 houses were dealt with ten years later. This swing away from clearance has been bound up with the development of area improvement policies which have often been seen as a preferable alternative to demolition.

*Improvement and Rehabilitation*

Improvement policies have been mainly related to the provision of basic amenities, such as a hot water supply, bath or shower and inside WC, where these have been missing in older houses. Thus the concept of improvement grants only became relevant when the government extended its concern from the minimum standards implicit in slum clearance to an attempt to ensure that all houses were of a reasonably modern standard. Improvement grants were introduced in 1949 but for some 20 years they were used on only a small scale. A weakness of the system was that there was no machinery to ensure that all the substandard houses in an area were improved, nor was much impact made on seriously unsatisfactory housing which was otherwise likely eventually to be demolished. Until the end of the 1960s improvement grants were mainly utilised by owner occupiers to upgrade individual houses which were usually far from being the worst. The more radical improvement of seriously inadequate houses, particularly those which fall below the tolerable standard, is usually referred to as rehabilitation.

A key event in the development of improvement policies was the publication in 1968 of *The Older Houses in Scotland: A Plan for Action*.[6] This white paper and the subsequent Housing (Scotland) Act, 1969 heralded effective policies for the improvement of areas of housing. The housing treatment area procedure introduced in 1969 proved to have defects and was replaced by housing action areas by the Housing (Scotland) Act, 1974.[7] The size of HAAs varies greatly from a handful of houses to some hundreds. Many local authorities in Scotland, including some in rural areas, have declared HAAs, and Glasgow and Edinburgh have taken them up on a particularly large scale. (It should be noted that HAAs in England and Wales are somewhat different.)

The change of emphasis in housing policy from slum clearance to improvement was motivated by a range of factors. Perhaps the most influential was work done by economists which demonstrated that in cost-benefit terms improvement is very often preferable to demolition and rebuilding. Particularly when interest rates are high it is cheaper, discounting future costs to their present value, to spend relatively large sums on modernisation. Another consideration was a widespread dissatisfaction with new council housing at a time when high flats and non-traditional building methods were in vogue. The desirability of preserving existing communities was also emphasised.

These arguments are undoubtedly valid though reservations may be made about them. The apparent cheapness of improvement in comparison with renewal depends a great deal on the assumptions which are made about the data that are fed into cost-benefit analyses. Over-enthusiasm for re-habilitation may have resulted in some wrong decisions about the better policy in particular cases. Attitudes to clearance are affected by the quality of alternative housing in the public sector. The building of massive blocks of flats has now largely been abandoned and the latest council housing is much more attractive to potential tenants. Renewal need not destroy communities if it is done on a phased basis so that many residents can be rehoused near by. In any case, there is evidence that improvement, by changing tenure patterns and increasing housing costs, can lead to the break-up of communities.

The provision of improvement grants is not enough to ensure that areas of the worst housing will be rehabilitated. A great deal of work is required on most houses; owner occupiers are often elderly and have low incomes; many houses are still privately rented whilst few landlords are interested in improvement; and incremental rehabilitation over a period of years may be too slow if an area is to be saved from demolition. For all these reasons a public agency, either the local authority or a housing association, has an essential role in HAAs. The local authority or housing association usually has to acquire most of the tenanted houses and many of the owner-occupied ones before they can be improved. Specialist staff are required to liaise with individual residents to discover their varying needs.

The number of improvement grants approved each year between 1972 and 1981 both for work in HAAs and outwith them is shown in Figure 5.1 (though it should be borne in mind that improvement by local authorities and housing associations is subsidised in the same way as their other activities and not by improvement grants). The large increase in the number of grants between 1972 and 1974 was due to their temporary increase from 50 per cent to 75 per cent of approved expense in order to counter unemployment in the building industry. After a sharp fall the number of grants rose again but to little more than half their peak level. Grants can be claimed by owner occupiers (who receive over three-quarters of the total), by private landlords and, since the Tenants' Rights, Etc. (Scotland) Act, 1980 under certain circumstances by tenants. As well as the installation of basic amenities, grants cover a wide range of work such as electrical rewiring or replacement of lead plumbing. Up to half of the improvement grants may be spent on repairs, and grants may also be made solely towards the cost of repairs which, if neglected, would threaten the future useful life of the house. The conversion of a large house into a number of smaller dwellings, or of a building used for some other purpose into living accommodation, may also be grant aided.

Grants are basically 50 per cent of 'approved expense' (which in 1983 was itself normally a maximum of £10,200 per house), though in certain circumstances the proportion may be higher. In most cases grants are paid at the discretion of the local authority (except for the now unimportant 'standard grants' for the installation of basic amenities only). In the case of a house in an HAA, however, the council must give a grant and the rate is 75 per cent of approved expense (or up to 90 per cent in cases of financial hardship). In 1982 grants for the installation of basic amenities, repairs, and replacement of lead plumbing were increased to 90 per cent of approved expense. This temporary measure, primarily intended to increase employment in the building industry, is intended to come to an end in 1984.

As can be seen from the statistics on possession of basic amenities and the number of sub-tolerable houses, these problems which have long been the concern of housing policy have to a considerable extent been solved. But a growing problem in recent years has been the disrepair of otherwise satisfactory houses. This affects both the owner-occupied and council sectors, and the latter is discussed below. But some owner occupiers, particularly the elderly, cannot afford properly to maintain their homes. In the future it seems likely that grants, for repair more than improvement, will be required on an increasing scale.

HOUSING SUBSIDIES

Subsidies are a complex topic which cannot be dealt with in detail here, but some general points can be made about them. The primary purpose of subsidies is to ensure that households are not prevented from obtaining adequate accommodation because they cannot afford it. Apart from anything else, decent housing benefits the community by, for example, preventing disease. But subsidies clearly go beyond this objective by encouraging the

FIGURE 5.1   Private Sector Improvement Grants Approved 1972-1981

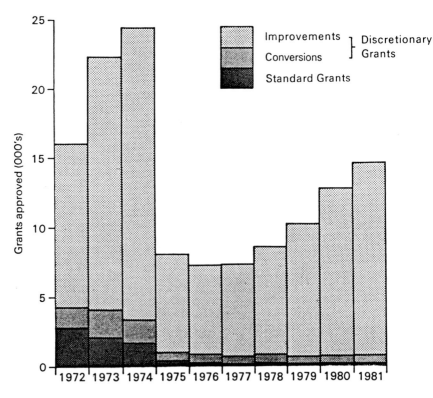

production and consumption of housing even where there is no question of inadequate accommodation. Subsidies can therefore also be seen as reflecting a view that more and better housing *per se* is socially desirable. It is difficult to see, however, that expenditure on housing over and above the achievement of the kind of basic standards outlined above — the avoidance of overcrowding, the availability of internal amenities and so on — has any external benefits to the community as opposed to individual households. A more realistic view may be that for largely historical reasons Britain has become accustomed to housing subsidies for which there is little objective justification but which it is politically almost impossible to end.

The great bulk of housing in Britain is subsidised by the taxpayer so that its full cost is not met by owners or tenants, though in entirely different ways depending on tenure. As far as tenants are concerned, a major form of subsidy is housing benefit (rent rebates and allowances, and payments to those receiving supplementary benefit) provided on a means-tested basis which is dealt with in chapter 2. This is the only subsidy available to tenants of private landlords. The cost of council housing to tenants is, however, also reduced by housing support grant from the exchequer and rate fund contribution from local authorities. The chief way in which owner occupiers are assisted is by a subsidy on mortgage interest payments. A large proportion of the costs of housing associations is met by housing association grant (and low income tenants are entitled to housing benefit).

*Public Sector Subsidies*

Exchequer subsidies have existed since 1919 and until 1972 they were usually paid as a fixed sum for 40 or 60 years for each house. The amount of contributions from the rates was (after 1957) at the discretion of local authorities. In most cases rate fund contributions were substantial and their relatively large size was the chief cause of the lower average rent levels in Scotland compared with England and Wales. It became increasingly clear that this system of subsidies was unsatisfactory in that their amount was related more to historical accident than differing local needs.

Public sector subsidies were radically altered by the Housing (Financial Provisions) (Scotland) Act, 1972. First, the existing exchequer subsidies were abolished and replaced by a range of new ones related to current levels of expenditure. Second, the amount of local rate fund contributions was fixed as a proportion of exchequer subsidies. Third, local authorities were obliged to charge rents which in total exactly met expenditure not covered by central and local subsidies. Fourth, a national rent rebate scheme was introduced. Previously not all local authorities had operated rebate schemes and the new one was on a more generous scale than most. Some aspects of the 1972 act, particularly the loss of local authority freedom to determine the level of rents (and mandatory annual rent increases during a transitional period) caused political controversy. A change of government led to the Housing Rents and

Subsidies (Scotland) Act, 1975. Exchequer contributions were modified and local powers to determine the level of rents were restored. But the 1975 act was only an interim measure. The green paper on Scottish housing reviewed the structure of subsidies and subsequently the Housing (Financial Provisions) (Scotland) Act, 1978 introduced housing support grant (HSG).

The aim of HSG is to provide a flexible subsidy which is related to local needs and capable of being adjusted as circumstances (and government policies) change. The 1978 act provides a framework for determining the level of grant rather than specifying the actual amounts; the system has some similarity with rate support grant. The level of grant is fixed annually by the Secretary of State in consultation with the Convention of Scottish Local Authorities and approved by the House of Commons. It was paid from the financial year 1979-80.

As well as subsidies for new building, HSG replaced other subsidies to council housing, for example for improvement, thus giving greater freedom to local authorities. The basis on which the grant is determined is as follows. A basic level of income is set which local authorities are deemed to provide from local resources, that is rents and rate fund contributions. Although the balance between these is decided by local authorities, the government announces an assumed rent increase each year. Councils which fail to implement such an increase, and therefore make a larger contribution from the rates than the government thinks appropriate, have been penalised by reduction of capital allocations. HSG covers 90 per cent of the difference between so-called 'assessed expenditure' (accepted as eligible by the government) and basic income.

The proportion of expenditure by local authorities falling within housing revenue accounts (relating to expenditure on the provision of council housing) met by exchequer subsidies increased from less than 30 per cent in the early 1970s to over 40 per cent in 1976-77 (Figure 5.2). It then decreased to some extent but a sharp fall began with the change of government in 1979. The policy of the Conservative government has been drastically to reduce the level of subsidies received by council tenants, except on a means-tested basis. In 1983-84 HSG was planned to meet only some ten per cent of expenditure, and 20 local authorities, covering about 40 per cent of council houses in Scotland, received none at all. If the policy of assuming rent increases greater than the rate of inflation is continued, more councils are likely to be excluded from HSG. The proportion of expenditure covered by rents before rebates rose from around one-half in the 1970s to about 70 per cent in 1983-84. The level of rate fund contributions varies widely depending on the political orientation of local authorities, and some do not make any.[8] As rents increase in real terms, however, more tenants become eligible for housing benefit. Taking into account housing benefit paid to recipients of supplementary benefit as well as through rent rebates, over half council tenants receive means-tested assistance.

Since 1974 the chief way in which housing associations have been

FIGURE 5.2 Housing Revenue Account: Sources of Income

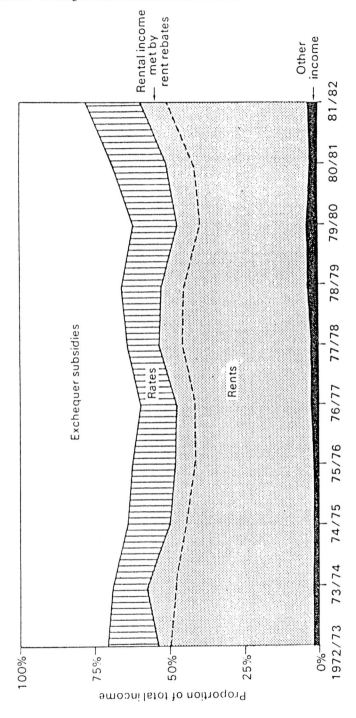

subsidised is through housing association grant (HAG) which meets a proportion (usually a very substantial one) of capital costs. The intention is that remaining debt together with maintenance costs can be covered by 'fair' rents. But under conditions of inflation HAG has proved to be an ill-conceived form of subsidy. Whereas some associations have required additional revenue deficit subsidy, over time, as rents rise and inflation erodes the real burden of debt, large surpluses could be achieved. The government has therefore taken steps to recoup HAG in these cases.

Another topic in the field of public sector housing finance is how local authority capital spending is controlled by central government. Councils cannot undertake capital expenditure without the consent of the Scottish Development Department (though permission to spend should not be confused with the provision of subsidies through HSG). Until recent years local housing authorities saw their role as being largely confined to building and managing council houses. Today, however, they are required to take a more comprehensive view of their responsibilities which have been extended to include the assessment of housing need within their areas and the ways in which it can best be met, whether by the public or private sectors. These responsibilities have been embodied in a system of housing plans which authorities have to submit to the Scottish Development Department. (Housing plans have similarities to housing investment programmes in England and Wales.)

The first housing plans were submitted in 1977 to cover a five year period and initially new ones had to be produced annually. Now, except in the case of Glasgow, new housing plans have to be prepared only every four years. In assessing housing needs factors taken into account include population trends and the condition of the housing stock. These needs may be met by new building or renovation and by the public sector or owner occupation, the desirable combination depending on local circumstances.

The system of housing plans is intended to give more freedom to local authorities to decide the details of their capital expenditure programmes. Instead of a number of separate capital allocations, covering improvement, new building, mortgage lending and so on, there are now only two expenditure blocks. One covers the public sector, including new building and improvement of council owned houses, and the other private sector improvement grants, house purchase loans and slum clearance. In making capital allocations the intention is to ensure that the resources which are available within the limits of public expenditure are deployed where they are most needed. The scope and approach of housing plans have varied a good deal depending, for example, on the size of local authorities and the character of their housing needs. Broadly, however, each housing plan is expected to include first, an analysis of local housing needs; second, a statement of objectives and policies (including the contributions to be made by the SSHA, other housing associations and owner occupation); and, third, a costed capital programme covering the following five years.

*Owner-Occupier Subsidies*

It is not easy to compare subsidies received by people in different tenures, owing to their very different form and to real problems of deciding precisely what should be included. Nevertheless, some broad comparisons can be made, particularly of the trend of subsidy levels over time. The sharp reduction in HSG to council housing has already been mentioned, and this has only been compensated for to a limited extent by increased expenditure on means-tested housing benefit. (In any case it is questionable how far this should be counted as a housing subsidy rather than an income support measure akin to social security.) In contrast subsidies to owner occupiers have not been reduced and they continue to rise in line with the house price inflation (though there are fluctuations reflecting interest rate changes). Whereas the capital debt on council housing (the servicing of which is on average about two thirds of recurrent costs) is only increased by new building or major improvements, mortgages get larger every time houses are resold at progressively higher prices.

A majority of owner occupiers are repaying mortgage loans and they receive substantial subsidies on the interest. Until 1983 this was in the form of income tax relief but it is now given mainly through equivalent exchequer payments to building societies or other lending agencies to reduce monthly charges. In effect this is an extension of option mortgages, which were designed to assist those who paid little tax. But higher rate tax payers still receive part of their relief through the previous system. As the exchequer payments might at some time in the future be counted as public expenditure, which tax reliefs are not, the high cost of subsidies to owner occupiers may come under greater political scrutiny. These subsidies are unrelated to need and are regressive in that the greatest benefit is received by the most affluent. They can afford the largest loans and as higher rate tax payers they receive the largest rate of subsidy. For example, someone paying tax at the highest rate (in 1983) of 60 per cent with a £30,000 mortgage (the maximum counting for subsidy) will receive six times the amount of subsidy as a more typical person paying tax at the basic rate of 30 per cent with a £10,000 mortgage. Furthermore, the favoured treatment of owner occupation encourages high expenditure on house purchase as an investment at the expense of investment elsewhere in the economy. Nevertheless, owner occupiers now constitute a majority of households in Britain and it would be politically extremely difficult for any government to alter their privileged position. In summary, subsidies to owner occupiers have grown so substantially larger than those to tenants that it is hard to see the situation as anything but grossly inequitable, while they have little economic or social justification.[9]

PROBLEMS OF COUNCIL HOUSING

The public sector has been seen as a solution to housing problems by making available good quality accommodation to people who otherwise would not have been able to obtain it. In terms of the conventional indicator of housing quality, the possession of basic amenities, the public sector is of uniformly high quality. Yet in reality some council housing is unsatisfactory and may be difficult to let. Increasingly, as sub-tolerable houses lacking amenities are dealt with, attention is being turned to the public sector. A variety of factors may make housing relatively less attractive, such as building type, location, state of repair and environment. Other things being equal, houses are likely to be preferred to flats (particularly those in large blocks), central to peripheral areas, modern to old-fashioned dwellings and residential to industrial surroundings. Some council housing is unsatisfactory by any standards but more would be considered acceptable in one area but not in another. A great deal depends on the alternatives which are available.

The acceptability of council housing is important when attention is widened from physical characteristics to the way in which it is used. Almost invariably unpopularity and difficulty in letting housing lead to a deprived and unstable population. Such estates tend to have a disproportionate number of larger families, high child densities and a concentration of 'difficult' tenants. These factors exacerbate and interact with the basic physical shortcomings of the housing itself: for example, blocks of flats do not provide a very satisfactory environment for children. A vicious circle of increasing unpopularity and population imbalance can be set up.

Attention is often drawn to grading of applicants according to their housekeeping standards or alleged 'dumping' by local authorities, but the preferences of applicants themselves are probably at least as important. In most areas applicants for council housing are permitted to choose where they will live. As a result the best housing tends to be pre-empted by applicants who are in a position to wait a substantial time for a vacancy. Those who require a council house as quickly as possible, usually because their existing accommodation is either very unsatisfactory or in danger of being lost altogether, are constrained to accept an offer in an unpopular area for which there is no waiting list. Such people are also likely to be disadvantaged in other ways as well: for example, to be large or single person families or simply to have low incomes.

It must be recognised that many of the problems which are found in less popular council estates are not really housing problems at all. The design and location of some council estates and the concentration of disadvantaged people through the operation of the allocation process simply make pre-existing problems worse. The availability of even the best housing solves only one problem of poverty. With the decline of the privately rented sector the poorest have increasingly been moving to council housing. A combination of policies is required in fields such as social security and employment as well as housing.

Action can, however, be taken in the housing field to alleviate some of the problems. Housing which is in a poor state of repair can be rehabilitated. In some cases buildings can be modified to make them less unsatisfactory.

Amenities such as shops and pubs can be provided in estates where they are absent. It should be borne in mind, however, that lack of amenities is only one cause of unpopularity and that providing them is unlikely of itself to transform the situation. But some housing will always be more popular and some less popular. As well as action to alter physical conditions, therefore, allocation policies need to be changed if the concentration of disadvantaged people and the restriction of their housing opportunities are to be substantially alleviated. Allocation procedures could give more emphasis to housing need as against waiting time in determining who obtains popular accommodation, as has been done by some local authorities such as Glasgow. More specifically, councils could endeavour to ensure that families with children as far as possible do not have to live off the ground and to reduce child densities where these are exceptionally high in any estate.[10]

After many years of growth when it has met the needs of a wide section of the Scottish population, the role of council housing may now be changing. The proportion of public sector houses in the total stock ceased to grow significantly in the late 1970s, and in 1981 sales exceeded completions for the first time so that the absolute number fell. This change is caused by two factors. First, under the impact of sharp reductions in public expenditure on housing there has been a decrease in the number of houses completed (Table 5.2). Second, there are council house sales.

Until recently there were relatively few sales of council houses in Scotland compared with south of the border, in part owing to the opposition of many local authorities. But the Tenants' Rights, Etc. (Scotland) Act, 1980, which was brought in by the new Conservative government, introduced a 'right to buy' for most tenants of three years' standing. The terms of purchase are very favourable with substantial discounts depending on length of residence and the right to a local authority mortgage. It is impossible to say how popular the right to buy will be in the long term, but in 1981 nearly 11,000 houses (including new towns and the SSHA) were sold, over one per cent of the public sector stock. The average discount on market price was about 44 per cent.

The property purchased was not typical of the total stock. Less than 1000 flats or maisonettes were sold, confirming previous research evidence that it is overwhelmingly houses with gardens in more popular estates which are bought. This is always likely to be the case, both because they are more attractive to potential owner occupiers, and because it tends to be longer established and better off tenants who live in them owing to the operation of the allocation and transfer systems. The distribution of sales throughout Scotland is also very uneven. Relatively few have been sold in industrial Clydeside or Dundee where council housing is dominant. In rural areas, however, applications are running at a very high level, over ten per cent of the stock in some cases. In these areas there is already only a limited supply of council houses, and once in the owner-occupied sector the high prices paid for holiday homes mean that they are likely to be out of the reach of local residents.

Council house purchase at a discount is obviously advantageous to the buyer, but is seems likely to be costly to the community as a whole. As well as diminishing the quality of the public sector (and in some rural areas going a substantial way towards eliminating it altogether), the cost in housing subsidies to the taxpayer will be increased. No serious commentator would now claim that sales will save public money. Nevertheless, the policy of the Conservative party, and this has not been effectively challenged by Labour, is that owner occupation is a superior form of tenure which should be encouraged at almost all costs. In the past owner occupation has expanded partly through the sale of privately rented houses but this source of supply is drying up. If in the future it is to expand at all rapidly, especially if the objective is that the proportion of owner-occupied houses in Scotland should approach anywhere near that south of the border, this can only be achieved with a substantial rate of sales.

The future role of the public and private sectors in Scotland is an important issue in housing policy. On the one hand, sales might fall away once the initial demand to buy has been met, and council housing may continue to provide for the majority of Scottish people. But, on the other, over a period of years owner occupation may substantially expand and leave a much smaller public sector to cater primarily for specific groups: the elderly, the handicapped, the single and the poor. Inevitably the housing chances of those who are economically unable to achieve owner occupation will be diminished. It is not so much that there is likely to be an absolute shortage of council houses (though this may happen in some areas) as that they will nearly all be in environmentally unattractive estates or in blocks of flats. The rehousing of families with children in houses with gardens, for example, would become more difficult.[11]

HOMELESSNESS

Homelessness is the most acute form of housing need. In numerical terms it is a relatively small problem but, for those directly affected, a very acute one. The provision made for homeless people raises the question of how far housing is a right, in the same way as education or health care, regardless of ability to pay for it. Important changes were made in provisions for the homeless by the Housing (Homeless Persons) Act, 1977 which came into force in Scotland in April 1978. It strengthened local authority responsibilities and transferred them from social work to housing departments. The change recognised the fact that homelessness is basically a housing problem.

Under the act an applicant has to be 'homeless or threatened with homelessness'. This means that the applicant, or anyone who normally lives with him or her as a member of the family, has no accommodation that he or she is entitled to occupy, or has accommodation but is unable to use it (for example because of a risk of violence). If a household is in 'priority need' the local authority must at least provide temporary accommodation. Priority need means that the applicant or a member of his or her household has dependent children; is pregnant; is vulnerable because of old age or mental or physical disability; is the victim of a fire, flood or other disaster; or has 'other special reasons' for being homeless.

Housing authorities can, however, declare an applicant to be 'intentionally homeless' if, in the words of the 1977 act, he (or she) 'deliberately does or fails to do anything in consequence of which he ceases to occupy accommodation . . . which it would have been reasonable for him to occupy'. This is the most controversial aspect of the legislation, and it has been used by some local authorities to classify all those in rent arrears as intentionally homeless, thereby evading a duty permanently to rehouse evicted families.

Finally, there is the question of whether a 'local connection' exists with the area in which an application is made. This is defined as having a job in the area, having lived there previously, or having family associations there. If an applicant does not have a local connection with the district to which he or she applies, and is in priority need and not intentionally homeless, the local authority is normally entitled to refer the case to another where there is a local connection. If none exists the first authority must rehouse the applicant.

In 1980/81, the last year for which figures are available at the time of writing, there were over 14,000 applications to local authorities, and in 58 per cent of cases accommodation was provided. About 12,000 applicants were assessed as being in priority need, the majority of them households with dependent children. These statistics had not changed dramatically during the three years that the 1977 act had been in force. The bulk of applicants were staying temporarily with parents, other relatives or friends or in lodgings. The most common reason for homelessness was that those with whom applicants were staying could no longer accommodate them. This, of course, is rarely an absolute inability and is one explanation why the extent of provision affects the apparent size of the problem. The absence or unacceptability of provision reduces the flow of applicants but increases what has been called 'hidden homelessness'.

Some six per cent of applicants were classified by local authorities as intentionally homeless, though this proportion varied widely between areas. The districts most vigilant to root out imposture, or possibly with the least deserving citizens, were Edinburgh (36 per cent intentionally homeless), Midlothian (31 per cent), Kirkcaldy (29 per cent), Inverness (27 per cent), and Aberdeen and West Lothian (26 per cent).

The act has undoubtedly improved provisions for homeless people. In particular, far less use is now being made of communal accommodation such as old poorhouses. But it has shortcomings. First, the act does little for the single homeless — men and women who usually have no contact with relatives and may have been discharged from residential accommodation such as mental hospitals — who are not specifically a priority need category. They have been largely dependent on voluntary organisations which have insufficient resources adequately to fill the gap left by local authorities.

Second, the provisions concerning intentional homelessness are being interpreted harshly by a few local authorities, and attempting to enforce rights through legal action can be both difficult and costly. Nevertheless, even had parliament wished to place rigid obligations on local authorities, it would have been difficult to administer legislation that allowed no local discretion in dealing with varied individual circumstances. Unfortunately councils sometimes use discretion in a way which is out of keeping with the spirit if not the letter of the act.

In many respects housing conditions in Scotland are better than at any time in the past, as long-standing problems of shortage, slums and substandard dwellings have been largely overcome. But new problems and inequalities are emerging. There is the increasing disrepair of otherwise good housing, and the extension of owner occupation may make this worse. There is difficult-to-let council housing which resulted from the urgency of dealing with appalling slums, with desperate post-war shortages and, less justifiably, from the mania for system-built flats in the late 1960s and early 1970s. There is the profligate expenditure of scarce resources on subsidising owner occupation while at the same time investment in the public sector is drastically reduced even where needs are acute. It is a fallacy to believe that there is any such thing as *the* housing problem, still less that it is capable of a once and for all solution. Rather, there will always be a changing agenda of problems and needs which require a flexible response from both central and local government. This is not to suggest that government should be all-powerful, but to recognise that, both in its own activities and in setting the framework within which individuals themselves act, it inevitably has a crucial role in housing policy.

*References*

1.  *Scottish Housing: A Consultative Document*, Cmnd. 6852, HMSO, 1977.
2.  *Report of the Royal Commission on the Housing of the Industrial Population of Scotland, Rural and Urban*, Cd. 8731, HMSO, 1917.
3.  See for example: M. Bowley, *Housing and the State*, Allen and Unwin, 1945; and D. Whitham, 'The First Sixty Years of Council Housing' in J. English (ed.), *The Future of Council Housing*, Croom Helm, 1982.
4.  Scottish Special Housing Association, *A Chronicle of Forty Years 1937-1977*, SSHA, 1977.
5.  Data on housing conditions are from: Scottish Development Department, *Scottish Housing Statistics*, HMSO (quarterly); *Scottish Housing: A Consultative Document*; and General Register Office, *Census Scotland 1981: Scottish Summary Bulletin*, GRO, 1981.
6.  Cmnd. 3598, HMSO, 1968.
7.  Scottish Development Department, *Housing Action Areas*, HMSO, 1980.
8.  C. Jones, 'Housing Support Grant' in *Public Sector Housing in Scotland: Some Current Issues*, Occasional Papers in Housing Administration No. 1, University of Stirling, 1983.
9.  A. Grey, N.P. Hepworth and J. Olding-Smee, *Housing Rents, Costs and Subsidies*, The Chartered Institute of Public Finance and Accountancy, (2nd edition) 1981.
10.  J. English, 'Access and Deprivation in Local Authority Housing' in C. Jones (ed.), *Urban Deprivation and the Inner City*, Croom Helm, 1979.
11.  J. English (ed.), *The Future of Council Housing*.

## FURTHER READING

J.B. Cullingworth, *Essays on Housing Policy*, Allen and Unwin, 1979.
An introduction to some issues in housing policy which pays a good deal of attention to Scotland.

D. Donnison and C. Ungerson, *Housing Policy*, Penguin, 1982.
An up-to-date overview of the field.

J. English (ed.), *The Future of Council Housing*, Croom Helm, 1982.
A survey of the present position of public sector housing and of prospects for the future.

*Roof*, Shelter, bi-monthly.
This magazine takes a fairly radical position on housing issues, but it includes very useful information on recent policy developments and often has material on Scotland.

*Scottish Housing Statistics*, HMSO, quarterly.
The main source of statistics on Scottish housing from the Scottish Development Department.

# 6

## *Personal Social Services*

The personal social services, which in Scotland are the responsibility of the regional social work departments, include domiciliary, residential and day care services as well as social work itself. Before discussing these services as they exist today, it may be useful to relate how unified social work departments came to be created at the end of the 1960s.

Three very different sources contributed to the evolution of the personal social services. First in time came the poor law, which finally bequeathed to local authorities (under the National Assistance Act, 1948) responsibility for the provision of welfare services for such groups as the elderly and the homeless. Second, the concern of private charitable organisations for the 'deserving poor' played a part in creating a number of semi-professional social workers. Finally, and perhaps most importantly, a number of groups of specialist workers were created, the result of legislation or of administrative decision, to respond to some specialised area of need. The origins of both probation work and medical social work ante-date the first world war, though their respective functions were conceived in ways very different from those of their present-day successors. The Children Act, 1948 required local authorities to set up specialist services for children who had been 'deprived of a normal home life'. In these early years of the welfare state the profession of psychiatric social worker also became more securely established; although the number of specialist workers involved was comparatively small their influence was considerable.[1]

The scale of these developments should not be overestimated. As recently as the late 1960's scarcely more than 100 professionally qualified social workers were in the employ of Scottish local authorities. In addition, the probation service in Scotland employed about 180 trained staff. Virtually all the work done by local authority welfare departments as legatees of the poor law was carried out by staff who lacked formal qualifications, as was a very substantial fraction of other personal social service activities.

But the qualified social workers in particular were not isolated from the mainstream of ideas and practice in their profession, and indeed made notable contributions to its development. During the late 1950s and early 1960s the most powerful trend in social work was the growing emphasis on those elements of theory and practice that were deemed to be common to all social work activities, irrespective of the particular client group to which they were directed or of the setting in which the work was done. Professional social work remained fragmented, carried out by small groups of specialists with circumscribed responsibilities and distinctive training; but increasingly the notion of common principles, methods and objectives in all work with individuals and families gained ground.[2] Professional training courses, especially those based in the universities, began to shift towards a new, 'generic' pattern. The move towards the recognition of generic principles in the organisation of social work practice, however, came about earlier in Scotland than in England, and in a curiously roundabout way.

## THE ESTABLISHMENT OF SOCIAL WORK DEPARTMENTS

The establishment in 1961 of the Kilbrandon Committee on Children and Young Persons is described elsewhere (see chapter 7) as are the main features of the committee's report. The report[3] was little concerned with theoretical principles of delinquency and penology or with more general problems of the social services. It was limited almost exclusively to setting out in some detail an original set of proposals for dealing with children 'in need of compulsory measures of care'. A key feature of these plans was the establishment in each major local authority of a lay children's panel which would reach decisions on appropriate measure of care, while responsibility for providing supportive social services to the new panels was to be in the hands of a group of specialist social workers attached to the local authority education department. The committee considered the suggestion put to it by some witnesses that the social work service for children and their families ought to be incorporated in a comprehensive welfare and social service agency. They rejected the proposal, principally because it fell outside their terms of reference, but possibly also because they were not wholly convinced of its viability. But within a couple of years a white paper[4] had, in a sense, reversed the priorities. The government was aware, not only of the growing sense of unity among social workers, but also of the many criticisms that had been expressed — though not specifically in a Scottish context — of the wasteful and possibly even harmful effects of dividing responsibility for family care between different specialists. They were also conscious of the absence of preventive work when existing personal social services were geared to dealing with crisis and breakdown. It was therefore argued that, instead of implementing the Kilbrandon proposals in isolation the opportunity should be taken to re-shape quite fundamentally the personal social services of Scottish local authorities. The comprehensive social work departments that would emerge from these changes would take on responsibility for the provision of supportive services to the proposed children's panels, together with a wide range of other duties that had previously been carried out separately by children's departments, welfare departments, public health departments and the probation service.

The movement towards unification of the personal social services was now considerably ahead of that in England and Wales, where consideration of the future of the juvenile courts had not been linked up with any other issues. By the end of 1965, when the Seebohm Committee was appointed in England, the Secretary of State for Scotland had already made clear his commitment to a new comprehensive social work service. The white paper *Social Work and the Community*, published in 1966, is the fullest statement available of the government's intentions. Since the Social Work (Scotland) Act, 1968, which gave legislative expression to almost all of these proposals, consists principally of the specifications of formal structures, powers and duties, and does not incorporate any explicit statements of policy objectives, the white paper is of importance as a reference document.

The defects of the current organisation of local authority social work and welfare services were seen in the white paper as arising from their piecemeal development in response to 'the identification at different times of certain groups of people who needed social help'. But the inter-relatedness of human problems, the body of expertise common to all social workers, the shortage of trained and experienced staff and the bewildering array of agencies all point to one conclusion: 'the local authority services designed to provide community care and support, whether for children, the handicapped, the mentally and physically ill or the aged, should be brought within a single organisation'.[5] There are sensible if superficial discussions of the importance of co-operation between the proposed new social work department and other statutory and voluntary agencies and of the value of preventive work. The areas of responsibility of the new departments are briefly summarised. The main increase in cost, it is concluded, would be due to the appointment of directors of social work and some regrading of other posts, balanced by savings resulting from more efficient deployment of staff. It is perhaps unfortunate that the government did not commission some background studies. We find a complete lack of statistical information, an absence of even the simplest research, and no sign of any analysis either of the social and economic context or of possible lines of future development.

The Social Work (Scotland) Act, 1968 introduced few significant alterations in the principles laid down in the white paper. Perhaps the most important change was the decision to increase the number of social work departments. The original intention had been for the then counties and four cities to form the new social work authorities. Political pressure rather than considerations of principle dictated the inclusion of the large burghs, bringing the number of the new departments to 50, some of them smaller in population than a Glasgow housing estate. A specialist branch, the Social Work Services Group, had been established within the Scottish Education Department in the previous year. The new social work departments came into being in November 1969, although the implementation of Part III of the act (that is the operation of the children's hearings system) was delayed until April 1971.

The principal objective of the new departments was expressed in somewhat global terms in section 12(1) of the act: 'to promote social welfare by making available advice, guidance and assistance on such a scale as may be appropriate for their area'. The social work departments were made responsible for social work in the sense of personal, professional involvement with individuals and families with problems ('fieldwork'), and also for a wide range of other services. These include residential services, of which homes for children deprived of a normal family life and homes for old people unable to live on their own in the community account for the greater part; day-care services, such as day nurseries and special centres for disabled or mentally disordered people; and domiciliary services, such as the provision of home helps and 'meals on wheels' schemes. Few qualified social workers were employed outside the fieldwork services, although the other provisions involved substantial staffs and large numbers of clients. One notable feature of the new act was the duty it gave to social work departments (under section 12) to provide assistance in cash. Cash payments had previously been permitted under child care legislation, but now became more widely applicable as one of the ways in which social welfare might be promoted. It is interesting to note that neither the general power to promote social welfare nor the general power to give financial help is provided for in the English legislation.

EARLY PROBLEMS OF THE NEW DEPARTMENTS

One early but recurrent problem was that of an unforeseen level of demand for personal social services. The act had been seen — in spite of the generous terminology of section 12 — as essentially a tidying-up operation, providing a new service that would cater more efficiently for the existing pattern of needs at little additional cost. Not for the first time in the history of welfare legislation, little serious consideration was given to the possibility that the very creation of a new service might itself help to influence the way in which people thought about their problems and the demands they would consequently make on the service. Behind the assumption that the new departments would discharge responsibilities not very different from the sum-total of those of the former specialised ones that they replaced lay the notion of needs and demands as somehow existing in fixed quantities within the community. In fact, the demand for social services is of course extremely elastic, since the concept of need is largely a subjective one and very variable over time. What at any given time people think of as needs justifying a demand for services depends on a complex state of public awareness, which is itself in part influenced by the current state of professional opinion and the nature of service provision.

It was certainly the case that, in the urban-industrial districts in particular, the new service brought to light areas of need not previously recognised, which created very heavy demands. Much of the new demand stemmed from problems in which financial and environmental factors played a large part. Although the local authorities quickly began to improve their staffing levels, the latter always seemed to fall short of the level of demand. There was no easy way of drawing boundaries and excluding certain areas of work. The almost inevitable consequence was a heavy emphasis on work in crisis situations as they arose, rather than the carefully planned long-term preventive work to which the white paper had looked forward.

The white paper had also stated the case for close collaboration between the social work department and other statutory agencies, and had seen the social work director functioning as an adviser on social matters to housing and planning authorities. Whether social work training and experience provide the ideal foundation for such consultative functions is debatable; but in any case there was nothing in the tradition of local government to facilitate such trans-departmental alliances. In practice, in most areas, separate departments pursued their separate and sometimes conflicting ways.

The introduction of children's hearings in 1971 involved important new responsibilities for social workers, who were required to provide social background reports for reporters and panel members and to undertake the supervision of those youngsters in respect of whom such an order was made at a hearing. The priority necessarily accorded to these statutory responsibilities inevitably reduced still further the scope for that careful assessment and long-term intensive work with vulnerable individuals and families that had been seen as a major objective of the unification of personal social services.

The creation of unified departments imposed heavy demands on their staff, who were expected to lose old allegiances, to overcome old inter-departmental suspicions, and to adapt their specialised skills to the needs of client groups with which they were not familiar. To create a new sense of unity and cohesiveness was a challenge to which not all social work directors could respond equally effectively. In the end the problem was not so much solved as swamped, as the rising demand for new staff resources led to enlarged training programmes and an influx of young professionals into the beleaguered departments.

A new dimension of uncertainty was added when it became clear that existing social work departments were soon to be amalgamated as a consequence of the reorganisation of local government in the early 1970s (see chapter 1). The location of social work was seriously debated but the arguments of those who saw it as essentially a community-based service, responsive to local needs, and therefore more appropriately defined as a district responsibility, were outweighed by the claim that the amalgamation of resources at the regional level would make for a more comprehensive range of provision and access to more high-powered specialist services. But in addition to the regions the three all-purpose islands authorities also became responsible for social work. Thus within five years of coming into existence 50 social work departments were reduced to twelve.

PRESENT SCALE AND STRUCTURE

Both before and after local government reorganisation the new social work departments grew rapidly. The recurrent demands for additional staff were met to a substantial extent — at least as far as field social workers were concerned — by the creation of new training courses and the expansion of existing ones. The work of the Central Council for Education and Training in Social Work, established for the whole of the United Kingdom in 1971, gave a powerful impetus to the promotion of training. The number of staff (on a whole-time equivalent basis) employed by social work departments almost doubled between 1971 and 1981, but the proportion of different kinds changed little except for a marked increase in that of fieldwork staff (Table 6.1). The overall rate of growth was, however, by no means consistent throughout the decade. During the first three years of the period the increase in staff numbers ran at about twelve per cent per annum, but between 1974 and 1979 annual growth was on average about seven per cent (though that for fieldwork staff was in excess of ten per cent per annum). Even in 1980, when there was strong central government pressure on local authorities to restrict expenditure, expansion continued though at a very much reduced rate. It was only in 1981 that the total staff complement of local authority social work departments actually fell (by 600). This smaller overall total conceals the fact that some categories of staff continued to grow during the year (for example, main grade field social workers from 1712 to 1780); the principal cause of the reduction was a further substantial cut in the number of home helps.

The organisation and professional responsibilities of the various staff groups are considered later in this chapter. Before examining these it may be useful to review briefly the current staffing pattern of social work authorities.[6]

TABLE 6.1
Staff of Social Work Departments 1971 and 1981

| Grade and location | 1971 Number* | % | | | 1981 Number* | % | | |
|---|---|---|---|---|---|---|---|---|
| Headquarters and fieldwork staff | 8,294 | (56) | | | 15,234 | (54) | | |
| Managerial and administrative | | | 307 | (2) | | | 661 | (2) |
| Fieldwork | | | 1,168 | (8) | | | 3,290 | (12) |
| Home Care | | | 5,828 | (39) | | | 9,230 | (33) |
| Clerical and domestic, etc. | | | 991 | (7) | | | 2,053 | (7) |
| Staff in day centres | 1,512 | (10) | | | 2,720 | (10) | | |
| Staff in residential establishments | 5,132 | (35) | | | 9,711 | ( 35) | | |
| Staff on secondment | — | | | | 384 | (1) | | |
| Total | 14,938 | (100) | | | 28,049 | (100) | | |

*Whole-time equivalents.

Source: Social Work Services Group, *Staff of Scottish Social Work Departments 1981 (SWSG Statistical Bulletin)*, SWSG, 1982

It is important to bear in mind that although social work gives its name to the departments concerned (unlike England and Wales, where the term 'social services' is used), social workers in the strict sense account for only a relatively small fraction of the total staff complement. The 'practitioner' grades (main grade and senior social workers) amount to less than ten per cent of all staff — perhaps just ten per cent if unqualified social work assistants are also included. The category 'fieldwork staff' also includes community workers and welfare rights officers — whose responsibilities many would see as an integral part of social work practice — as well as occupational therapists, whose profession is generally classified as supplementary to medicine.

The personal social services do not give the impression of being top-heavy with managerial and administrative staff; indeed, it could be argued that in some respects a more substantial investment in the forward planning and development of services would be beneficial. For example, the 'managerial and administrative' total includes all staff responsible for research and training. These amount to less than 100 workers: a small force, if one bears in mind the complex and constantly changing problems that the personal social services are obliged to confront, the prevailing uncertainty about the effectiveness of various forms of service provision, and the large numbers of wholly untrained staff, particularly in the residential sector.

Leaving training implications to one side, however, it is important to recognise not merely that social workers (in the sense of those who hold the Certificate of Qualification in Social Work or its equivalent) form only a small proportion of social work department staff, but that those with formal qualifications of any kind are very much in the minority. If qualified social workers, occupational therapists, teachers and nurses are added together, they amount to only about one quarter of the work force. Home helps are by far the largest single group, and to these may be added domestic workers in day centres and residential establishments, and unqualified care staff in both, as well as secretarial and clerical staff.

The Scottish personal social services on their present scale are obviously a far cry from the modest redeployment proposed in the mid-1960s. They employ more than 40,000 people (well over half of them on a part-time basis), control well over 300 residential establishments and about 250 day centres. For public resources of this scale to be deployed with even a minimum of effectiveness or accountability, it is essential to have formal structures which allow for the formulation of broad policies and their implementation as well as for the oversight of more or less routine activities. Since the personal social services are a responsibility of local government, both political and administrative processes must be involved.

Each regional and island authority is required by the 1968 act to appoint a social work committee, and in principle it is that committee that has the ultimate responsibility for the oversight of the authority's social work services. In practice, as is the case throughout local government, the position is a good deal more complex.[7] The elected members of local authorities almost always have other occupations or interests, and very rarely have either the time or the detailed knowledge that would be necessary if they wished to familiarise themselves with the workings of a complex and many-sided service. Inevitably, committee members are heavily dependent on the director of social work and his senior colleagues for a regular appreciation of current trends and emerging problems. It is after all the director and his staff who largely shape the agenda of committee meetings and prepare the papers that present committee members with policy choices. In keeping with the strong tradition of professionalism among local authority principal officers, the director of social work maintains a high degree of autonomy in the management of the service. The committee tends therefore to be concerned with broad questions of staffing levels and budgetary requirements, and with major policy decisions such as a shift away from residential child care. There are some important exceptions to the general dissociation of social work committees from the specifics of practice. Most noticeable is the rapid response of elected members to unfavourable publicity. If, for example, there are allegations in the press of malpractice in any of the local authority's own establishments, or if the death or serious injury of a child at the hand of his parents brings out the suggestion that this might have been prevented by closer supervision or more rapid intervention by a social worker, elected members tend to be galvanised into action. Searching enquiries are set in train and new guidelines are rapidly drafted, but the wider implications of such events for management and the maintenance of professional standards often go unstudied.

Another and more positive type of exception is that exemplified by the creation in Strathclyde Region of a series of working groups made up jointly of social work committee members and senior departmental staff. These groups have tended to concentrate on the problems of client groups whose needs are admitted to have been inadequately met (for example alcoholics or the mentally handicapped). Initiated at least in part as a means of conveying to elected members a deeper sense of specific social problems, these groups have with few exceptions generated considerable enthusiasm and produced reports containing many practical recommendations for the improvement of services. In some instances 'monitoring groups' have been set up to check and report on the implementation of recommended changes.

Beneath the political level, the pattern for management and delivery of personal social services depends on considerations of scale; both the size of the population and the terrain served have administrative implications. The regions with large concentrations of population and large social work departments need fairly complex management structures. On the other hand, a region such as Highland, with a population no bigger than that of Dundee but covering an area as large as Strathclyde and Grampian combined, faces special organisational problems in ensuring the delivery of personal social services. While recognising therefore that it is difficult to generalise about the structure of Scottish social work departments, we may say that the key unit in the delivery of field services is the area office.

Differences in pattern arise from regional policy, historical accident and population density, but most area offices serve populations of between 30,000 and 60,000. The area officer who is in overall charge is in his turn accountable to higher authority within the regional department; the different forms that this can take will be considered later in the chapter. In a typical area office there may be a dozen or so qualified social workers, organised into two teams each with a senior worker and one or two social work assistants; a small group of occupational therapists and assistants; and a home help organiser and a fairly large team of home helps. Depending on regional preferences, area offices may also provide working bases for community workers and welfare rights officers. And, of course, in order to function with even minimal efficiency, an area office will need some provision for typing letters, maintaining records, taking incoming telephone calls and receiving members of the public.

There are several different ways of deploying social work services for the population of a particular district. The most common practice is for the district to be divided into a number of areas, each of which is served by its own team. In recent years there has been increasing interest (though perhaps to a greater extent in England than in Scotland) in the reduction of an area office's territory to several small 'patches', with a very small sub-team of social workers assigned to each.[8] It has been claimed that the 'patch' method enables the professional workers to understand their territory intimately, and puts them in a better position to mobilise local resources and make more effective use of volunteers and of less highly trained staff. Like most innovations in social work, the method is forcefully advocated by some and sharply criticised by others, without the benefit of much objective research evidence concerning its advantages and shortcomings. One might speculate that the patch approach is most effective in areas characterised by a strong sense of community identity, long-established families and well developed informal supportive networks, and may be less appropriate in districts where there is a good deal of population turnover and where there are few social bonds between households.

There is too a professional dimension to be considered. If a particular district is to be served by two or three social workers, they will need to have a high degree of general professional competence. In a large team there may be opportunities for individual social workers to develop some degree of specialisation in the use of a particular social work method or in work with a particular client group, while in a very small team the concept of the multi-purpose social worker is carried to an extreme. Nevertheless, the difference is of degree, for it is very unusual anywhere to find social workers in area teams with clearly defined and formally recognised specialist roles.

In a number of offices, however, there is to be found an interesting variant which cuts across both the traditional specialist divisions and the dif-ferentiation by geographical boundaries. This is the use of an 'intake team' and a 'long-term team'. The former deals with all new referrals and retains cases which appear to be capable of being carried through within perhaps three months. The long-term team takes over cases where there is an initial expectation of protracted work — including those (for example, supervision orders made by children's hearings) where there is a statutory obligation that will continue for a longer period — and those which, whatever the forecast when contact was first made, turned out in practice to require social work involvement over a considerable period. In addition to statutory cases, a long-term team would inevitably have on its books a considerable number of families with multiple problems and complex needs.

The area office is an extremely important unit in the structure of the social work department, and the social worker in charge has both a very influential management role and some direct professional responsibilities, although not having his or her own caseload. It normally falls to the area officer to decide, for example, when to call a case conference in cases of suspected child abuse, and to chair the proceedings when one is convened. Much of what the social work department provides, however, is not generally organised through area teams. Residential services are usually controlled from departmental headquarters, or, in the case of the larger regions, by a unit somewhere between the area office and regional headquarters. The same generally applies to day care services, though it is by no means unknown for some to be area-based.

As was pointed out above, social work authorities in Scotland vary considerably in the size of population and area served, so that there are differences in their management structures. In a small region the area officers may be directly responsible to the director of social work, while at the other extreme Strathclyde region is made up of five divisions which in their turn are broken down into more than 20 districts and into more than 60 areas. District managers in Strathclyde have a considerable measure of operational autonomy, including responsibility for residential as well as community services. There has for some years been discussion about the possibility of eliminating the divisional layer in Strathclyde, thus creating a 'flatter' management structure with district managers being directly accountable to the regional directorate. There are certainly good arguments in favour of reducing the number of links in the management chain; and although it is difficult for really small social work authorities to provide a comprehensive range of services, there is no reason to assume that quality improves indefinitely as size increases.

To most front-line practitioners, especially in large and organisationally complex authorities, 'management' seems remote and largely irrelevant. Such judgements, though understandable, should not be taken at their face value. By no means all styles of management are equally constructive or imaginative, but given the scale of public resources involved and the vulnerability of most social work clients there are essential roles for management in ensuring accountability, monitoring the implementation of major policy decisions and providing specialist advice. The problem of how best to draw upon specialist knowledge and skills is a serious one in a service where the great majority of practitioners have been trained as generalists. For many client groups, effective social work intervention may require access to practice skills and specialised knowledge of a kind not acquired without advanced training and substantial experience in a particular field of work. It is usual therefore for the social work department to include in its staff a small group of specialist advisers — for example, in mental health or in social work with offenders — but because they tend to be few in number and located at headquarters it is easy for them to become heavily involved in providing policy guidance to directors and committees at the expense of consultation and advice to practitioners.

THE WORK OF THE PERSONAL SOCIAL SERVICES

If we want to know how many people, in the course of a year, are treated in hospital because of appendicitis or an inflamed gall bladder, the necessary information is not difficult to obtain. Published national statistics are readily available and do not on the whole present major problems of interpretation. If, however, we ask questions about the size and make-up of the clientele of social work departments we immediately run into difficulties. Some of these arise from the fact that maintaining detailed records and compiling statistical returns are not always highly valued activities in social work departments. The Social Work Services Group has struggled for several years to implement a comprehensive system of statistical information and, although many of the early difficulties have been overcome, there are still significant gaps. But with the best will in the world problems of definition and classification still have to be faced, especially as many contacts between members of the public and social work offices are of a very short-lived nature. On the whole we would expect to find statistically firmer information about residential services and about areas of work where the local authorities have statutory responsibilities (for example, children in care) than about the generality of personal social services provided in the community. Bearing in mind then the limitation of existing information, we turn to review some of the major aspects of the work of the personal social services.

*Residential Care*

The residential sector of the local authority social work departments is both large in scale and of considerable importance, and the demands made upon it are changing rapidly. As far as staffing is concerned it involves nearly 10,000 people throughout Scotland. Residential care for children who are permanently or temporarily deprived of a normal home life is a significant component of this work. About 170 children's homes are provided, with an increasing tendency towards smaller units; the average number of places in each is now about 15. The occupancy rate is around 80 per cent, so on any one day there will be about 2000 children in residence. Local authorities also operate a number of residential assessment centres, mainly for children referred through the hearings system. These provide several hundred places, and deal with about 3000 short-term admissions each year. The ordinary children's homes also have a high proportion of short-term and medium-term admissions; more than 70 per cent of those discharged have been in residence for less than six months.

Local authorities, however, do not take direct responsibility for the whole of residential child care; voluntary organisations such as Barnardo's and Quarriers' Homes currently have about 1200 children in their care, nearly all of whom are maintained with the financial support of the local authorities. But it is noticeable that while the total number of children in residential care in Scotland has been falling steadily since 1976, the reduction has been much more marked in the registered voluntary homes than in those directly controlled by local authorities. Changes in social attitudes and in child care policies, discussed later in this chapter, have led to reductions in the demand for residential places, and the local authority social work departments have preferred to see empty beds in voluntary homes than in their own.

While the number of children in residential care has been decreasing, this has not been the case at the opposite end of the age scale. The problems of the growing elderly population are discussed in detail in chapter 10. It may be sufficient to note here that local authority homes for the elderly deal with more than 4000 admissions a year. These are old people who cannot satisfactorily look after themselves or be looked after in the community, but whose condition is supposed not to warrant hospital admission; at any given time we would expect to find between 8000 and 9000 old people living in local authority homes in Scotland. There are also nearly 200 registered voluntary homes for the elderly, many of them run by the churches, the clients of which account for more than one-third of all old people in residential care. Unlike the other services of the local authority, residential care operates on a round-the-clock basis. Its potential impact on the quality of life of its clients is therefore very great, and it is perhaps the more surprising that it employs such a low proportion of qualified staff.[9] We should remember also that although there are now fewer children in residential care, the proportion with emotional or behavioural problems is high. It would of course be absurd to suppose that all or even most of the staff of residential homes need to have formal qualifications, but it is a little disturbing to note that approximately one in three of the officers in charge of both children's homes and old people's homes, and about one half of their deputies have no professional qualifications of any kind. While nursing qualifications are fairly common, social work qualifications are distinctly unusual. There is little doubt that the emphasis on training for field social work staff has been accompanied until very recently by a neglect of the training needs of the residential services.

*Services for Children*

Child care services must figure prominently in any account of the personal social services. The residential provision referred to above is of course a significant component of child care, though most social workers would hold to the view that taking a child into residential care should generally be thought of as a last resort. A considerable amount of skilled social work activity is therefore devoted to trying to prevent family breakdown with a consequent need for children to be taken into care; child care in this preventive sense thus becomes inseparable from casework with families, and concern for their housing and financial needs. Even when a residential solution becomes unavoidable, it would generally be hoped that this will be temporary rather than permanent, and a period of intensive work with the parents may be required in the hope of making it possible for the child to return home. Because of the prevailing high rates of marital breakdown and divorce, and because unmarried mothers more often than in the past prefer to bring up their own children, single parent families have become increasingly common. They often require a good deal of help of many kinds, though it would be optimistic to assume that these needs are always met.[10]

In the most extreme cases children may need to be actively protected from one or both of their parents. There has in recent years been an intense development of interest in what is now usually referred to, euphemistically, as 'non-accidental injury'. It has come to be accepted, very painfully and reluctantly, that each year a number of children die and very many more are injured at the hands of their parents. Social work departments have powers to intervene in cases where it is clear that children are seriously at risk, and to take them compulsorily into care. Such cases can be referred to the reporter to the children's panel and brought before a children's hearing. For social work management the problem of child abuse is extremely sensitive politically, and there is a tendency to seek safety in laying down elaborate procedural arrangements. But for social workers this may require very complex professional judgements and sometimes genuine moral dilemmas. This area of work also requires the sharing of information between several agencies — the social work department, health visitors, general practitioners, hospital specialists, the police and voluntary bodies — and the co-ordination of decision-making.[11]

Between 1500 and 2000 adoption orders are made each year by the Scottish courts, and in a large proportion of cases important responsibilities fall to the social work department. Investigating applications from prospective adoptive parents, and handling the sensitive relationship that develops when a natural mother is plagued by doubts about whether it is right to part with her child, demand both human understanding and professional expertise. In recent years there has been a rapid growth of interest in finding 'new families' for children who have been in residential care. Making suitable arrangements for older or 'hard to place' children — often with physical or mental handicaps — is a complex professional task. In this field, as in many aspects of child care, Barnardo's have been pioneers.

## Social Work and Children's Hearings

The children's hearings system is the subject of chapter 7, but here our concern is specifically with the social work contribution to it. Scotland is unusual in having a juvenile justice system that is controlled by social work legislation. Indeed, as has been explained, the proposal to reorganise Scottish social work services on the lines with which we are now familiar was originally a by-product of the Kilbrandon plan for the replacement of the juvenile courts by a system of children's hearings. Since the latter have as their goal the promotion of the interests of the children who appear before them, and since they deal equally with children in need of care and protection as with those who have committed offences, it would be perfectly justifiable to discuss this aspect of social work practice under the heading of services for children rather than in the context of the justice system. However, it would by hypocritical to pretend that children's hearings have no connection with law enforcement; children who make their appearance there do so under compulsion, and the decisions reached by panel members carry legal force. They are not interesting suggestions for the children and their parents to accept or reject as they think fit.

Social workers have a number of extremely significant responsibilities in relation to young offenders. When such children are brought to the notice of the reporter he will usually ask the social work department to provide a preliminary social background report; we know from research findings that these reports have an important influence on the reporter when he decides whether or not to bring a given child before a hearing. If the reporter decides that the child does indeed appear to be in need of compulsory measures of care, either the same or a new, fuller social background report will be provided for the guidance of the panel members, generally with a recommendation about the disposal of the case. These reports in their turn help to shape discussion in the hearing and also have a good deal of influence on the outcome.

When that outcome is a supervision requirement (as is more often than not the case) social workers are given a central role. The great majority of such supervision orders allow the child to continue to live at home, but social workers may also be required to maintain contact with the minority of young people who are required to spend perhaps a year in a List D school. A supervision requirement differs in many ways from a probation order, although the two are often confused. Essentially it is an opportunity for a young person to form a relationship of trust with a social worker; and for the latter to use that relationship to help bring about greater self-awareness, and a move towards more mature attitudes and more responsible behaviour. There has in the last few years been a marked interest in developing programmes for young offenders which are somehow more exacting than supervision alone but do not involve removal from home. Many social work departments and voluntary agencies have begun to construct schemes of 'intermediate treatment', as it has come to be called, always involving group activity and ranging from discussion and drama to camping and climbing.[12]

## Social Work and the Adult Offender

Social work connections with the sheriff courts are more limited than with children's hearings. When probation orders are made it falls to the social work departments to carry them out, but such disposals account for only a very small fraction of sheriff court cases. Some sheriffs regret the demise of a specialised probation service and are reluctant to involve social workers in duties that many of the latter find uncongenial. The preparation of reports for the courts is, however, a large-scale activity, mainly because the Criminal Justice (Scotland) Act, 1980 requires the courts to obtain reports about young adult offenders (that is under the age of 21) in order to decide whether any method other than detention is appropriate, as well as about older offenders who have not previously been sentenced to imprisonment or detention.[13]

In the search for alternatives to imprisonment, the concept of the community service order has attracted widespread interest. Offenders — usually young adults — may be required to spend a fixed number of hours on some practical, socially constructive task. Several pilot schemes have been established in Scotland. The supervision of community service orders falls to the social work department, and the staff undertaking this work generally specialise in it.

One of the more neglected areas of social work practice is the after-care of discharged prisoners. Once the responsibility of the probation service, it is perhaps a field of work that has suffered more than most from the elimination of a corps of specialists. It is an area of practice with even more than the customary level of disappointment and frustration, and it is not altogether surprising that it receives little priority. Useful work is done by a voluntary body, the Scottish Association for the Care and Rehabilitation of Offenders, though inevitably its scale of operation is comparatively small.

## Health-Related Social Services

Medical social workers (or almoners as they were originally called) began to be appointed to the staffs of major hospitals before the 1914 war. They were at first largely concerned with the assessment of patients' means, but they became increasingly involved with a wide range of social and domestic problems associated with illness — exclusively so after the creation of the national health service. For some years social work within the NHS remained separate from the local authority services, and when the latter assumed responsibility in 1975 there was some anxiety that the hospital-based practitioners would all be absorbed into area teams. In fact they have generally retained a high degree of independence, working with varying degrees of co-operation with the area offices and for the most part having their closest links with the medical and surgical consultants.

One area of social work which many writers believe to have considerable potential but which has not been very highly developed is in health centres. A number of studies have indicated that social workers attached to primary care teams do more than provide a valuable ancillary service for general practitioners; they build up caseloads of individuals with often substantial personal and family problems who are not known to the area social work services and would be unlikely to approach them.[14] There are currently about 20 social workers employed in association with general practice teams in Scotland, compared with 450 working in general and psychiatric hospitals.

Not all patients leave hospital cured. Many have varying degrees of disability, and usually become the responsibility of the local area social work office rather than of the hospital-based service. The responsibilities of local authorities for people with long-term handicap were strengthened by the Chronically Sick and Disabled Persons Act, 1970, and the Chronically Sick and Disabled Persons (Scotland) Act, 1972. Within the limits of available financial resources, social work departments can meet the cost of various adaptations in the home and provide aids to daily living (from handrails to ramps for wheelchairs) as well as pay for telephone installations. The assessment of clients for 'aids and adaptations' is essentially the responsibility of occupational therapists and their aides, with social workers being drawn in only when there seem to be serious housing, financial or domestic problems. Some social workers have become particularly knowledgeable about the complex rules governing the various types of benefits to which disabled people may be entitled.[15]

The role of the personal social services in provision for the mentally ill and the mentally handicapped is discussed more fully in chapter 4. Here we may note that although the slower rate of run down in hospital provision for these client groups in Scotland than in England might have been expected to provide a better opportunity for a compensating build-up of community services, this was not in fact what happened. The development of community-based mental health and mental handicap services has in reality been extremely slow; it was not until 1981, for example, that an attempt was made to launch the first multi-disciplinary service in Glasgow for severely mentally handicapped children and their families, or that the first hostel for discharged psychiatric patients was opened. Until very recently social work departments had little to offer either the mentally ill or the mentally handicapped, whether as alternatives to institutional care, or by way of supportive services for those leaving hospitals or other residential institutions with some degree of residual disability.

*Other Aspects of Social Work Practice*

Elderly people make up a substantial proportion of the clientele of social work departments, principally when they are isolated, frail or disabled. Residential provision by local authorities has already been mentioned; in addition they are major beneficiaries of the home help service, of various day care services and of the community occupational therapy service. It must be said that they are not the favourite client group of many social workers, who perhaps tend to see them — erroneously — as offering only limited opportunities for achieving significant change. It is striking that when elderly clients become involved with area teams, they are generally allocated to untrained social work assistants.

There remains an area of work which is substantial, inevitably poorly defined, and overlapping in varying degrees with the other categories outlined above. It is made up of the miscellaneous requests for advice and assistance that come the way of the social work departments. Some of these are misdirected and need only to be re-routed to another agency (for example, the local Department of Health and Social Security office). Others require information or advice, or a straightforward form of help which need not involve any long-term relationship. In other cases, however, the problem may turn out to be complex; it may involve, for instance, negotiations with housing departments or public utilities to stave off eviction or the withdrawal of fuel supplies, some direct financial help in meeting arrears, and, it may be hoped, the beginning of rather more protracted professional work with the client in the hope of preventing similar crises in the future. Just how frequently the various client groups figure in the collective caseload of local authority social work, what is the time-scale of the services provided in response to their needs, and what proportions of available staff resources are absorbed by each group, are questions that cannot be answered until better statistical information becomes available. Still further questions about comprehensiveness of coverage and about the consequences of social work intervention must remain unanswered until major research studies are undertaken.

*Community Work*

Most of the activities of the social work departments reviewed in this chapter have involved the provision of personal services, whether simple or complex, to individual clients or to families. The professional activities usually brought together under the heading of 'community work' do not conform to this pattern or indeed to the general public image of social work, and therefore merit some special comment. The community worker's focus of interest is most commonly the neighbourhood, with the object of encouraging residents to identify their collective problems and to try and find ways of resolving them. Most community workers — of whom there are now about 100 employed in Scottish social work departments — are in either run-down inner city areas or deprived council housing schemes. Environmental, economic and personal problems tend to be widespread in these areas and there is little natural sense of interdependence and community identity. Around 1970 community work attracted a number of people with unrealistic, at times almost messianic, expectations of achieving far-reaching changes in the social order. The accumulation of experience, sometimes painful, has made clear the limitations of what can be achieved at the local level, but has also drawn attention to the possibility of bringing about comparatively modest but significant advances in community development. The skills and persistence required are considerable. Although community workers and 'traditional' caseworkers have often seen their respective priorities as polarised, there are in fact some interesting parallels between their objectives. Both aim to help their clients — whether individuals or community groups — to attain greater insight into the nature of their problems and to mobilise their resources so as to deal more effectively with them. In community work, this commonly involves patient discussion and supportive work with local groups (such as tenants' associations) to initiate campaigns, for example for housing or environmental improvements or to establish community industries. While it would be absurd to suppose that most of the problems of deprived areas can be solved within their boundaries, the gains in community integration, self-esteem and self-confidence that good community work can help to bring about may notably strengthen their capacity for survival, even development, in the face of adversity.[16]

THE FUTURE OF THE PERSONAL SOCIAL SERVICES

Retired generals collect their state retirement pensions, well-known political figures send their children (perhaps a little ostentatiously) to comprehensive schools, and the patients in the general practitioner's waiting room may be drawn from every social class. But while many social services are used almost universally, the personal social services directly affect only a minority. And it is a minority made up, leaving aside the elderly and the handicapped, largely of the despised and the rejected, the casualties of our society. If social workers often seem overly passionate advocates of their clients' cause, it is partly because they know that delinquents and alcoholics, homeless people and multi-problem families do not command a great deal of sympathy within the community at large. The personal social services, which grew rapidly in a time of economic expansion and tolerant, liberal attitudes, are particularly vulnerable when recession sets in, public expenditure is closely scrutinised and the level of social generosity may decline rapidly.

Yet there is nothing to support the view that the volume of demand is likely to go down. Indeed, the very shifts in our national economic fortunes that create pressure on local authority and voluntary agency budgets will in all probability themselves generate, indirectly, more problems for the personal social services to deal with: more disaffected youth, more offenders, more broken families. Even more firmly predictable is the changing age structure of the population. The total number of people aged over 65 will not vary greatly between now and the end of the century, but within that total the total number aged 75 and over in Britain will go up by half a million. So far, as we have seen, the effect of the recession has been to halt the expansion of, and then slightly reduce, the scale of the personal social services. It is going to be very difficult to ensure that there are no major further reductions, and the prospect of any growth in the foreseeable future seems extremely remote.

Perhaps the largest single problem in these circumstances is that of delineating boundaries. In the days before the 1968 act, the specialised departments dealing with aspects of social welfare were criticised because of their segregation and their limited conception of their respective responsibilites. The situation was not without some counter-balancing advantages: specialist workers gained deep experience in their particular areas of responsibility, and lines of communication tended to be well defined. It might be argued that we have now gone to an opposite extreme, and that we have no clear sense of where the responsibilities of the personal social services begin or end. This has made it very difficult to determine priorities rationally in circumstances where demand outstrips the availability of resources, to lay down realistic objectives for social work training courses in terms of the knowledge and skills that newly-qualified workers should possess, or to provide any systematic basis for decisions about appropriate staffing levels. To allow the scope of the personal social services to be defined by the level and pattern of spontaneous public demand is to risk the level of provision always falling short of the current level of expectation.

One special aspect of the problem of boundaries is that of the relations between the personal social services and other social services. However wide-ranging and ill-defined the role of the personal social services, they remain a departmental function of local government. They are therefore clearly segregated from the NHS, which is outside local government, from housing, which is the responsibility of districts rather than regions, and even from education. Although education is also a regional service it may well find itself in competition with social work departments for influence and resources, and possibly at variance with social work in its values. Inescapably, it seems, provision for client groups tends to be considered and planned within the limits of each established service, even though it is impossible to imagine a pattern of comprehensive care for deprived children, the mentaly ill, the mentally handicapped, the physically disabled or the high-risk elderly that does not cut across at least one existing service boundary. Exhortations to collaborate are common; examples of successful joint planning and collaborative practice are a good deal harder to find. Central government itself does not set a very good example. Co-operation between services at the local level might be easier to achieve if it could be carried through in the framework of co-ordinated national plans which deliberately took account of the interdependence of the separate services. To take a simple example: the home help service makes it possible for many elderly people to remain in their own homes, so that a reduction in that service is very likely to lead to an increase in demand for expensive hospital facilities. No one disputes this, but the different bases of financing make it seem quite reasonable for the social work committee to reduce its costs by throwing an additional burden on the NHS.

Uncertainty about the scope and limits of the social work department is reflected in uncertainty about the knowledge and skills that the individual social worker should possess. Social workers are engaged in tasks that vary greatly in their complexity and in the demands they make on the expertise and depth of understanding of the practitioners. The mix no doubt varies from area to area, but there are probably few basic grade workers who work only at the high level of professionalism for which their training is intended to equip them.

We may need to move towards a more explicit recognition of the fact that the social work department is in fact a multi-purpose social services agency, and that as far as fieldwork is concerned a fair proportion of the public's demand for services can be met by less highly trained personnel. This would involve a careful delineation of the role and functions of the professionally qualified social worker and a greater opportunity for him or her to function as a planner of services, rather than necessarily as their direct provider.

Social workers practise not only at varying levels of sophistication, but also with a considerable variety of client groups. Inevitably, the practice skills, the theoretical understanding and the legal knowledge needed to work effectively with a client will not be the same in the case of a neglected child, an adolescent persistent offender, a middle-aged housewife with a serious depressive illness, or an isolated old man. The temperament and native talents of the social worker may also greatly influence preferences for one client group or another. There have been criticisms from many quarters of the lack of that knowledge and experience in depth which collaborators in other professions claim that they used to be able to count upon in the days before it came to be assumed, quite incorrectly, that generic training should necessarily lead to generic practice. Talk of specialisation is now no longer taboo in social work circles, although there are very few within the profession who would seek to return to an era of segregated training and employment. Basic social work training is likely to be seen increasingly as a necessary foundation for practice, but one on which many workers will wish to build further, specialist training after acquiring sufficient work experience to find out where their own specific talents and interests lie. Such a move, however, would have major implications for the deployment of staff, and would require a degree of shared thinking between social work authorities and training establishments. Some encouraging signs of the latter have recently begun to emerge, but it is unlikely that the future of specialised training will receive proper consideration until there is a major change in the economic climate.

Finally, it should be said that the work of the personal social services is gravely handicapped by the virtual absence of any systematic knowledge of their successes or failures. To make better use of scarce resources, we need to have clear thinking about the objectives of intervention, about the methods of intervention and above all about the consequences of intervention. Until we know what types of social work activity achieve what results for what sorts of client, far too many decisions will be made on the basis of unvalidated assumptions. This implies a substantial development of relevant research; the area of study is certainly difficult but by no means impossibly so.[17] No less necessary than the growth of research itself, however, is the need for sensitivity to research findings and their implications on the part of social service managers and practitioners.

The personal social services should be clear both about their goals and their limitations, and provisions should be planned so that a sensitive response can be made to areas of need in a way which effectively and imaginatively utilises the available human and material resources. Fortunately, an increasing number of practitioners now recognise that a systematic and rational approach is fully compatible with — and can indeed enhance — the deeply-rooted concern of social work and the other caring professions to prevent human suffering to the fullest possible extent, and where prevention is not possible to alleviate it and to minimise its consequences.

*References*

1. For the history of personal social services see: K. Woodroofe, *From Charity to Social Work*, Routledge and Kegan Paul, 1962; and P. Seed, *The Expansion of Social Work in Britain*, Routledge and Kegan Paul, 1973.
2. See for example: E. Younghusband (ed.), *New Developments in Casework*, Allen and Unwin, 1966.
3. *Report of the Committee on Children and Young Persons, Scotland* (Kilbrandon Committee), Cmnd. 2603, HMSO, 1964.
4. *Social Work and the Community*, Cmnd. 3065, HMSO, 1966.
5. *Ibid.*, para 8.
6. Social Work Services Group, *Staff of Scottish Social Work Departments (SWSG Statistical Bulletin)*, SWSG, annual.
7. See for example: R.G.S. Brown, *The Management of Welfare*, Fontana, 1975.
8. R. Hadley and M. McGrath, *Going Local: Neighbourhood Social Services*, Bedford Square Press, 1981.
9. See for example: P. Brearley, *Residential Work with the Elderly*, Routledge and Kegan Paul, 1977; and L. Davis, *Residential Care: A Community Resource*, Heinemann, 1982.
10. J. Packman, *The Child's Generation*, Basil Blackwell and Martin Robertson, 1975.
11. C. Hallett and O. Stevenson, *Child Abuse: Aspects of Interprofessional Co-operation*, Allen and Unwin, 1979.
12. F.M. Martin and K. Murray (eds.), *The Scottish Juvenile Justice System*, Scottish Academic Press, 1982 (especially V. Hiddleston, 'Using Reports'; and R. Ford, 'Consequences').
13. G. Moore and C.J. Wood, *Social Work and Criminal Law in Scotland*, Aberdeen University Press, 1981.
14. E.M. Goldberg and J.S. Neil, *Social Work in General Practice*, Allen and Unwin, 1972.
15. See for example: J. Casserley and B. Clark, *A Welfare Rights Approach to the Chronically Sick and Disabled*, Strathclyde Regional Council, 1978.
16. P. Henderson and D.N. Thomas, *Skills in Neighbourhood Work*, Allen and Unwin, 1981.
17. E.M. Goldberg and N. Connelly (eds.), *Evaluative Research in Social Care*, Heinemann, 1981.

## FURTHER READING

J.D. Cooper, *The Creation of the British Personal Social Services 1962-74*, Heinemann, 1982.
An account of the emergence of unified social services departments in England and Wales, and Social Work Departments in Scotland.

M. Davies, *The Essential Social Worker*, Heinemann, 1981.
An interesting and pragmatic review which is described as 'a guide to good practice'.

E.M. Goldberg and R.W. Warburton, *Ends and Means in Social Work*, Allen and Unwin, 1979.
One of the few attempts to analyse systematically the transactions of a social work agency.

C. Hallett, *The Personal Social Services in Local Government*, Allen and Unwin, 1982.
Usefully places the personal social services in the political and administrative context of the local authority.

E. Sainsbury, *The Personal Social Services*, Pitman, 1977.
A useful general introduction to the personal social services with references to the Scottish situation.

# 7

## *Children's Hearings*

In a broad sense, the emergence and development of a separate juvenile justice system may be seen simply as one strand in a growing recognition of social welfare objectives in public policy during the late nineteenth and twentieth centuries. Changing beliefs about the nature of youth and its problems have been an important set of specific influences. Within early industrial society children were viewed as minature adults and those who broke the law were subject to adult procedures and penalties. Their cheap labour was a source of wealth, and protection by the state from abuse and neglect was virtually unknown. Gradually children came to be seen as individuals with needs and rights of their own, and as personalities still in the process of development. Society's increasing concern for their welfare was reflected in new approaches to child offenders, while new theories of criminality also influenced penal policy. The emphasis on adverse life experiences as predisposing factors gave added impetus to the move away from punitive attitudes and towards an increased recognition of the scope for reform and prevention. The new disciplines of psychiatry and psychoanalysis highlighted the importance of childhood experiences in the development of the personality and redrew the picture of the child offender as someone needing help and support.

Changing policy towards juvenile delinquents was gradually reflected in the segregation of children from adults in prisons, in the provision of separate institutions where children would receive appropriate training and education, and in the scaling down of certain offences committed by juveniles to a less serious category. But the most significant development was the provision in the Children Act, 1908 for a separate system of juvenile courts. Clearly the emphasis on punishment was beginning to shift towards a policy aimed at reform or, considerably more recently, prevention.

CHANGES IN LEGISLATION 1908-75

While the creation of juvenile courts proved an important landmark it gradually became clear that children were not receiving the special consideration which their situation demanded. The 1908 act made no provision for the selection of special justices to sit in juvenile courts and by the 1920s this had come to be regarded as a major weakness. Following their review of the treatment of young offenders, the Morton committee[1] recommended that jurisdiction over children and young persons be transferred to specially constituted juvenile courts conducted by justices with knowledge and experience of juvenile cases. The committee also recommended that the age of criminal responsibility, which under common law was seven years, be raised to eight. These recommendations were given effect in the Children and Young Persons (Scotland) Act, 1932. The welfare of the child was expressly stated to be one of the major objectives of a juvenile court. Separate juvenile courts were introduced in the counties of Ayr, Fife and Renfrew and in the city of Aberdeen but they covered only 16 per cent of the juveniles coming before the courts in Scotland.

During the 1940s social reforms were aimed increasingly at the welfare of children and the improvement of relevant public services. The reports of the Clyde committee[2] in Scotland and the Curtis committee[3] in England resulted in the Children Act, 1948 which created local authority children's departments with an obligation to consider the needs of childlren in their care. The problem of the neglected child and of the young offender were seen as being rooted in broadly similar circumstances and it was felt that efforts to prevent neglect could also lead to the prevention of delinquency.

During the 1950s the incidence of social problems generally and of crime and delinquency in particular became a matter of increasing public concern. Successive governments set up a seies of committees to look into the problems of youth, the management of delinquency and the need for personal social services. The work of the Ingleby[4] and McBoyle[5] committees was followed by the Children and Young Persons Act, 1963 which placed a duty on local authorities to give such advice, guidance and assistance as was necessary to keep young offenders out of court: no changes were made to the structure and procedure of the juvenile courts.

*The Kilbrandon Committee*

In 1961 the Secretary of State for Scotland appointed a committee under the chairmanship of Lord Kilbrandon to review the arrangements for dealing with juvenile delinquents and juveniles in need of care or protection. The committee's remit was:

> To consider the provisions of the law of Scotland relating to the treatment of juvenile delinquents and juveniles in need of care or protection or beyond parental control and, in particular, the constitution, powers, and procedure of the courts dealing with such juveniles, and to report.

The findings were published in 1964. The committee began with the assumption that children appearing before the juvenile court, whether for offences or as being in need of care or protection, were all exhibiting symptoms of the same difficulties. These were felt to arise from a failure in the upbringing process — in the home, in the family environment and in the school. The committee chose to approach these problems by 'social education' which would involve working closely with the parents in order to strengthen 'those natural influences for good which will assist the child's development into a mature and useful member of society'.[6]

The committee found that the existing juvenile court arrangements failed to give full effect to the educational principle. They proposed instead a separate structure for each of the court's dual functions — determining guilt or innocence and making decisions about treatment. This would involve removing all juveniles under the age of 16, except those who committed serious offences, from the jurisdiction of the criminal courts and bringing them before 'juvenile panels'. (The term 'panel' was used to describe both the lay body authorised to deal with juvenile offenders, and the group of three persons drawn from an area list on any given occasion.) Disputed issues of fact would be settled by a court of law and not by panels.

### The White Paper and the 1968 Act

In October 1966 a series of proposals for legislation was set out in a white paper.[7] While this accepted the principles of the children's panel system and most of the Kilbrandon committee's detailed recommendations on machinery, it did in one important sense reverse the priorities. Instead of a specialised family casework service being set up within the education authority the white paper proposed the creation of a comprehensive social work department which would among many other functions provide support for the children's panels (see chapter 6).

The white paper also significantly broadened the basis of panel membership. The Kilbrandon committee had intended this non-legal body to be comprised of 'persons who either by knowledge or experience were considered to be specially qualified to consider children's problems'. The white paper advocated drawing members from a wide variety of occupation, neighbourhood, age and income groups as well as those whose occupations or circumstances had hitherto prevented them from taking a formal part in helping and advising young people.

The new method of dealing with children in need of compulsory care proposed by the Kilbrandon committee and endorsed in the white paper appeared as Part III of the Social Work (Scotland) Act, 1968. The reformed system came into force in April 1971. It thus took an entire decade from the time the Kilbrandon committee was appointed to the inception of the new system. A few minor amendments have been made by subsequent legislation but the legal and administrative framework remains in all important respects that of the 1968 act and the Children's Hearings (Scotland) Rules, 1971 made under it. A continuing oversight of the system is exercised by the Secretary of State for Scotland through the Social Work Services Group, a specialised sub-department of the Scottish Education Department.

*Corresponding Developments in England and Wales*

At this point it may be interesting to note the changes that were occurring at the same time in England and Wales. The Children and Young Persons Act, 1969 also endorsed a social welfare approach to children who offend. This was preceded by a number of committee reports. First, the Ingleby committee was set up in 1956 to inquire into the operation of the juvenile court and to make recommendations for its improvement. The committee recognised the conflict between the court's judicial and welfare functions but still argued in favour of its retention. It recommended raising the age of criminal responsibility from eight to 12 and below that age replacing criminal proceedings with care and protection proceedings. These recommendations did not become law except that the age of criminal responsibility was raised to ten in England and Wales.

While in opposition the Labour Party set up a study group which produced radical proposals with some similarity to Kilbrandon's ideas. As an alternative to the juvenile court this suggested a 'family service' in which the child, family and social worker would discuss the treatment of the child and only where agreement could not be reached or where the facts of the case were disputed would the child be referred to a new 'family court'.

Shortly after the formation of the 1964 Labour government a white paper[8] was published which followed the ideas of the study group except that the 'family service' was replaced by a 'family council' consisting of social workers and other persons selected for their understanding and experience of children. This was strongly opposed by the lay magistrates and the probation service. The family council was itself abandoned by the 1968 white paper[9] which retained the juvenile court.

Children between the ages of 14 and 17 could be subject to criminal proceedings but only after mandatory consultation between police and social workers, and after application to a magistrate for a warrant to prosecute. Social workers were given the power to vary, as well as responsibility for implementing, orders made by the courts. Magistrates were no longer to be involved in detailed decisions about the kind of treatment appropriate for the child. Thus, although the composition and constitution of the juvenile court were virtually unchanged, its jurisdiction was radically altered. This formed the basis of the Children and Young Persons Act, 1969. Following criticism of the working of the 1969 act in England and Wales changes were incorporated in the Criminal Justice Act, 1982. This restored to magistrates the power to commit children to residential care and has also given them additional powers in relation to supervision.

THE STRUCTURE AND OPERATION OF THE CHILDREN'S HEARINGS SYSTEM

Three agencies can be identified as the principal components of the hearings system: the reporter, the children's panel and the social work department. Of these the office of reporter and the children's panel itself were created solely as instruments of the new system. The police are of course quite independent of the hearings system but it need scarcely be said that the functioning of the system is heavily dependent on their co-operation.

### The Reporter

The reporter is the administrator of the hearings system, its adviser on matters of law and procedure, and also a decision-maker with considerable discretionary powers. The act provides that 'Where any person has reasonable cause to believe a child may be in need of compulsory measures of care he may give to the reporter such information about the child as he may be able to discover'. Referrals come from police and procurators fiscal (80 per cent), from education departments (ten per cent) and social work departments (five per cent) of local authorities, and also from other sources such as voluntary bodies and private individuals. Children are referred if they are alleged to have committed an offence, on grounds of truancy, if they are believed to have been neglected or harmed by their parents, or because of solvent abuse.

After investigating the referral by inviting reports from the social work department and from the child's school the reporter can decide:

1. to take no further action; or
2. to ask the social work department to advise, guide and assist the child and family on a voluntary basis; or
3. to bring the child before a children's hearing:
   (i) if he is satisfied that there is sufficient evidence of at least one ground for referral;[10] *and* (ii) if it appears to him that the child is in need of compulsory measures of care.

The reporter refers only about a half of all juvenile offenders to a hearing and of those reported to him for the first time the proportion referred is only 25 per cent. His effectiveness as an intake official depends on his skill in assessing social and other evidence, on his links with statutory and voluntary agencies and on his legal abilities. In the 12 regional and island authorities the 97 posts for reporters and their deputies are filled largely by personnel with legal or social work backgrounds. No official requirements are laid down: the Secretary of State is empowered to prescribe the qualifications necessary for reporters but has not so far chosen to do so.

### The Children's Panel

The children's panel exists solely to provide the members of children's hearings. It is a striking example of voluntary activity which currently involves some 1700 people, ranging from approximately 900 in Strathclyde to ten in Orkney. In each region and islands area members of the children's panel are appointed by the Secretary of State from a list of applicants who have been nominated by the children's panel advisory committee (CPAC), a committee created for the main purpose of recruiting and selecting panel members. Each CPAC consists of five members: two nominated by the local authority and three, including the chairman, appointed by the Secretary of State. In Strathclyde region four members are nominated by the local authority and six by the Secretary of State. Generally appointments to a panel are made for a five year period but a few regions make them for two or three years. Appointments may be renewed on the recommendation of the CPAC but rarely continue beyond a total of ten years.

The aim of the recruitment and selection process is to achieve within each panel a blend of members with appropriate personal characteristics and a proper mix of community representation. There is an approximate balance of the sexes and an age range from about 20 to a maximum of 60. In the early stages there were some criticisms about the composition of panels. True community representation was difficult to achieve, lower income groups and manual occupations being particularly hard to recruit. Considerable efforts have been made to increase panel membership among manual workers. It may, however, be unrealistic to suppose that perfect representativeness can ever be achieved.

It is at least equally important that the selection procedure identifies people with the personal qualities needed to meet the heavy demands made upon them. They must be able to maintain an informal atmosphere during hearings while keeping to the detailed rules of procedure that have been laid down; they must deal responsively and coolly with information that is often sensitive and sometimes disturbing; and they must be competent to take decisons that can have serious implications for the lives of the families concerned. It is therefore essential to recruit people with a genuine concern for the welfare of children, and free from extreme attitudes either of punitiveness or of permissiveness.

Since the inception of the system considerable importance has also been attached to the training of panel members; all are required to attend a period of part-time training before commencing service and are encouraged to undergo regular in-service training thereafter. Training is at present organised by four university-based tutors, who are each responsible for a local authority region or group of regions. There has been some increase in the emphasis given in training to the development of practice skills which will enable panel members to communicate more effectively with the family in the hearing and to make constructive use of professional advice in their decision-making. It is, however, arguable that this has not gone far enough and that there could be greater use of a variety of educational methods, particularly audio-visual aids, role playing and other alternatives to formal instruction.

*The Social Work Department*

The social work department was also created by the 1968 act (see chapter 6). In each local authority area it took over responsibility for the personal social services formerly provided under the auspices of health, welfare and children's committees and for the work of the probation service. Since the children's hearings system was initiated one of the major commitments of the department has been to work in close conjunction with the hearings. It provides background reports on children and undertakes the supervision of those judged by the hearings to be in need of 'compulsory measures of care'. This responsibility applies whether the child is under supervision at home or in a residential establishment. Some time is also given to supervising children on a voluntary basis. Reporters currently send about five per cent of all children referred to them to the social work department for voluntary supervision. It is possible that reporters would make more frequent use of voluntary supervision if social work departments were under less pressure; as matters now stand it often seems unlikely that active supervision can be expected unless a compulsory order is made by a hearing.

The number of qualified field social workers has increased very substantially since the inception of the children's hearings system, but so have competing demands on their time. Whether there has been a corresponding improvement in the quality of the services provided to children's hearings is not a matter on which there is any evidence.

JURISDICTION

Jurisdiction is limited to children under 16 years who commit offences, truant, fall into bad associations or whose environment is deemed to be unhealthy. Care and protection cases between 16 and 18 years remain within the jurisdiction of children's hearings if they are already the subject of a supervision requirement. Until recently this provision also applied to offenders but the Lord Advocate has now instructed procurators fiscal to take steps to bring all offenders over 16 before the courts unless there are special circumstances indicating that they should be dealt with by hearings. The Lord Advocate retains the power to direct the prosecution of children of any age in serious cases. These are taken in the sheriff court or High Court and generally involve offences against the person except in cases where a court hearing is technically necessary for proof (as in some cases where offences have been committed jointly with adults).

The children's hearing cannot proceed unless jurisdiction is established. If the grounds are not accepted by child and parent, or if the child is unable to understand the grounds, the case must be dismissed or sent to the sheriff court for proof. The reporter has authority to abandon the referral but should he proceed and the sheriff finds it established the case will return to a hearing for consideration. Before reaching a decision the hearing considers the grounds for referral and the reports obtained from the social work department and other sources. After careful discussion with the family, the hearing must decide on the course of action which is in the best interests of the child.

Challenges to the jurisdiction of a children's hearing are relatively infrequent. The Kilbrandon committee was encouraged to develop the concept of a decision-making body which did not concern itself with guilt or innocence by the fact that some 95 per cent of the children who appeared before the former juvenile courts entered a plea of guilty. Since the establishment of the hearings system, the proportion of children who deny the grounds for referral has generally been in the region of ten per cent. In the majority of such cases the matter is referred to the sheriff. Broadly speaking, sheriffs have agreed in about two-fifths of all such denials that the grounds for referral should be abandoned.

STATISTICAL PATTERNS

Statistics relating to the children's hearings system are published annually by the Social Work Services Group from records submitted by reporters. Table 7.1 shows, for each of the ten years 1972-81, the number of children coming into the system, the number of reports received by reporters in respect of these children, the percentage of reports referred to hearings and their subsequent disposals. Since a child may be referred to the reporter on more than one occasion in any one year, the number of reports is greatly in excess of the number of children reported. The number both of children and of

TABLE 7.1

Children Dealt with by Reporters and Hearings 1972-1981

| Year | Total children reported (all ages)* | Number of reports received | % reports referred to hearings | % home supervision requirement (in relation to all cases referred to hearings) | % residential requirement (in relation to all cases referred to hearings) |
|---|---|---|---|---|---|
| 1972 | 17,950 | 24,219 | 52 | 50 | 14 |
| 1973 | 21,017 | 29,566 | 51 | 47 | 12 |
| 1974 | 21,907 | 31,876 | 48 | 48 | 11 |
| 1975 | † | 30,022 | 49 | 42 | 13 |
| 1976 | 18,637 | 29,514 | 53 | 38 | 16 |
| 1977 | 18,537 | 28,551 | 53 | 39 | 16 |
| 1978 | 17,308 | 26,583 | 53 | 38 | 16 |
| 1979 | 16,924 | 25,842 | 53 | 38 | 16 |
| 1980 | 19,035 | 28,950 | 53 | 3' | 15 |
| 1981 | 20,111 | 30,786 | 51 | 37 | 14 |

*Children in respect of whom one or more reports were received during the year.
†Reliable figures are not available for 1975 owing to local government reorganisation.

Source: Social Work Services Group, *Children's Hearings Statistics 1981 (SWSG Statistical Bulletin)*, SWSG, 1983.

reports shows an increase between 1972 and 1974 followed by a marked decline over the period 1975-79.

The decline in the number of children was rather more rapid than the fall in referrals, which implies a small increase in the average number of referrals per child in a calendar year. The downward trend was reversed in 1980 when both the number of children reported and of referrals increased by ten per cent.

While the police continue to be the main source of reports, the proportion of cases referred by them decreased from 88 per cent in 1972 to 59 per cent in 1981. The greater part of this difference is attributable to a large increase in the number of referrals routed through procurators fiscal rather than coming direct from the police. Offences are the grounds of referral in as many as 79 per cent of cases, truancy grounds amount to ten per cent of the total, and grounds where the child is alleged to be beyond control or to be in moral danger to four per cent. Grounds relating to cases of non-accidental injury amount to eight per cent of the total.

Boys very substantially outnumber girls, and about 61 per cent of all referrals to reporters concern boys in the 12-15 age group. The predominance of boys is largely confined to offence referrals.

Between 1972 and 1974 the rate of referral to hearings for Scotland as a whole fell from 52 per cent to 48 per cent, but it then rose slightly and from 1976 remained steady at 53 per cent (though dropping to 51 per cent in 1981).

There are, however, considerable regional variations, which may be explained by differences between reporters in the use made of informal supervision arrangements and of police warning schemes.

Striking differences are also recorded in the use made of different dispositions. During the first three years of operation the proportion placed by hearings on compulsory home supervision remained constant while residential requirements decreased. After 1974 a decrease in home supervision was accompanied by an increasing proportion of residential requirements until 1978 when the latter began to fall.

As mentioned above, not all young offenders find their way to hearings. In each of the years 1976 to 1981 more than 1000 children were prosecuted in court. Sheriffs have the power and, when a child is already on supervision, a duty to ask for the advice of a hearing on the disposition of a case although they are not obliged to take it. In 1981 Scottish courts made 695 references to hearings for advice, and remitted 257 cases for disposal by a hearing.

POWERS

The powers of children's hearings are strictly limited. They are not empowered to send a child to prison, a borstal establishment or a detention centre, or to impose a fine or any other financial penalty. The decisions open to a hearing are:

1. to discharge the referral which means that the child goes home and no further contact is made;

2. to make a supervision order which means that the child is not taken away from home but is required to remain under the supervision of a social worker; or

3. to make a residential supervision order which requires the child to enter a specified residential school or home.

If a supervision requirement is made, whether in an institution or in the community, it must be reviewed within a year and can be reviewed at any time if requested by the social worker, by the parent or by the child himself.

The child or his parents may appeal to the sheriff against the decision of a hearing and, from him, on a point of law or irregularity, to the Court of Session. Between 20 and 30 appeals are heard in a typical year, and in these cases it is unusual — but not unknown — for a sheriff to overturn an order made by a hearing. It is important that child and parents should be advised of their right to appeal and of the availability of legal aid. (Since children's hearings are classified as tribunals legal aid is not available for the hearing itself.)

In May 1981 the Secretary of State for Scotland announced the outcome of a major consultative exercise on the powers and procedures of children's hearings.[11] While rejecting the introduction of punitive measures he did suggest alterations with the intention of creating a broader framework for the activities of children's panel members. These included giving greater encouragement to the use by hearings of voluntary reparation as a suitable method of treatment; giving hearings the power to suspend the decision on a case for up to six months; extending the grounds for referral so as to bring children who engage in potentially dangerous practices such as solvent abuse ('glue sniffing') to the attention of reporters; giving hearings a power to order the forfeiture of weapons used in the commission of offences; and bringing all offenders over 16 before the courts unless there are special circumstances indicating that they should be brought before hearings. None of these proposed changes alters the welfare principles on which the hearings system is based but how effectively the new powers are used will depend on the readiness of panel members to develop their practice skills and to deepen their understanding of the families they serve.

STRENGTHS AND WEAKNESSES

During the first ten years discussion of the principles and practice of children's hearings was inevitably based on tentative knowledge gained by subjective and unrepresentative personal observation and experience. Information derived from research was restricted to one or two areas and touched on operational features in only a limited way. More recently the completion of large-scale research[12] has increased understanding of how the system works and has led to more informed discussion of its strengths and weaknesses.

### The Best Interests of the Child

If the over-riding concern of the hearings system is with the interests of the children who enter it, there are a number of complicated questions to be faced about the best ways of identifying and advancing those interests. When the system was being planned, it was widely believed that as many children as possible would be brought before panel hearings; if what they had to offer was beneficial, it made sense for those benefits to be widely distributed. Fairly rapidly, however, an alternative viewpoint began to develop: that many early offenders had sufficiently supportive backgrounds to protect them from getting involved in a long-term delinquent career, and that in the cases of such children there was a lot to be said for keeping formal intervention to a minimum. The responsibility for deciding whether a child has a high or low risk of becoming a serious delinquent falls to the reporter.

An analysis of reporters' discretion which formed part of the research study showed clearly that the decision to refer to a hearing is influenced in the case of first referrals by factors in the child's background: school attendance and whether or not there are problems at home or in school. In the case of second or subsequent referrals the reporter gives greater weight to the seriousness of the offence but is still significantly influenced by the child's social and family circumstances.

As indicated earlier, about half of all the offence cases referred to the reporter, and about three-quarters of those who come to his notice for the first time, have no further action taken. A substantial number of young offenders are thus being diverted even from the relatively informal proceedings of a children's hearing. The important thing to note about this is that three out of every four children so diverted do not come to the notice of the reporter on a subsequent occasion. It can be said therefore that reporters have developed considerable skill in identifying those children who have a good chance of getting through a patch of delinquent behaviour without recourse to compulsory measures of care.

When a child does come before a hearing, the sole concern of the panel members should be that child's need for care. The 1968 act defines care as including 'protection, guidance, treatment and control'. Unlike English magistrates and judges, panel members are not responsible for the protection of society in general. Neither are they supposed to be concerned with punishment. The aim of 'compulsory measures of care' is not to cause pain of any kind but to help the child develop more mature and socially constructive ways of living and of relating to others. The measures may indeed sometimes be experienced as restrictive, even as painful. But this is not the intention: the aim is to re-educate and rehabilitate, not to punish.

Of the alternatives open to children's hearings, only the residential supervision order, involving as it does compulsory removal from home, enforced intimacy with strangers and a more or less disciplined regime, could be seen as having punitive possibilities if punishment were the intention. Recent research leaves little doubt that panel members with rare exceptions see List D schools (formerly 'approved schools') as means of social education to be used sparingly, indeed reluctantly, as a last resort when home supervision has indisputably failed and parents are manifestly unable to cope. It is a notable achievement that over the last few years the number of children resident in List D schools has fallen from over 1600 to about 1000. Remarkably, the situation is different in England and Wales, where legislation intended to reduce the orientation of the juvenile court towards punishment appears to have led to a sharp increase in the number of children in custodial institutions.

The task of adapting the limited number of disposals available to panel members to the needs of individual children is a challenging one. If new, non-punitive powers are hard to come by, there is a pressing need for greater inventiveness in the use of those powers that now exist. Home supervision in particular is too frequently identified in only the most general terms; it should often be possible to consider with the social worker in the case the specific objectives to be pursued and styles of supervision to be employed. 'Intermediate treatment' covers a variety of group activities, and panel members should have sufficient knowledge of the provisions available to be able to recommend types of programme that they believe will be helpful in the individual case. Residential establishments should offer, and be known to offer, a wide range of environments and opportunities, and be selected for their special appropriateness. Such disposals are not unknown at present but they tend to be the exception rather than the rule.

It is clear that panel members in all their work with children depend heavily on the social work profession. Social workers are responsible for the preparation of reports on the children and their circumstances, and they also take on the supervision of children when the hearings decide that this would be an appropriate course of action. But reports vary greatly in quality. Important areas are sometimes omitted, and they seem too often to have been constructed with an insufficient awareness of the needs of those who will make use of them. Although there is very little systematic information about the quality of social work supervision, there is a widespread belief that its quality also differs from area to area and from one practitioner to another. Social workers tend to be burdened by heavy case loads so that new supervision orders or requests for reports must be weighed against competing demands on their time by a multiplicity of clients with needs that seem no less pressing.

*Family Participation and its Limits*

Involving the child and his parents in the proceedings of the hearing is an important goal of the system. Research findings show clearly that a notable measure of success is achieved in involving the family members in the hearing discussion, helping them to overcome their anxieties, their defensiveness and their lack of self-confidence, and occasionally even opening up sensitive and stressful areas of family life for honest examination. Children and parents in general respond very favourably, and see the panel members as genuinely interested in what they have to say, as trying to help them and as treating them with courtesy and respect. An honest exchange makes it easier for the hearing to assess what the child's needs are, and makes it possible to involve the family in the process of reaching a decision, so that at the end they too will agree that what is being done is in the child's best interests.

For the most part, however, discussion in hearings is contained within limits that exclude highly emotive areas. We know from research evidence that discussion is significantly influenced by the information contained in the social work, educational and other reports made available to the panel members in the case three days before the hearing. In general, references in reports to aspects of the child's home and school life provide conversational gambits; but when social background reports draw attention to specific domestic problems of a serious nature — psychiatric illness in a parent, or a criminal record or a history of violent behaviour — the references act instead as danger signals. Anxious to avoid what they see as stressful and potentially damaging confrontations with parents, panel members shift rapidly to the firmer ground of the child's school attendance and leisure pursuits.

Entering into and maintaining a dialogue in which one participant is confronted with his own shortcomings calls for great skill and self-confidence, and we should not be surprised if panel members shrink from such a task, settle for superficial topics of conversation, and sometimes even appear to collude with parents against the child. Yet in doing so they are contradicting their belief that parental failure and family breakdown are causal factors in delinquency. Perhaps more important, they may be missing an opportunity to prepare the way for the supervision process. Most social workers see supervision as requiring work with the whole family and not merely with the delinquent child, but few parents on emerging from the hearing would imagine that the supervision process has any connection with them.

### The Borderlines of Legality

To create an appropriate climate for the hearing discussion an informal atmosphere must be created. Many panel members tend to assume that informality cannot be combined with strict observance of procedural rules. The research evidence suggests that a significant proportion of hearings fall short of the by no means excessively demanding standards of procedure laid down in the 1968 act and the Hearing Rules. There is of course a familiar argument that a lack of concern for legal safeguards is an inevitable corollary of a welfare-oriented approach to juvenile justice. According to this viewpoint, the temptation to assume control of young offenders' destinies, doubtless with benevolent intentions, is so powerful that legal protections are perceived as irritating and irrelevant obstacles, to be ignored or circumvented whenever it seems necessary. But the research evidence shows that hearings are capable of maintaining the legal rights of children. Some hearings are impeccable in their adherence to the rules of procedure and, so far from being stilted and formal, these same hearings are often the most successful in achieving a high level of family participation. A marked improvement in procedural standards is essential if hearings are not to fall into disrepute for their lack of regard to legal rights, and new approaches to training and the monitoring of performance are needed to bring this about.

## Problems and Prospects

In the first few years of its existence the children's hearings system was the target of much ill-informed and often abusive criticism from people who were opposed to the whole idea of a non-punitive approach to young offenders. The tide seemed to turn after about five or six years. That is not to say that everyone in Scotland is fully attuned to or in complete sympathy with the welfare philosophy of children's hearings. But it does seem that 'the panel' has come to be accepted as an integral part of the Scottish scene, and even the return to power in 1979 of a Conservative government pledged to take firm measures in support of 'law and order' did not, in the event, lead to any significant changes in the structure or the powers of the established system. Of course, on close examination we find some blemishes. But these are shortcomings at the level of practice and not faults in the basic principles and structure of the system. These faults can all be remedied by careful attention to the selection and training of panel members and to the monitoring of their practice.

There is much that we still do not know. Since the children's hearings system justifies intervention in terms of the positive consequences that are expected to accrue, it is morally obliged to examine closely the impact upon children and parents of the measures it imposes. A sensitive study of supervision is much needed; so too is a careful examination of regimes, environments and social climates in residential establishments. While the reduced demand for List D places is a matter for cautious congratulation, few believe that they have no future. There is an additional need for knowledge about the longer-term careers of children who come through the hearings system: whether they come into conflict with the law as adults and, if so, at what age and for what reason.

Many panel members would like to see a growth in that side of their work that concerns the non-delinquent child. They are keen to assume additional welfare responsibilities, for example, for making decisions about the custody of children affected by divorce; and they have had encouragement from the Royal Commission on Legal Services in Scotland,[13] which saw a future role for both reporters and panel members in such cases. This could prove to be an exciting, although an immensely demanding extension of present responsibilities.

In the next few years the hearings system may well encounter a sharp renewal of criticism. If current economic trends continue, we might see a growth of disaffection and alienation among young people who see no future for themselves, with a consequent increase in law breaking. Economic pressures also tend to create intolerance and prejudice, and there is a distinct possibility that children's hearings could again come under fire from the exponents of harsh punishment. If the hearings system is going to remain strong in the face of such threats it will be important for the key participants to stay true to their principles, and to spread knowledge and build friendships and alliances outside the system. Above all, they must avoid becoming inward looking and self-satisfied, but remain ready to profit from experience and to acquire a deeper awareness of the significance and the difficulties of their task.

*References*

1. *Report of the Departmental Committee on the Treatment of Young Offenders* (Morton Committee), HMSO, 1928.
2. *Report of the Committee on Homeless Children* (Clyde Report), Cmd. 6911, HMSO, 1946.
3. *Report of the Care of Children Committee* (Curtis Report), Cmd. 6922, HMSO, 1946.
4. *Report of the Committee on Children and Young Persons* (Ingleby Report), Cmnd. 1191, HMSO, 1960.
5. *Report of the Prevention of Neglect of Children* (McBoyle Report), Cmnd. 1966, HMSO, 1963.
6. *Report of the Committee on Children and Young Persons, Scotland* (Kilbrandon Report), Cmnd. 2306, HMSO, 1964, para. 17.
7. *Social Work and the Community*, Cmnd. 3065, HMSO, 1966.
8. *The Child, the Family and the Young Offender*, Cmnd. 2742, HMSO, 1965.
9. *Children in Trouble*, Cmnd. 3601, HMSO, 1968.
10. See: Social Work (Scotland) Act, 1968, S.32(2) (a-h) (and (gg) inserted by Solvent Abuse (Scotland) Act, 1983).
11. *Consultative Memorandum on Part III of the Social Work (Scotland) Act, 1968*, Social Work Services Group, 1980.
12. F.M. Martin, S.J. Fox and K. Murray, *Children Out of Court*, Scottish Academic Press, 1981.
13. *Report of the Royal Commission on Legal Services in Scotland*, Cmnd. 7846, HMSO, 1980.

## FURTHER READING

N. Bruce and J.C. Spencer, *Face to Face with Families*, MacDonald, 1976.
An account of the hearings system drawing on studies of two urban and two rural areas.

F.M. Martin, S.J. Fox and K. Murray, *Children Out of Court*, Scottish Academic Press, 1981.
The findings of a major research study of the working of the hearings system.

F.M. Martin and K. Murray (eds.), *The Scottish Juvenile Justice System*, Scottish Academic Press, 1982.
A collection of essays drawing on research findings.

A. Morris and M. McIsaac, *Juvenile Justice?*, Heinemann, 1978.
The report of an early study of children's hearings in two districts.

P. Parsloe, *Juvenile Justice in Britain and the United States*, Routledge and Kegan Paul, 1978.
A comparative review of the juvenile justice systems in Scotland, England and the United States.

# 8
## Education

Education is perhaps the most controversial of the social services: no-one doubts that it has significant consequences both for the individual and for society as a whole, but opinions differ sharply both as to the nature and extent of its influence. We may see education as enhancing every child's (and even every person's) development, and at the same time as transmitting values that maintain cohesion and order in society. But education can also be seen as an agency for the selective and unequal distribution of opportunities — or life chances — and it is therefore open to criticism for perpetuating social divisions, for reinforcing the position of the disadvantaged and for legitimising privilege.

Until recently education in Scotland has been widely praised both at home and abroad, not only because of the broad-based content of what is taught in Scottish educational institutions, but also for its pursuit of excellence and rationality. Despite the optimism heralded by the comprehensive school, however, it is now felt by many that the present schooling system is not as effective as it should be. Some believe that it does not sufficiently maintain a paramount allegiance to traditional standards, excellence and rigour, authority and discipline; some that it is not keeping pace with the changing values and norms of modern society; and some that it fails to tackle acute social problems such as poverty and deprivation. Increasingly people are beginning to wrestle with the underlying issues and search for ways in which the system can better meet the challenge of a rapidly changing social context.[1]

THE EDUCATIONAL SYSTEM IN SCOTLAND

With the exception of independent schools and the universities, the Scottish educational system is controlled centrally by the Scottish Office through the Scottish Education Department (SED). However, the administration of the system (except for colleges of education and the colleges known as central institutions) is the responsibility of regional and islands councils.

The SED has the overall task of formulating and implementing policy within the framework laid down by acts of parliament. For instance, parental choice of school and the assisted places scheme were introduced under the Education (Scotland) Act, 1980. The act requires regional and islands councils

143

to allow parents more flexibility in the school to which they send their children, and to co-operate in the scheme for the admission to independent schools of able children from families with relatively low incomes. Similarly, local authorities are required to establish school councils with the duty of discharging such functions of management and supervision of educational establishments under their control as the former may determine. Despite the fact that the structure of the education system is centrally controlled, the SED has little jurisdiction over the school curriculum. The only area of the curriculum that is mandatory is religious education. Even so, most secondary schools adhere to a standard curriculum with only minor variations in the subjects on offer.

The other major function of the SED is the oversight of schools and other educational establishments through the inspectorate service, known as Her Majesty's Inspectors of Schools (HMIs). In recent years inspection has tended to diminish and to be replaced by a consultation role, so that HMIs are now more active in curriculum development and the implementation of SED policy than in the monitoring of standards.

Regional councils through their education committees are responsible for the running of all educational institutions under their jurisdiction: schools, colleges, adult and community education centres, child guidance clinics and youth centres, as well as schemes such as school to work projects. The education committees appoint staff, administer buildings and works, purchase equipment, supervise school meals and have powers to influence such pedagogical matters as the curriculum, the grouping of children and the size of schools. The allocation of children can be particularly problematic owing to the falling number of pupils and financial pressures to close smaller schools.

SCHOOLS

The law requires that all children between the ages of five and 16 should be educated. A parent may, however, opt out of the state system, either by using an independent school or by proving his or her capacity to educate the child by other means. Nevertheless, over 96 per cent of children in Scotland attend state schools. Compulsory education was introduced into Scotland by the Education (Scotland) Act, 1872 which marked the transfer of educational matters from the church to the state. The church had previously been the principal body providing education for the ordinary people. The main concept of education in the new state schools was the provision of the 'three Rs', although it was widened somewhat to cover the social and physical wellbeing of children by the Education (Scotland) Act, 1908.

Though the idea of 'secondary education for all' had been discussed since the 1920s, it was initiated in practice by the Education (Scotland) Act, 1945. The act laid down that all children up to the age of 15 should be educated according to their age, aptitude and ability. It also provided for the school leaving age to be raised to 16 when practicable (which was done in 1974). In Scotland a bipartite system of secondary schools was set up which many critics saw as socially divisive. Children who attained a certain standard in a qualifying examination, taken at age 11, had the chance to attend a senior secondary school or academy. Those children whose performance fell below the stipulated level, which fluctuated depending on the distribution of ability in a particular year, were required to attend a junior secondary school.

Between 1946 and 1965 research findings confirmed the suspicions of the critics of the bipartite system. Even with comparable intelligence, children from poor backgrounds tended to be allocated to junior secondaries whilst their more privileged peers attended senior secondary schools. In 1965 the SED under a Labour administration issued Circular 600 which instructed local education authorities to submit plans for comprehensive reorganisation. The qualifying examination (or eleven plus) was abandoned, as was the distinction between junior and senior secondary schools. All children living within the zone of the newly formed comprehensive schools were given a place irrespective of ability.

Also in 1965 the SED issued the Primary Memorandum,[2] the purpose of which was to promote both a wider curriculum in the primary school, including subjects such as language, arts and environmental education. It also sought to encourage more progressive teaching methods, so that children were encouraged to progress at their own pace through a process of exploration rather than by rote learning of facts.

Since the issuing of Circular 600 and the Primary Memorandum, a number of changes have occurred in both the primary and secondary sectors. The following discussion is a brief outline of the present position.

*Primary Schools*

Over the 15 years after 1965 there was a significant move to introduce so-called progressive education through a broader curriculum and less traditional methods of teaching for children between the ages of five and 12. Whilst instruction in the 'basics' of schooling, that is reading, writing and arithmetic, was still afforded top priority, new areas of activity were introduced such as environmental health and science education. Classroom organisation also changed: instead of the traditional rows of desks facing the teacher, children were allocated to smaller groups. Thus, teaching methods moved away from an exclusive emphasis on instruction to the management of children's learning experiences through guided discovery. To assist teachers to adjust to these changes, local authorities appointed primary advisers with the specific remit of curriculum development. In addition, in-service training courses were expanded in the colleges of education to which teachers were seconded.

The extent to which these changes both in curriculum and method have been implemented is, however, a source of debate. A recent report by the inspectorate criticised the primary schools for spending too much time on the 'basics' to the detriment of creative arts, language and science.[3] Nevertheless, many primary schools have changed a great deal over the past decade. The system abounds in interesting and lively schools with hard-working and committed teachers. That we need more of these schools and teachers is perhaps the message of the report, and to this end there has been an attempt to strengthen in-service training through the introduction of school-based activity. A fresh impetus for in-service training seems likely, and it is proposed to introduce a formal award system for teachers who successfully complete courses.

## Secondary Schools

After leaving primary school children attend the local comprehensive school at least till the age of 16. Although the majority of children leave school at 16, about 40 per cent stay on until they are 17 and 18. For the first year of secondary schooling, children in most schools are placed in mixed-ability groups. Streaming or setting does not take place till the second year and in many schools not until the third year. The curriculum is traditionally based on 'subjects', with children learning the rudiments of a broad range in the first and second years. At the end of the second year children are allocated to classes on the basis of ability assessed on their performance. In general, three broad clusters of ability are identified by the school: those who will follow non-examinable courses; those who will take less than five 'O' grades; and those who will take between five and nine 'O' grades.

The curriculum and the assessment process in the third and fourth years of the secondary school have each been the subject of a major report. The Munn Report[4] on the curriculum, whilst retaining an emphasis on a subject-based approach, recommended a more balanced curriculum based on modes of activity. This involves a 'core' set of subjects and a series of options. The chief recommendation of the Dunning Report[5] on assessment is the introduction of 'certification for all'. In other words, each pupil on leaving school should be given a certificate of performance based on the course taken at one of three levels (foundation, general and credit). The SED is now involved in implementing the Munn and Dunning proposals, using pilot schools throughout Scotland.

## Other Schools

In addition to primary and secondary schools for children between the ages of five and 18, the system also contains special schools and List D schools. Under the Education (Scotland) Act, 1969 local authorities must make provision for children with special educational needs such as physical disability, mental handicap and emotional maladjustment. This provision is available through special schools, the majority of which are day schools though there are also a number of residential schools, particularly in rural areas. Children with special educational needs were the subject of the Warnock Report[6] which recommended a policy of integration. Progress in implementing this recommendation is inevitably constrained by the availability of resources.

Juvenile offenders in Scotland may be sent by children's hearings (see chapter 7) to List D schools, which are now the responsibility of social work departments rather than education departments. Changes in policy in favour of more community-based provision has meant that some schools have been closed whilst others have been reduced in size.

*School Councils*

The Local Government (Scotland) Act, 1973 made provision for the establishment of school councils. Following local government reorganisation in 1975, the new regional and islands authorities began establishing school councils, and 302 had been set up by 1977. School councils were intended to replace the former area education sub-committees, in order to fulfil such functions of management and supervision of the schools attached to them as determined by the local authority. Membership includes teachers, parents, pupils, ministers of religion, and sometimes representatives of further education and the local community. In determining the coverage of councils, most authorities decided that the unit should be a secondary school and its feeder primary schools, though some grouped two or more secondary schools and their associated primaries.

In a recent research report on school councils, their functions were allocated to six categories: school and community, school and home, non-educational in-school issues, curriculum, staffing, and accountability.[7] On the first of these, the councils have been concerned with school letting and transport arrangements. In only rare cases have councils addressed themselves to broader matters such as learning and teaching in the wider context of the community.

The predominant issue in the field of school and home taken up by councils has been the non-attendance of pupils, often referred to as 'truancy', a phenomenon considered serious enough to merit a special enquiry.[8] Cases have been dealt with through the attendance sub-committees of the councils (with the exception of Grampian region which deals with truancy issues directly) after referral by the school. Often parents are interviewed by sub-committee members and, on occasion, prosecution is initiated via the procurator fiscal. The attendance sub-committee also deals with requests for 'exceptional transfer' where a parent can ask the council for his or her child to be transferred to a school outwith the zone of the local school. The parent making the request is not required to give a reason for the request; the decision on it generally depends on the availability of a place at the school desired.

Under non-educational in-school issues, matters such as holiday dates, promotion of extra-curricular activities and uniforms are the items most often discussed, although the councils are empowered only to advise the education departments and have no direct control over individual schools. Some councils were consulted about the Munn and Dunning proposals referred to earlier. By and large, discussion of curriculum matters is very rare in the councils, either because it is thought to be outwith their remit or because the professional members consider such issues to be the exclusive domain of the teachers.

On staffing, some councils have been given executive power to appoint non-teaching staff whilst others have only advisory functions. The responsibility for the appointment of teaching staff, however, still remains with the regional and islands authorities, though Lothian region has introduced a system of involving parents in the selection process for senior school staff.

Accountability is only a peripheral activity of school councils and mainly involves the dissemination of information about individual school matters. The councils have encouraged schools to become more active in communicating with the public and in promoting more parental interest in education.

Overall, it is often felt that school councils are relatively powerless in influencing basic aspects of schooling such as curriculum and assessment. The councils may be seen as token bodies with no real powers. Others take the view that the councils are yet in their infancy and that they should be gradually given wider functions. Some recommend that each school should have its own council. There seems to be little doubt, however, that school councils have been successful in controlling levels of truancy. Whilst statistical evidence is not available, most of those involved in the councils regard the control of truancy as one of their more successful functions.

*Parental Choice of School*

During recent years there has been mounting pressure to give parents more say in the operation of the education system. In particular, the 1979 Conservative government considered it desirable that parents be allowed to choose the school their child attends instead of being restricted by zoning arrangements. The Education (Scotland) Act, 1980 extended the existing exceptional transfer mechanism by permitting parents to make a 'placing request' direct to the local authority for their child to attend a different school than that proposed by the authority. A parent may now exercise the right to make a placing request with respect to any state school, providing that he or she is prepared to finance transport to and from that school if it is not the one to which the authority allocated the child in the first instance. Should an authority refuse to grant a placing request, the parent may refer the decision to an appeals committee in the first instance and subsequently to the sheriff.

Both to assist the minority of parents who wish to exercise this right, and to equip all parents to support their child throughout his or her schooling, the Education (Scotland) Act, 1981 requires local authorities to make certain kinds of information about schools available to parents. This information is divided into three categories:

1. Basic information: for example, brief details of the authority's policy and practice with regard to placing in schools, school commencement arrangements and transport provision.

2. School information: in particular the school's examination results for the Scottish certificate of education in terms of the number of pupils achieving each grade for each subject.

3. Supplementary information: for example, information about nursery schools, special schools, primary-secondary transfer arrangements and appeal procedures.

All this information, which is revised annually, is set out in booklet form and copies are available from the local authority on request.

As yet it is too early to assess the impact of these new procedures though they will undoubtedly increase pressures on schools to be more accountable to parents. Some parents may take the view, however, that undue pressure is being placed on schools to prepare pupils for external examinations by the requirement to publish results, to the detriment of other worthwhile but non-examinable activities. The new procedures could precipitate the closure of particular schools if sufficient numbers of parents were successful through their placing requests in transferring their children elsewhere. At the same time, we may see a wide variety of schools emerging, some specialising, for instance, in traditional academic subjects, and others in sports and others in community affairs. The new procedures might even eventually re-introduce a form of the bipartite system which was displaced by the comprehensive school.

In theory, parents now have more choice in the schooling of their children than ever before. Whether the introduction of greater choice will in fact motivate more parents irrespective of social background to give greater support to their children's education, or whether it will only be taken up by those groups in society which already benefit most from the present school system, will only emerge in the years ahead.

PRE-SCHOOL EDUCATION

The 1972 white paper, *Education in Scotland: A Statement of Policy*, gave a new emphasis to pre-school education:

> There has been a statutory duty on education authorities in Scotland since 1945 to make adequate provision for nursery education but because of the demand on resources successive Governments have been unable to let education authorities carry out their duty. The present Government believes that the time has come to remove the restrictions imposed in this field and to make nursery education available as widely as possible without charge, to children whose parents wish them to benefit from it.[9]

Following this government pronouncement, the number of nursery places, either in purpose-built nursery schools or nursery classes attached to primary schools, rose by a factor of three, from just over 10,000 in 1972 to over 30,000 in 1977. This expansion was based on a belief in the value of nursery schooling for children whose early experiences were limited and narrow because of deficiencies in the environment.

Research had an important role to play in this area of education. For instance, the pre-school field formed a major component of the educational priority area schemes which were set up in the expansionist period of the late 1960s.[10] Some of the research was equivocal, however, on the issue of whether early schooling was the best way to assist young children. A new awareness began to arise of the value of working with parents and other professionals such as health visitors.

Many parents were already active in providing pre-school support for their children through the Scottish Pre-School Playgroups Association (SPPA). At the beginning of 1972 over 22,000 playgroup places were being provided in Scotland. The SPPA rejected in principle schooling for the under-fives in which the parent, most often the mother, was excluded from the education of her child. The association promoted the view that the interests of children would be best served through shared experiences of mother and child, with the mothers themselves organising and running the playgroup.

In some areas, as new nursery schools were built, tension emerged between the state and voluntary sectors. New ideas arose such as children's centres in which professionals and parents co-operated; and more recently there was the Stepping-Stone Project in Glasgow which has pioneered alternative ways of working with the under-fives.[11] During the 1970s new energy in the pre-school field was released and regional councils took up the challenge. As well as expanding provision for the under-fives, other experimental schemes such as the Lothian Home Visiting Project and the Govan Project were set up to assist in policy making.

In the Lothian project, home-visiting teachers (a new idea in Scotland) were attached to a small number of nursery and special schools. Their job initially was to visit families with children under three years of age, and support the mother in her role as informal educator by showing her how to stimulate her child intellectually through language and play. As a direct result of the project the number of home-visiting teachers has grown rapidly.[12]

The Govan Project was not solely concerned with the pre-school field, and adopted a rather different approach to parents. The pre-school co-ordinator attached to the project visited all the families in the area covered by the project, first to provide information about the value and availability of pre-school education in the area; second, to support and strengthen the existing provision; and, third, to set up new activities such as a toy library.[13]

Not surprisingly, with expenditure cut-backs this phase of expansion has come to an abrupt end. Since 1980 the increasing financial pressure experienced by local authorities has meant that pre-school education has suffered severe cuts. Nursery schools have been closed and confusion is widespread. In response, authorities are now struggling to rebuild a more comprehensive pre-school strategy involving greater co-operation between the professionals.

*Universities*

In the decade following the Robbins Report[14] the number of universities in Scotland increased from the original four — Aberdeen, Edinburgh, Glasgow and St Andrews — to the present complement of eight, the new ones being Dundee (formerly a constituent college of St Andrews), Heriot-Watt, Stirling and Strathclyde. (The Open University of course also has students in Scotland.) This massive expansion attempted to fulfil the philosophy of Robbins, that a university place should be available to every qualified school leaver who wanted one. The Scottish Universities are financed through the University Grants Committee, which covers the whole of Britain, and are not the responsibility of the SED.

Scottish universities encourage a broad-based higher education (as opposed to early specialised education in the English universities). Nearly all students for the first two years follow a general course in arts, engineering, law, medicine, science or social science. Students (except in medicine) then opt to take an ordinary degree (requiring a further year) or an honours degree (a further two years).

Universities have been subject to severe financial constraints, and they are all now engaged in a process of shedding staff and restructuring their courses. The consequence of the reduction in the number of university places available will mean that it will be more difficult for qualified school leavers to be admitted until there is a fall in their numbers in the late 1980s. The cut-backs may also curtail the relatively recent innovation of admitting mature students who do not necessarily possess the formal minimum entry qualifications required of school leavers.

*Colleges of Education*

Recently the colleges of education have undergone a major restructuring process owing to the dramatically reduced demand for teachers. School rolls will have fallen by over 20 per cent between 1978 and 1988, and the ten colleges existing in 1980 have been reduced to seven.

Teacher training for primary schools is carried out at present either as a three-year course leading to the certificate of education or as a four-year degree course leading to a bachelor of education degree. It is planned to abandon the certificate in favour of an all-graduate entry into the profession. The route to secondary school teaching is predominantly through a university degree followed by a post-graduate one-year certificate course. There are, however, a small number of teachers entering secondary schools via the BEd degree, though it is likely to be discontinued for intending secondary school teachers in the near future.

*Central Institutions*

There are 14 central institutions in Scotland, which provide specialist courses in subjects such as agriculture, art, domestic science, music and drama, and town and country planning. Some offer more general courses in science, engineering and social sciences. In addition to the central institutions, which are directly financed by the SED, a few of the larger local authority colleges also offer courses up to degree level. As with the universities, the central institutions have seen a large expansion since the 1960s.

*Colleges of Further Education*

These colleges provide a wide range of vocational preparation on both a full-time and day-release basis. They also offer SCE courses for those who left school at 16 and who subsequently wish to obtain 'O' or 'H' grade qualifications.

*Adult and Community Education*

A range of leisure-time courses in both academic and non-academic subjects for people of all ages and interests is provided by the education authorities, the Workers' Education Association (WEA) and extra-mural departments in universities. Following the publication of the Alexander Report[15] on adult education, the existing youth and community service, which made provision for the leisure-time needs of young people, was combined with the adult education service into a new community education service. In addition, a council for community education in Scotland was set up in 1979. Many people now look to community education as a means of introducing new ideas into the education system. In particular, this part of the system is in direct contact with many current social problems such as unemployment and poverty. Adult education provides training in literacy skills through the basic adult education scheme which is an extension of the original adult literacy scheme. Unfortunately, community education is often referred to as the 'Cinderella' of the system, being relatively ill-financed. It also attracts criticism for not being sufficiently concerned with local issues, such as poor facilities in disadvantaged areas, and for stressing the needs of individuals rather than issues affecting groups such as the unemployed and ethnic minorities.

EDUCATION AND SOCIAL CHANGE

The challenge now facing out education system is perhaps the most profound since the introduction of compulsory schooling in 1872. The source of this challenge is the rapidly changing nature of society. Changes in social organisation, in particular the distribution of work, are now well under way and, coupled with falling school populations, they require a reappraisal of the education process. We are rapidly moving away from a society in which the focus of human endeavour has been predominantly geared to the manufacturing process. With the shift towards the service sector, the introduction of automation in the production process and the growth in unemployment, a decreasing number of people are engaged in productive work. The emerging 'post-industrial' society could be one in which power and resources are divided with unprecedented unevenness between workers and non-workers. Conceivably, however, the society of the future might be characterised by a more equitable distribution of opportunities and rewards. How far and in what way education can and should react to these rapid social changes, and attempt to influence their outcome, is both controversial and politically contentious. Even if one accepts that education is concerned with the transmission of fundamental human values and the struggle to create a more just, humane and civilised society, there are very different views as to how the education system should be changed.

How far any education system has the capacity to influence the speed and direction of social change is itself uncertain, but most educationists now accept the view that it is a relatively weak agent of change. The system responds slowly to the wider society rather than being the engine of social change. The argument that education has a role to play in social change has, however, been restated in a recent book, *Education, Politics and the State*.[16]

One immediate challenge brought about by changes in society is the growing incidence of youth unemployment. The response of successive governments has been to support the Manpower Services Commission (MSC) in its efforts to improve the employability of young people between the ages of 16 and 19 who are without work. Increasingly, the MSC's special programmes have overlapped with traditional educational activity, and have heightened rather than resolved the tension between the 'training' and 'education' elements. The whole field of the 16 to 19 year old is now the focus of attention both in political and educational circles (see chapter 9). In Scotland a comprehensive approach to the problem is being adopted by Strathclyde regional council, in that it is now recognised that a new strategy for post-compulsory education and training is required involving all the agencies with responsibilities in this field: industry, colleges of further education and the MSC.[17]

But if youth unemployment is beginning to have effects on further education, it has not yet led to major changes in secondary schooling. There is convincing evidence that many young people now see little advantage in striving for certificates which they believe to be of little value, and that general disaffection from school is now a growing problem.[18] The kind of response which the schooling system should make is a source of fierce contention and ideological debate. The various ideological stances have been grouped into four categories: conservative, liberal, radical and Marxist.[19] Conservatives criticise schools for not being sufficiently concerned with the maintenance of academic standards and they place a strong emphasis on the teaching of traditional subjects. They claim that the teaching profession has directly contributed to the lowering of standards by being over-concerned with progressive methods and 'pastoral' matters such as guidance and counselling. Their remedy is that both government and parents should assert greater control over what is taught and how it is taught. Teachers must regain their authority and be made more accountable through greater parental choice; hence the 1979 Conservative government has promoted parental choice of schools. An extension of parental choice is the proposal for an educational voucher system currently under debate in some Conservative circles.

It is often claimed forcefully that standards of achievement in basic subjects have fallen, and equally vigorously denied. The evidence is by no means clear-cut, and there is a tendency for selected data to be deployed to support either current practices or proposed changes. In general, conservative critics are inclined to use the 'falling standards' argument as a means of exerting pressure on schools to pay more attention to basic subjects and perhaps to become more amenable to SED policy. It is arguable therefore that the fundamental issue is that of the distribution of control over schooling.

Liberal ideology also regards freedom as an important consideration, and it sees the education system as restricting many individuals from achieving their full potential. Liberals are often concerned with the under-utilisation of talents, particularly within the lower status groups in society. This 'waste' is regarded as socially unjust and blame is attributed to an inappropriate school curriculum, maladministration and insufficient resources. The key slogan of liberal ideology during the post-war period has been 'equality of educational opportunity'. To create wider opportunities for all, educational hurdles within the schools such as selection tests and limited access have been abandoned; support services such as compensatory and remedial education, guidance facilities and more effective management of schools have been promoted; and higher education has been greatly expanded following the Robbins report.

A recent innovation to tap more effectively the under-utilised talents of the working class children has been the development of the community school, which in Scotland has been pioneered by Lothian and Grampian regional councils.[20] In most instances these schools are purpose-built and provide a wide range of activities including the publication of a community newspaper (for example, *Commune* in Craigroyston in Edinburgh), certificate classes for adults and leisure and recreation facilities for all. They represent one of the more interesting developments in Scottish education in the 1980s.

Another issue that is of concern to liberals is poverty and the related phenomena of disadvantage and deprivation. Attempts to offset the problems of poverty through the education system have met with varying degrees of success since the first major American initiative, Project Headstart, in the 1960s. Although early results from this 'war on poverty' were disappointing, longer-term findings show distinct educational advantages for positive discrimination. In Scotland the EPA project in Dundee also produced mixed results, though the more recent area-based initiative in Govan succeeded in generating a high level of community participation in novel educational activities. Nevertheless, our society is still seriously affected by the social implications of poverty. The effects of disadvantage remain as acute as ever, as indicated in the recent work of the National Children's Bureau.[21] It is not surprising therefore that liberal ideology, which has dominated educational policy since the second world war, is now under attack.

Although radical educational ideas have been in existence for some time they have met with considerable resistance from virtually all existing power bases in Scottish education: the professionals, the administrators and the politicians. The radicals claim that the education system is more concerned with social control than with freedom and liberation for all, and that this control is a consequence of our particular social organisation which they believe to be unnecessarily hierarchical. Schooling is seen as a socially divisive agency, in that it is claimed to be oppressive, manipulative and exploitative, particularly for the working class.

The radical critique of education takes more than one form: 'liberation' is a central notion, but is not always interpreted in the same way. Some writers are concerned with liberation in the sense of a development of critical consciousness.[22] Their solution to the problems of the school is to dismantle the institutional nature of schooling so that the whole community becomes the context for education and every member a potential 'teacher'. One such attempt was the free-school in Barrowfield in Glasgow, which attracted considerable attention when it existed some years ago. Another manifestation of these ideas is the growing number of parents who opt to educate their children other than by sending them to school, though usually they are middle class.

The libertarian radicals are criticised from both ends of the political spectrum. Those of conservative outlook attack them for promoting anarchy. Marxist socialists, on the other hand, see them as naive for failing to recognise the political and economic forces at work under capitalism. Whilst both groups see schooling as an exploitative and dehumanising process, the Marxists locate the solution firmly in the revolutionary overthrow of capitalist institutions — of which schools are but one example — whilst libertarians see the future in terms of individual awareness. Marxists view schools as agencies for the reproduction of social relations required for the efficient production of goods and services, a process which they regard as immoral. For Marxists, the ultimate solution, of educational as of all other human problems, is to be found only in the overthrow of capitalism. The extent of such beliefs among Scottish teachers is, however, extremely limited.

The struggle for change in Scottish education, which is currently being fought in the schools with ammunition from Munn and Dunning reports and the parents' charter, is piecemeal and lacking in any real appreciation of the present crisis. The ideological scales are now tipping in the direction of liberal-conservatism and away from the ideas of the socialist-liberal reformers of the post-war era, but whether this shift in direction will be maintained depends to a large extent on how much the issue of unemployment affects the schools. The proposal to introduce a new examination for young people who return to school after failing to find employment is a clear bid from schools to become more involved in the education of the 16 to 19 year olds.

The plan for new degree courses in community and leisure education is a further indication that they will have a key role to play in coping with unemployment in the years ahead. Whether these proposals are sufficient to meet the challenge of the social upheaval now taking place remains a matter for speculation.

*References*

1. For a recent discussion of the problems facing Scottish education see: N.D.C. Grant, *Crisis in Scottish Education*, Saltire Society, 1982.
2. Scottish Education Department, *Primary Education in Scotland*, Cmnd. 3216, HMSO, 1966.
3. Scottish Education Department, *Children in Primary 4 and Primary 7*, HMSO, 1981.
4. Scottish Education Department, *The Structure of the Curriculum in the Third and Fourth Years of the Scottish Secondary School* (Munn Report), HMSO, 1977.
5. Scottish Education Department, *Assessment for All: Report of the Committee to Review Assessment in the Third and Fourth Years of Secondary Education in Scotland* (Dunning Report), HMSO, 1977.
6. Department of Education and Science, *Special Educational Needs: Report of the Committee of Enquiry into the Education of Handicapped Children and Young People* (Warnock Report), Cmnd. 7212, HMSO, 1978.
7. For an account of school councils see: A. Macbeth, M. MacKenzie and I. Breckenridge, *Scottish School Councils: policy-making, participation or irrelevance?*, HMSO, 1980.
8. Scottish Education Department, *Truancy and Indiscipline in Schools in Scotland* (Pack Report), HMSO, 1977.
9. See: *Education in Scotland: A Statement of Policy*, Cmnd. 5175, HMSO, 1972.
10. For an account of the educational priority schemes see: *Educational Priority*, Vols. 1-5, HMSO, 1972-74. (The Scottish scheme, based in Dundee, is described in Vol. 5.)
11. J. Overton, *Stepping Stone Projects*, Scottish Pre-school Playgroups Association, 1982.
12. J. Raven, *Parents, Teachers and Children*, Scottish Council for Research in Education, 1981; and G. McCail, *Mother Start*, Scottish Council for Research in Education, 1981.
13. J.E. Wilkinson, D. Grant and D. Williamson, *Strathclyde Experiment in Education: Govan Project: Public Report*, University of Glasgow, Department of Education, 1978.
14. Department of Education and Science, *Higher Education* (Robbins Report), Cmnd. 2154, HMSO, 1963.
15. Department of Education and Science, *Adult Education: Challenge of Change* (Alexander Report), HMSO, 1975.
16. B. Tapper and E. Salter, *Education, Politics and the State*, Methuen, 1982.
17. Strathclyde Regional Council, *Discussion Paper: A Strategy for Post-Compulsory Education and Training*, Strathclyde Regional Council, 1981.
18. L. Gow and A. McPherson, *Tell Them From Me*, Aberdeen University Press, 1980.
19. G. Grace, *Teachers, Ideology and Control*, Routledge and Kegan Paul, 1978.

20. J. Nisbet, L. Hendry, C. Stewart and J. Watt, *Towards Community Education: An Evaluation of Community Schools*, Aberdeen University Press, 1980.
21. P. Wedge and J. Essen, *Children in Adversity*, Pan Books, 1982.
22. P. Freire, *Pedagogy of the Oppressed*, Penguin, 1972.

## FURTHER READING

N.D.C. Grant and R.E. Bell, *Patterns of Education in the British Isles*, Allen and Unwin, 1977.
S.L. Hunter, *The Scottish Education System*, Pergamon Press, 1972.
Descriptions of the education system in Scotland.

G. Kirk, *Curriculum and Assessment in the Scottish Secondary School*, Ward Locke, 1982.
An analysis of the proposals of the Munn and Dunning reports.

M. Young and G. Whitty, *Society, State and Schooling*, The Falmer Press, 1977.
An important book for those interested in the current debate on the political and social aspects of education.

# 9

## *Manpower Services*

The three main aspects of manpower services are the provision of training, the organisation of labour market information and the implementation of a series of special measures for dealing directly with the problem of unemployment. They are designed to improve the competitive edge of individuals in the labour market or to increase the efficiency of that market. Though they have major economic functions, manpower services can also be regarded as part of the social services. Other services, such as social security and health care, have to cope with the casualties of labour market competition and, to the extent that manpower policies are successful (say in reducing the level of unemployment), the demands on social services in general may be reduced. There are, however, links between the manpower and social services which run in the opposite direction. For example, at the policy level it is often argued that social security schemes for the unemployed generate higher rates of unemployment than would otherwise prevail. At a more immediate level an individual's health, education and so on are known to be important influences on pay levels, unemployment experience and other indicators of success in the labour market.

In the first section of this chapter there is a general discussion of the relationship between manpower problems and policies on the one hand, and social problems and policies on the other. The next section looks at the facts on employment problems in Scotland and where relevant considers the extent to which certain problems are more prevalent within Scotland than in the rest of Britain. The third section examines the principal manpower services and assesses their contribution towards the solution of specific problems. Finally, there is a discussion of some general issues surrounding manpower services as an arm of social policy.

EMPLOYMENT PROBLEMS AND SOCIAL PROBLEMS

Most people have to sell their labour in order to generate the incomes necessary to support themselves and their families. Although the market for labour is very different from the market for goods and services there are also common characteristics. First, some types of labour fetch higher prices than others. In part this reflects differences in the qualities of labour between individuals. For example, some have undertaken more education and training than others. Second, as in the case of commodities, surpluses and shortages are common in the labour market. The surpluses manifest themselves as unemployment in particular occupations or regions; and throughout the 1970s there was a growing *overall* surplus. In the early 1980s the economy is in the grip of a severe recession with levels of unemployment unprecedented in the post-war period.

The basic problem arising from the operation of the labour market is the inability of certain groups of individuals to generate a reasonable level of income over a given period of time. This is the proximate cause of many phenomena which we would label social problems. Low income means that access to goods and services is limited. This influences the consumption of essential commodities like food, clothing and housing by reducing the quantity and the quality of goods and services enjoyed. Apart from the direct problem of poverty as measured by income levels, the low levels of consumption of certain necessary goods and services lead to secondary problems; for example, poor housing conditions generate health problems, educational problems and general family stress. Problems such as these are treated by various social service organisations, though in some instances the cause lies one step back.

Low income does not simply influence the ability to consume goods and services sold in the market-place. Many of the services which help to raise the welfare of individuals and families are provided by the state and its various agencies. It is known that the consumption of health and education services is disproportionately large among the higher income groups when differing morbidity rates are taken into account.[1] Although there are many explanations for this, one is that public sector facilities tend to be inferior in the poorer areas which contain disproportionate numbers of people with disadvantageous labour market characteristics.

The failure to generate adequate incomes in the labour market can arise from a number of circumstances. First, it may reflect low wages whilst in employment. Although individuals may be in regular employment their jobs simply do not pay enough to sustain a reasonable standard of living. Second, unemployment creates a situation where incomes are depressed. For many people experiencing unemployment this may be a relatively short-lived phenomenon. However, there are two problem groups. First, there are the long-term unemployed consisting of people who have been out of work for substantial periods of time. As a consequence they suffer considerable loss of income. In addition, many studies have suggested that long periods out of work can lead to medical problems of a physical and a psychological nature. The loss of income understates the cost of long-term unemployment to the individual and the social problems it creates. The problem is further aggravated inasmuch as long periods out of work may lower the income-generating capacities of the individual over the longer term. Partly this reflects the physical and mental damage resulting from unemployment and partly the skill loss resulting from long periods of idleness. This problem was neatly summarised in a famous pre-war study of unemployment:

> [U]nemployed men are not simply units of employability who can, through the medium of the dole, be put in cold storage and taken out again immediately they are needed. While they are in cold storage, things are likely to happen to them.[2]

A second problem group consists of those who suffer recurrent spells of unemployment. If we consider a sufficiently long period of time the problem of recurrent unemployment can be seen more easily. In a period of, say, three years many workers will experience no unemployment at all; others may experience one or two long periods out of work amounting to, say, one year of unemployment in total. A similar amount of unemployment can result where workers experience many spells of unemployment; say 12 spells of one month each. Serious income losses can result although less is known about the side-effects of this type of unemployment.

One crucial aspect of the problem of unemployment follows from these considerations. The incidence of unemployment falls heavily on a minority of the labour force. Those with lengthy durations or recurrent spells account for a very large proportion of the weeks lost through unemployment in any one year. A second consideration is that the unemployed are not 'chosen at random'. Certain groups have higher probabilities of becoming unemployed and of experiencing extensive periods of unemployment. Groups such as the young, the old and the unskilled experience consistently higher unemployment rates than the average for the labour force as a whole.

So far we have described how the labour market can generate social problems. It is also the case that the problems people bring to the labour market will influence their likelihood of unemployment and low income. Health problems, including disability, are a good example of this. Such difficulties may prove an impediment to getting a job. Where people already have a job they may be more prone to dismissal or be forced to quit because their health difficulties place too great a strain on their ability to carry it out. Similar labour market disadvantages apply to individuals with, for example, limited education and prison records. We should also note the strong possibility of interaction between social and labour market difficulties. Reference has been made already to the impact of unemployment on health. Consequent health problems then influence future labour market success.

Fierce arguments have raged over a more contentious link between social and manpower policy. The debate revolves around the influence of the level of benefits for the unemployed on the overall extent of unemployment. It is argued that the higher the ratio of benefit income to expected earnings the longer will be the duration of unemployment, because the more attractive is unemployment relative to employment. This argument received much of its impetus from the observation of a large jump in the potential benefit-earnings ratio in 1966 with the introduction of the (now abolished) earnings related supplement to unemployment benefit, which was coupled with a significant upward shift in the level of unemployment.

A number of studies have investigated the issue and the following seeks to be a fair summary of their findings. Workers with a high benefit income (relative to their potential earnings) experience longer spells of unemployment than those with a low ratio. However, the effect of benefits tends not to be large and when attention is centred on those who have already been unemployed for some time benefits no longer appear to influence the remaining time out of work. So there is some evidence that the variation in the ratio of benefit income to earned income explains why some *individuals* are unemployed for longer than others. Whether there is a relationship between benefits and the *aggregate* level of unemployment is less clear. If benefits were to be raised would unemployment in Scotland rise still further? It is more likely that if some job searchers were to turn down offers they would have accepted before the rise in benefit some other unemployed individuals will snap these offers up. Employers now have a range of highly acceptable candidates to choose from for most vacancies. In this instance a rise in benefits would have no influence on the level of unemployment. A similar argument can be applied to the effect of a fall in benefits.

EMPLOYMENT PROBLEMS IN SCOTLAND

The problems of unemployment and low pay are clearly not confined to Scotland. In this section an attempt is made to assess the extent of these problems in Scotland relative to Britain as a whole. These relativities are examined over a period of time to assess the direction and magnitude of change. The emphasis is placed on the problem of unemployment which has grown in significance in the last decade. Recent trends in Scottish unemployment are also examined.

*Earnings*

Historically the incidence of low pay was relatively higher in Scotland, largely because average earnings were lower in Scotland than in Britain as a whole. However, we can see from Table 9.1 that average earnings in Scotland moved closer to the British average in the course of the 1970s. By 1982 there was no difference in average male earnings, although the gap for females had not yet closed.

Several other points not illustrated in Table 9.1 are worth noting. First, if we consider manual workers only, males in Scotland now have earnings significantly higher than the British average. Second, the less satisfactory performance on non-manual earnings is partly accounted for by the very high earnings for this group in the south-east of England. The concentration here of administrative functions for the public and private sectors produces a disproportionate number of high-level and high-paying jobs. Nevertheless, male non-manual workers in Scotland come second in the regional earnings league after south-east England.

TABLE 9.1

Average Weekly Earnings for Full-Time Adult Workers

|  | Males | | | Females | | |
|  | Scotland £ | Great Britain £ | Relative* | Scotland £ | Great Britain £ | Relative* |
| --- | --- | --- | --- | --- | --- | --- |
| 1970 | 28.3 | 30.0 | 94.3 | 15.3 | 16.3 | 93.9 |
| 1975 | 60.3 | 60.8 | 99.2 | 35.9 | 37.4 | 96.0 |
| 1980 | 123.1 | 124.5 | 98.9 | 74.7 | 78.8 | 94.8 |
| 1981 | 140.0 | 140.5 | 99.6 | 87.1 | 91.4 | 95.3 |
| 1982 | 154.5 | 154.5 | 100.0 | 95.0 | 99.0 | 96.0 |

*The 'relative' expresses Scottish average earnings as a percentage of the British average. Relatives equal to 100 indicate average earnings in Scotland which are equivalent to those for Britain as a whole.

Source: Department of Employment, *New Earnings Surveys*, 1970-1982.

## Unemployment

Scotland has suffered from relatively high unemployment for many decades. As in the case of earnings, the position of Scotland relative to Britain has improved over the last decade. For much of the post-war period Scotland's unemployment rate was roughly twice the British level. Over the last ten years or so the situation has improved dramatically although the Scottish unemployment rate is still roughly one third higher than the British rate. The movement of the Scottish unemployment relative (the Scottish unemployment rate expressed as a percentage of the British rate) through time is plotted against the British unemployment rate in Figure 9.1.

The graph illustrates the dramatic improvement in Scotland's relative unemployment position through time. However, we can also see that this improvement is generally associated with a worsening in absolute terms of both the British and Scottish unemployment problem. Unemployment in Scotland has simply grown less rapidly than in Britain as a whole. Nonetheless, there has been a real improvement in relative terms, as can be seen by comparing years when the British unemployment rate was at roughly the same level. For example, the British unemployment rate was 2.2 per cent in 1963 and 2.5 per cent in 1974, while the relative fell from 201 to 156 over the same period.

A number of factors explain this relative improvement. First, the application of regional policy since the mid-1960s has undoubtedly improved the employment position in Scotland relative to Britain as a whole. Second, oil developments have generated jobs which would not otherwise have been created although the absolute level of job creation has been relatively low.

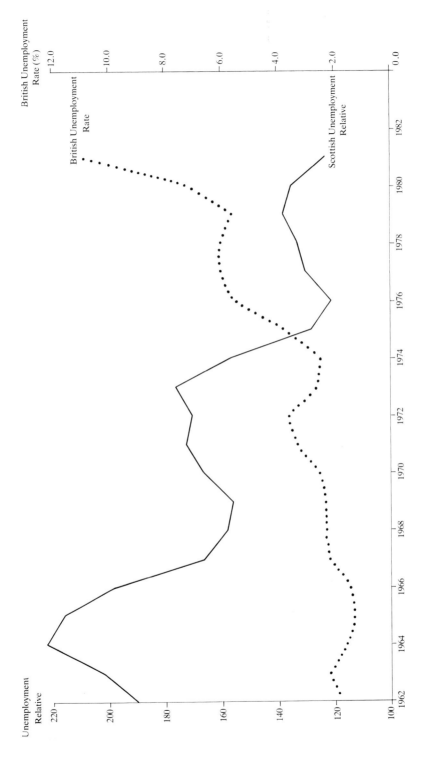

FIGURE 9.1: Scottish Unemployment Relative and British Unemployment Rate 1962-1981

Third, in recent years the government has subsidised temporary employment creation through a variety of schemes, from which Scotland has benefited disproportionately.

It is misleading simply to compare Scottish and British unemployment rates. The variation in unemployment rates within Scotland is itself substantial. Some of the flavour of this variation can be captured by looking at the unemployment rates for the local authority regions. These figures are presented in Table 9.2.

At the extremes the unemployment rate for the Western Isles is over three times as great as that for the Shetlands. Between these extremes there is considerable variation. The variation in unemployment rates within Scotland is much greater than that between Scotland and Britain as a whole. We should not be surprised by this. Scotland is a relatively large land mass with a number of communities which are relatively isolated from each other. In theory mobility of labour between different areas can lead to a narrowing of the differentials in unemployment rates. It has been suggested that labour mobility within Scotland is low because of the high level of reliance on council housing.[3] The argument is that people are reluctant to move in case they are sent to the end of the council house queue in their new area of residence. There is little evidence to support this view. However, we will discuss the contribution of the employment service towards the stimulation of labour mobility in the next section.

Table 9.3 presents a variety of figures relating to unemployment in recent years. The overall numbers unemployed have nearly trebled between 1975 and

TABLE 9.2

Unemployment Rates for Scottish Local Authority Regions and Islands Areas, January 1983

| Region | Unemployment Rate* % |
|---|---|
| Shetland | 7.5 |
| Grampian | 9.5 |
| Borders | 10.5 |
| Orkney | 13.2 |
| Lothian | 13.0 |
| Fife | 14.2 |
| Tayside | 14.7 |
| Highland | 15.7 |
| Central | 16.4 |
| Dumfries and Galloway | 15.0 |
| Strathclyde | 18.0 |
| Western Isles | 26.1 |

* Rate for males and females combined.

Source: *Employment Gazette*, February 1983.

TABLE 9.3    Recent Unemployment Trends in Scotland

|       | Rate % | Total (000s) | Women (000s) | School Leavers at July (000s) | Long-Term* at July (000s) | Vacancies (000s) |
|-------|--------|--------------|--------------|-------------------------------|---------------------------|------------------|
| 1975  | 5.2    | 112.4        | 27.2         | 16.0                          | 21.5                      | 16.9             |
| 1976  | 7.0    | 154.4        | 43.0         | 22.7                          | 27.7                      | 14.4             |
| 1977  | 8.1    | 182.8        | 57.1         | 27.8                          | 38.7                      | 16.4             |
| 1978  | 8.2    | 184.7        | 61.0         | 26.9                          | 52.8                      | 20.6             |
| 1979  | 8.0    | 181.5        | 62.8         | 24.7                          | 48.8                      | 21.5             |
| 1980  | 10.0   | 225.7        | 78.6         | 32.5                          | 49.0                      | 16.5             |
| 1981  | 13.6   | 307.2        | 99.0         | 30.0                          | 79.9                      | 12.6             |
| 1982† | 14.6   | 318.0        | 94.1         | 34.8                          | 118.6                     | 13.3             |

* Out of work for over 52 weeks.
† Number of unemployed calculated on new basis (benefit claimants).

Sources: *Scottish Abstract of Statistics* and *Employment Gazette*.

1981. However, the numbers of female and long-term unemployed rose by a factor of four. The rise in the number of unemployed school leavers was disguised by the introduction of the Youth Opportunities Programme which is discussed later in the chapter.

An additional point worth noting (but not in the table) is that Scotland has a relatively high proportion of the very long-term unemployed, with 25 per cent of its unemployed out of work for one year or more in July 1981. Comparisons with more prosperous regions show stark differences. Only 9.3 per cent of the unemployed in the south-east of England had been out of work for over a year.

So far we have presented various descriptions of the unemployment problems in Scotland. Although descriptive material can be of use to policy makers, it is more important to be able to analyse the nature of the unemployment problem. One convenient analytical device is the decomposition of unemployment into various components. At the simplest level there are three important categories of unemployment.

1. *Demand-deficient*: This reflects the overall lack of jobs due to a generally low level of activity in the economy as a whole. It is conventionally measured as the excess of the numbers unemployed over the number of unfilled vacancies.

2. *Frictional*: The labour market is a complex and imperfect mechanism. Information about jobs and workers is not always readily available and is often imperfect. As a result it takes time to match up unemployed individuals with job vacancies which they are capable of filling. At any point in time there will be some proportion of the unemployed who match existing vacancies and who will eventually fill these.

3. *Structural*: Structural unemployment exists where there are job vacancies which cannot be filled from the stock of the unemployed. There are

two dimensions to this. First, there may be many vacancies but few unemployed in particular skill classifications. In other skill categories the numbers unemployed may greatly exceed the volume of vacancies. Second, there may be many vacancies in one area but few unemployed; and in another area the situation may be reversed. Thus, if some of the unemployed were to train for the skill-shortage occupations, or move to labour-shortage areas, the overall level of unemployment would be reduced. As we shall see in the next section, the manpower services can play a role in attempting to reduce structural unemployment.

How does this decomposition of unemployment relate to the Scottish unemployment problem? Undoubtedly, Scotland and the other depressed regions have experienced high levels of demand-deficient unemployment for many decades. The object of regional policy has been to correct this regional imbalance in the level of employment opportunities. However, several studies have suggested that the Scottish labour market is more inefficient than the labour markets in other regions.[4] This is measured by trying to estimate the amount of frictional and structural unemployment.

It should be borne in mind that, even if the Scottish labour market could be made more efficient the level of unemployment in Scotland would still be extremely high. In 1981 there were on average over 300,000 unemployed in Scotland. The corresponding number of vacancies notified to the Employment Service was under 13,000. Roughly there are three actual vacancies for every vacancy notified, so there were approximately 40,000 vacancies. If all vacancies were filled instantaneously there would still have been an average of around 260,000 unemployed.

The overall lack of jobs is traditionally the responsibility of national government through budgetary and regional policy measures. However, the manpower agencies have taken on some responsibilities for this problem, as well as carrying out more detailed intervention in operations of the labour market to deal with particular problems of unemployment and the difficulties of particular groups.

THE MANPOWER SERVICES COMMISSION

The provision of most manpower services in centralised in a national body, the Manpower Services Commission (MSC). The MSC is made up of a number of divisions. There have been three main operational divisions:

1. the Employment Service Division (ESD);
2. the Training Services Division (TSD); and
3. the Special Programmes Division (SPD).

In April 1983, however, the TSD and SPD were amalgamated. Although the MSC is devolved organisationally, and its operations in Scotland have been the responsibility of the Secretary of State for Scotland since 1979, it is fair to say that manpower policies are designed to apply to the whole of Britain. But some regions and areas receive disproportionate shares of the resources allocated to particular policy instruments.

In this section we describe the main manpower policies and consider their contribution towards ameliorating the problem of unemployment within Scotland.

## General Placing Services

It is the stated objective of the ESD 'to help people choose, train for and get the right jobs, and employers to get the right people as quickly as possible.'[5] This objective relates directly to reducing the level of frictional unemployment. If the skills of individuals and the requirements of jobs can be matched more accurately, unnecessary job changing will be reduced. The quicker the matching process is carried out the lower will be the level of frictional unemployment.

We noted in the last section the problems of gathering information in the labour market. These problems have been recognised for some time and one of the reasons for setting up the first labour exchanges was the desire to systematise the matching of workers and job vacancies. In the modern employment service this objective is pursued in a number of ways. First, in many areas local employment offices have been replaced by jobcentres where vacancies are on open display. These vacancies can be consulted by unemployed and employed alike. This 'self-service' approach is a characteristic feature of jobcentres, and the MSC hope that the modernisation of the service will attract more job seekers as well as more vacancies from employers. The notification of vacancies by employers is not compulsory and it is thought that only about one vacancy in three is notified.

Second, the more traditional service of matching job seekers to vacancies continues. Here employment advisers interview men and women registered with the employment service. They may submit them to what are considered to be suitable job vacancies. Alternatively, they may advise the registrants to consider training or some other specialist service provided by one or other of the manpower agencies. It is in this last area that the employment service differs most clearly from private employment agencies which also provide information on job vacancies and attempt to match-up the requirements of job seekers and employers.

There is little evidence to suggest that the labour market in Scotland is more complex or more deficient in information than in Britain as a whole. Therefore, it is unlikely that these services make a particular contribution to solving Scotland's employment problem. This is more so given the very high levels of unemployment now prevailing and the very low level of vacancies. We will return to the information and placement services later but now we turn to consider policies — assisted geographical mobility and training — which influence the level of structural unemployment.

*Assisted Geographical Mobility*

For a number of years the employment service has run schemes to promote the mobility of workers between different areas. The major instrument has been the Employment Transfer Scheme which gives financial aid to workers taking a job beyond daily travelling distance from their home, provided the workers are unemployed or liable to redundancy within a given period.

The rationale for such a policy is clear. Vacancies may exist in some regions which cannot be filled from the local stock of unemployed. In other regions suitably qualified unemployed may have little prospect of finding work locally. Thus the policy of 'taking the workers to the work' may reduce the overall level of unemployment by cutting the amount of structural unemployment caused by geographical mismatches. Scotland is large enough to include a number of fairly distinct labour markets. We have already noted the suggestion that geographical mobility is low within Scotland because of the predominance of council housing as a tenure form. It might be thought that assisted mobility schemes are, therefore, of great importance in the Scottish context. However, there have been substantial cuts in provision; in 1980-81 only 1500 moved under the scheme compared to around 8000 in 1977-78.[6]

There are two problems to note with the schemes for assisted mobility. First, there is evidence that a large proportion of those moving under the scheme would have moved in any event.[7] In this circumstance the financial aid provided by the government is more of a bonus for moving than an inducement to move. Second, the contribution of geographical mobility towards a reduction in the level of unemployment falls as the overall level of unemployment rises. When unemployment stands at generally high levels there are few localities where existing vacancies cannot be filled from the local pool of unemployed. In these circumstances assisted mobility will do little to reduce the overall level of unemployment. Migrants into a given area will simply take jobs that would otherwise have gone to residents of that area; that is, the migrants displace the local unemployed. Indeed it is a fuller recognition of this problem which has led to a substantial cut in the numbers assisted.

*Training*

Training programmes seem an obvious solution to the difficulties experienced in the labour market by those who have few skills or whose skills are redundant. There are two principal components to the national training effort. First, the MSC is involved in training within industry through the Industrial Training Boards (ITBs), whose activities are partially funded by the MSC's Training Services Division. However, the government announced in 1981 that it would remove statutory backing from the majority of ITBs, and MSC support for their activities has been curtailed drastically. Second, the

Training Opportunities Scheme (TOPS) is available to certain categories of individual. The bulk of this training is carried out in colleges of further education or skillcentres. Cuts are taking place here as well. Whereas there were over 9000 TOPS trainees in Scotland in 1979-80 the figure will fall to 7000 by 1983-84. The cuts are concentrated in clerical and commercial training.

The role of the training measures in reducing the level of unemployment in Scotland is limited for reasons similar to those restricting the utility of the policy of assisted mobility. The reduction in unemployment resulting from training programmes will be greater the larger the number of vacancies which cannot otherwise be filled. Where there are few vacancies and many unemployed the chances are that most of these vacancies could be filled by some unemployed person without the need for training. In the final analysis training does not create jobs in any direct sense. Where the underlying problem is one of an overall shortage of jobs the successful placement of trainees in jobs will generally be at the expense of other people who are unemployed. That is the trainee takes a job that would otherwise have been filled by an unemployed individual already possessing the requisite skills. In any case as unemployment rises trainees become difficult to place, as Table 9.4 demonstrates.

There has been a rise in the proportion (from one-third to one-half) of ex-trainees who simply become unemployed. Even within Scotland there are variations reflecting local unemployment conditions. Nearly 56 per cent of ex-trainees from the north and east found employment compared with only 46 per cent in the west of Scotland.[8] Where labour is plentiful and unemployment is high, trainees are difficult to place.

*Special Programmes*

With the advent of high unemployment levels and the growth of the problem of youth unemployment types of manpower policy new to Britain were introduced. These Special Programmes encompass job creation, work experience, employer subsidies and training measures. The commitment to

TABLE 9.4

Post-Training Experience of Scottish TOPS Trainees

|  | 1978 % | 1979 % | 1980 % |
|---|---|---|---|
| Working and Using Skill | 50 | 49 | 39 |
| Working and Not Using Skill | 17 | 14 | 12 |
| Not Working | 33 | 37 | 49 |

Sources: Manpower Service. Commission, *Annual Reports 1978-79, 1979-80 and 1980-81*, MSC, 1979, 1980 and 1981.

provide employment of a temporary nature began with the introduction of the Job Creation Programme in October 1975. It was designed to provide temporary jobs in labour-intensive projects which would be of benefit to the community. The programme was renamed the Special Temporary Employment Programme (STEP) and, latterly, the Community Enterprise Programme (CEP). The costs of this kind of job creation are relatively low, partly because of an emphasis on labour intensity which reduces the need to utilise expensive capital equipment. In addition, the costs of job creation are further reduced when deductions are made for the various benefits that would otherwise have been paid to those taking part in the schemes.

With the continuing rise in unemployment and the emergence in the 1980s of a serious problem of long-term unemployment it became clear that the scale of these job creation schemes was inadequate. For example, CEP had places for 5700 long-term unemployed adults in Scotland in 1982. At the beginning of 1982 over 100,000 Scots had been unemployed for a year or more. In an attempt to reach a larger number of the long-term unemployed a new Community Programme was introduced in October 1982. This added 100,000 new places to the 30,000 already available in Britain under CEP. The innovation was that most of these new places were to be part-time. As with previous programmes the target groups are those out of work for a year or more. For the younger unemployed (aged 18 to 24) the qualification period is six months out of work. Again in line with earlier programmes full-time and part-time participants receive a wage equivalent to the local 'going rate'.

The Youth Opportunities Programme (YOP) is a much more extensive undertaking. YOP was funded to take 630,000 youngsters in Britain in 1982-83; Scotland has about 15 per cent of this total. YOP provides a variety of different opportunities to youngsters and it is intended to be a training programme and not a job creation programme. The various components of YOP are briefly described in Figure 9.2. It is clear that Work Experience in Employers' Premises (WEEP) is by far the most important component. Whilst on YOP youngsters receive a standard weekly allowance (£25 per week in 1982) in contrast to the wage paid to CEP participants.

YOP has been the subject of extensive criticism. First, the work experience element of YOP has been criticised at a number of levels. It is argued that a high proportion of youngsters receive no training but are used simply as free, unskilled labour by employers. Apart from the issue of the exploitation of these youngsters, the effect of this abuse is to raise the level of unemployment amongst adult unskilled labour; in other words, more people would have been employed in ordinary jobs if free labour under YOP had not been available. This process is known as substitution.

Second, and related to the previous point, there is no evidence to suggest that being on YOP improves a youngster's 'competitive edge'. That is it does not seem to make it more likely they will find normal employment. This suggests that the training content of YOP is very low. In general there has been a growing problem with the fate of youngsters leaving YOP. Of those entering

WEEP in September–October 1978, 78 per cent found work at the end of the programme. This figure had fallen to 39 per cent for those youngsters entering the scheme in the first three months of 1980.[9]

In the light of these and many other detailed criticisms a new Youth Training Scheme (YTS) is to begin in September 1983. The new scheme differs from YOP in a number of ways. First, whereas YOP was a temporary programme the new YTS will constitute a permanent bridge between work and school. Second, the new scheme is supposed to provide a stronger training content than existing YOP initiatives. Each youngster will spend up to one year on the scheme. The training year will be made up of elements already in operation under YOP (for example, work experience and further education). Third, the new scheme will be open to both employed and unemployed school leavers whereas YOP catered only for the unemployed. It remains to be seen whether these changes will eradicate the weaknesses of YOP discussed above.

In addition to the job creation and youth training efforts there are a number of other specific schemes which endeavour to reduce the level of unemployment. The Young Workers' Scheme provides for subsidies to firms employing youngsters in relatively low-paying jobs. To encourage short-time working rather than redundancy the government offers subsidies under the Temporary Short-time Working Compensation Scheme. In an attempt to reduce unemployment by cutting the size of the labour force the Job Release Scheme offers inducements to early retirement. Finally, a new and experimental 'job-splitting' scheme has been introduced. Grants will be given to employers who split full-time into part-time jobs on the assumption that this directly or indirectly reduces the level of unemployment.

The major strength of the various special measures is that they can be targeted towards disadvantaged groups and/or areas. The government can concentrate its resources on the young rather than the old, and on the longer-term rather than the short-term unemployed. A boost of equivalent size but activated through the medium of, say, reduced taxation is less predictable in terms of its influence on the employment of specific labour force groups living in particular areas.

*Service for Disadvantaged Groups*

So far the discussion has concentrated on the relatively mainstream activities of the MSC, and on the effects of various programmes on unemployment in Scotland. In this section some consideration is given to those manpower services which are directed towards the problems of particular disadvantaged groups.

The disabled are catered for by a range of services which mirror the overall pattern of services provided by the MSC; that is, there is assistance with placement, training and employment. Specialist staff (disablement resettlement officers) are employed by the ESD to attempt to place disabled people in employment, recommend suitable training opportunities and help

FIGURE 9.2    Youth Opportunities Programme: Summary of Schemes Available

| Type Opportunity | Name of Scheme (No. of entrants 1980-1981) | Objective | Duration | Provider and Location | Progression |
|---|---|---|---|---|---|
| *Work Preparation* | Short training courses† | Training for a specific though broad occupational area up to operator or semi-skilled level. | Most 13 weeks | TSD Skill centres, Colleges of Further Education, Employers' Establishments. | Many to normal employment. Some to further education or a work experience opportunity. |
| | Remedial and preparatory courses† | Participants should reach basic level of literacy and numeracy and basic entry requirements. | Up to 13 weeks | Colleges of Further Education Employment Rehabilitation Centres. | Most to other opportunities in programme. A few to normal employment. |
| | (Mainly work introduction courses and young people's work preparation courses) | | | | |
| | Assessment and employment induction courses (4100) | To improve young people's employability by assessing work they are most suited for and interested in, improving their knowledge of the world of work and improving basic social skills. | Most 2-3 weeks | Mainly Employers' Establishments. | Some to normal employment. Most to basic skill courses. Some to work experience opportunity. A few to further education. |

† 51,400 entrants to these two schemes.

FIGURE 9.2  (continued)

| Type of Opportunity | Name of Scheme (No. of entrants 1980-1981) | Objective | Duration | Provider and Location | Progression |
|---|---|---|---|---|---|
| *Work Experience* | Employers' premises (WEEP) (242,000) | To give first hand experience of different kinds of work on employers' premises. | Up to 6 months | Employers' Premises. | Many to normal employment. Others to work preparation courses or further education. |
| | * Project-based (20,100) | To provide a range of practical experience of project work of benefit to the community. | 6-12 months | Various sponsors, including local authorities, voluntary organisations, community groups. | Most to normal employment. Others to work preparation courses of further education. |
| | * Community service (30,200) | To provide experience of different kinds of community work. | 6-12 months | Various sponsors, including local authorities, voluntary organisations, community groups. | Most to normal employment. Others to work of further education. |
| | Training | To give first hand experience of different kinds of work in a work group producing goods or services. | 6-12 | Various sponsors as above using vacant factories and other premises or sites. | Many to normal employment. |

* Amalgamated in April 1981 to become Community Projects.

Source: Manpower Services Commission, *Annual Report, 1980-81*, MSC, 1981, Table 12.

with post-training employment placement. Training for the disabled is available under TOPS. As an aid to placement the MSC has administered a quota scheme which requires firms to employ three per cent of their labour force from the ranks of the registered disabled. The MSC argues that the existing quota provisions are unworkable because of the falling number of registered disabled, and it has recommended that the quota system be abandoned although the three per cent figure would remain as a guideline.[10]

About 4000 disabled persons completed TOPS courses in Britain 1980-81. In 1980-81 there were about 14,000 severely disabled people in Britain working in the various forms of sheltered employment. The bulk of these worked for Remploy which is organised as a series of small undertakings receiving annual subsidy from the government, with local authorities and voluntary bodies providing other facilities.

The employment rehabilitation centres (ERCs) provide courses for the disabled, others with sickness or injury problems, the long-term unemployed and younger workers with particular disadvantages. The aim here is to provide assessment and courses of work preparation to acquaint or re-acquaint the participants with the work environment. The numbers involved are extremely small; in 1980-81 just over 1500 people completed courses at the four Scottish ERCs.

Young people under the age of 18 who are socially or personally disadvantaged can find a placement with Community Industry. Although run by voluntary bodies this receives a government grant administered by the MSC. The scheme seeks to give young people work experience on projects producing goods or services of use to the community, and resources are concentrated in areas of high unemployment and the inner cities. Around 7000 places were available for youngsters from all parts of Britain in 1981-82.

These schemes for the disadvantaged can have little impact on the overall unemployment problem. Partly this reflects the fact that the numbers covered are relatively small. More importantly the unemployment rate is not high because of the existence of disadvantaged workers. Rather, when unemployment is high the disadvantaged are placed in a difficult situation as the competition for jobs become fiercer. Possession of some labour market disadvantage raises the likelihood that an individual will be unemployed. The policies outlined above seek to reduce the gap between the disadvantaged and the 'average' worker. Any success that such policies have in a climate of high overall unemployment largely results in redistributing unemployment between individuals.

CONCLUSIONS

In this chapter we have examined the relationship between unemployment problems and social problems, described the problem of unemployment in Scotland, and discussed the major manpower policies in operation. As the current unemployment problem reflects primarily an insufficient demand for labour, traditional manpower policies such as placement and training can do little to reduce its level. There also seems to be limited scope in Scotland or elsewhere for reducing unemployment through subsidising labour mobility and training for shortage occupations. With over 300,000 unemployed in Scotland and roughly 25 unemployed for every vacancy, there are few areas or occupations where labour is in short supply.

If manpower policies do have such limited effect should they not be cut back in times of recession and expanded when the economy is bouyant? Similarly, does it not make more sense to concentrate the resources used by manpower policies in the more prosperous regions where structural unemployment is likely to be a relatively greater problem? In practice the reverse tends to occur.

In effect there is a tension between the social and economic objectives of manpower policy. We noted earlier that ex-trainees from the low unemployment areas within Scotland tend to find work more easily than their counterparts in the high unemployment west of Scotland. At the level of individual characteristics it is also true that the employed can be trained more effectively than the unemployed, the previously skilled more effectively than the unskilled and so on. If economic costs and benefits were the criteria for evaluation there would certainly be good grounds for reducing the volume of resources devoted to manpower policy and for concentrating these resources on the more prosperous areas and the 'better prospects' in the labour force.

The case for a greater emphasis on the social objectives of manpower policy must rest partly on the value society places on spreading the burden of unemployment over a greater number of individuals. Continuing to upgrade the unskilled will lead in the current situation to a rise in the unemployment rates for the skilled relative to the unskilled. Special placement efforts on behalf of the disabled will, if successful, lead to the placement of the disabled at the expense of other groups of unemployed, such as the long-term unemployed. In neither case is there likely to be much impact on the overall level of unemployment. Thus the extensive resources being devoted to manpower policy may simply reshuffle the unemployed. This may be a valued objective of society. Alternatively society may decide that it is simpler to give the victims of unemployment good financial compensation for the costs which they incur.

*References*

1. J. Le Grand, *The Strategy of Equality*, Allen and Unwin, 1982.
2. Pilgrim Trust, *Men out of Work*, Cambridge University Press, 1938.
3. C. Mulvey, 'Labour Market Policy', in D.I. Mackay (ed.), *Scotland 1980: The Economics of Self Government*, Q. Press, 1977.
4. These studies are reported in Mulvey, 'Labour Market Policy'.
5. Manpower Services Commission, *Annual Report 1977-78*, MSC, 1978.
6. MSC, *Annual Report 1977-78* and *Annual Report 1980-81*, MSC, 1981.
7. P.B. Beaumont, 'Assessing the Performance of Assisted Labour Mobility Policy in Britain', *Scottish Journal of Political Economy*, Vol. 24, No. 1, 1977.
8. MSC, *Annual Report 1980-81*.

9. House of Commons: Committee on Scottish Affairs, *Youth Unemployment and Training: Vol. 2, Minutes of Evidence.* HC 96-II/1981-82.
10. Details of the MSC's recommendations can be found in the *Employment Gazette,* July 1981.

### FURTHER READING

Manpower Services Commission, *Review of Services for the Unemployed,* MSC, 1981.
An excellent critique by the MSC of their own policies for the unemployed.

Manpower Services Commission, *Review of the Second Year of the Special Programmes,* MSC, 1981.
A good review and discussion of the various special programmes.

B. Showler, *The Public Employment Service,* Longman, 1976.
A study of the public employment service in Britain which is critical of the lack of emphasis given to the social objectives of the service.

A.P. Thirlwall, 'Government Manpower Policies in Great Britain: Their Rationale and Benefits', *British Journal of Industrial Relations,* Vol. 10, No. 2, 1972.
A readable discussion of the economic aspects of manpower policies.

*Employment Gazette,* HMSO, monthly.
The standard source of statistics on the labour market which also has short, non-technical articles on manpower problems and policies.

# 10

## *Services for the Elderly and Physically Handicapped*

In this chapter we turn our attention to two large groups in the population, the elderly and physically handicapped, who make more than average demands on the income maintenance, health, housing, manpower and personal social services. These services are discussed fully in earlier chapters, and here we focus on provisions of particular relevance to these groups. Special cash benefits and services have grown up, often in a more or less haphazard manner, to meet some of the particular needs of the elderly and the handicapped: policies of 'positive discrimination' to use the phrase originally coined by Richard Titmuss. The result is a bewildering array of provisions made by central and local government, involving professionals from a wide range of disciplines, and by voluntary organisations and volunteers. Some of the consequences of this diversity have already been touched on elsewhere in the book.

Take-up of benefits is, for example, far from complete. Potential beneficiaries may not be fully informed of their entitlements or may be deterred from applying by the complexity of the provisions. In some cases benefits are available only on a test of means that may be seen as an affront to independence and personal pride. With the exception of social security benefits, the services available often vary from area to area. For historical reasons some areas may be better provided than others with hospitals or residential homes, and local authorities vary in their political and financial commitment to developing personal social services. Individuals with like needs may receive very different levels of service according to where they happen to live. In other cases diversity of provision may result in wasteful duplication of services, or in discontinuities of service as when the community health and personal social services are not advised of the needs of patients being discharged from hospital to their own homes. At the same time, the provision of services and cash benefits for such large groups of recipients raises difficulties of demands on public expenditure.

THE ELDERLY

For many purposes the elderly population is defined as men and women of pension age, that is men of 65 and over and women of 60 and over. Much of the information we will be using, however, covers a somewhat different group, men and women of 65 and over; this applies particularly in the case of the health and personal social services. Scotland, in common with other parts of the developed world, has an ageing population. Men and women of pension age, nearly three quarters of a million in total, make up some 17.5 per cent of the population compared with about six per cent at the beginning of the century. The demographic problem of the 1980s and 1990s, however, will not be the increasing size of the elderly population; men and women of pension age will in fact decline somewhat in numbers. But the elderly population itself will age, as Table 10.1 shows. By 1991, of the population aged 65 and over,

TABLE 10.1

Size and Composition by Age of the Elderly Population
(65 and over), Scotland, 1976-1991

|  | Number | 65-74 % | 75-84 % | 85+ % |
|---|---|---|---|---|
| 1976 | 698,200 | 65.4 | 28.7 | 5.9 |
| 1981 | 728,000 | 62.4 | 31.3 | 6.3 |
| 1986 | 727,000 | 59.1 | 33.4 | 7.4 |
| 1991 | 731,000 | 58.3 | 33.4 | 8.3 |

Source: Office of Population Censuses and Surveys, *Population projections* (Series PP2, no. 8), HMSO, 1978.

some two-fifths will be 75 and over (300,000 men and women), and eight per cent will be 85 and over (60,000). It is these older age groups which make the heaviest demands on the health and personal social services. Women far outnumber elderly men and it is among very old women, particularly if single or widowed, that some of the most acute problems of poverty, loneliness and disability arise. A further complication is the uneven spread of the elderly population between different parts of Scotland, to a large extent the result of the emigration of younger people from the remoter rural areas in search of employment in the central belt of Scotland, England or overseas. People of 65 years and over range from about 12 per cent of the total population in the Central and Strathclyde regions to over 20 per cent in the Western Isles, the Borders, Shetland and Orkney, with considerable variations between areas within these regions.

Obviously we are dealing here with a cross-section of society from all social, occupational and income groups who have little in common except that they have reached a certain age. At one end of the spectrum are active, healthy men and women in their early and mid-sixties, while at the other are frail old people in their nineties who may have substantial dependency needs. Age in itself is not the problem and the surprising thing perhaps is that the majority of elderly people, nearly 95 per cent, are able to live independent lives in their own homes or in those of their children or other relatives. Only 15 per cent of these make any calls on the personal social services to substitute for or to supplement the care provided by themselves or by their families. However, health and the capacity for self-care do decline with advancing years, and it may be that families, even if willing, will be unable to give the support that their ageing parents need or may be placed under considerable difficulties in doing so. Family resources are already being stretched by increasing social, occupational and geographical mobility. With rising standards of living the different generations want to live independent lives in homes of their own. More and more married women, who still provide the bulk of care for elderly relatives, have taken up employment outside the home. The decline in family size means that there are fewer children to share the task of caring, and in future increasing numbers of the 'children' of the very old will be past prime working age and may even be in need of support themselves. Nearly one in three of the present generation of pensioners are in any case childless.

The stated objective of provisions for elderly people is to enable them to live independent lives in their own homes for as long as possible, which is also the preferred option of the vast majority of the elderly themselves. For this to be possible an adequate income, suitable housing and appropriate health and personal social services are essential.

*Income Provisions*

From sample surveys of the elderly population, it appears that the majority of pensioners attach most importance to good health and adequate social contacts as a basis for a satisfactory old age. The drop in income which most people experience when they give up work causes less concern although large numbers of elderly people would give an increase in income high priority.[1] After retirement incomes decline still further as savings are used up and the real value of income from investments falls in times of inflation. Elderly women have particularly low incomes. In the case of widows, even if their husbands had occupational pensions, these may have ceased on their death. If single they may never have had a job which carried occupational pension rights. Future generations of the elderly, including women, will have better income protection in their old age.

The main source of income for the great majority of the elderly today is the basic national insurance pension. As we have seen already, this provides an income below the poverty line as defined by the supplementary benefits level. Over one in five pensioners are having their contributory pensions supplemented on a means-tested basis. Though they are not in poverty they are living at the poverty line. There are, however, considerable numbers of pensioners — an estimated 25 per cent of those who are eligible for supplementary benefit — who do not claim their entitlements and therefore have incomes below the poverty line (though the sums unclaimed however are relatively small). More important, those who are receiving supplementary benefit have incomes only between a third and two-fifths of average post-tax manual earnings if single and about a half if married.

On the other hand, one in two of retirement pensioners have an additional pension from their place of work, and many have other income from assets such as bank or building society deposits or investments. The size of these varies very considerably and there are wide inequalities of income within the elderly population. Taken as a group it is estimated that pensioners' incomes are a third or more below the post-tax incomes of the working population. But even if the objective of income maintenance programmes for old age is to maintain standards of living, it does not mean that incomes need be as high as during working life. Family commitments are generally completed, income tax liabilities are lower, and work expenses are no longer relevant. Research on income requirements in old age suggests a figure of 70 to 80 per cent of pre-retirement earnings as a realistic pension objective. This figure is by no means reached by the majority of British pensioners today but prospects for the future are very much brighter. More and more people will retire with two pensions: the basic pension and an additional pension either from an occupational scheme or the state earnings-related scheme. The target for the basic pension plus state additional pension is only of the order of 50 per cent of average gross pre-retirement earnings, but lower income workers will enjoy a higher replacement ratio. Those who receive occupational pensions will have higher incomes on retirement, but problems are likely to arise as pensions in excess of the equivalent entitlement under the state scheme are not guaranteed to rise in line with inflation. The basic issue here is the extent to which the working population and their employers will be willing to forego income in order to finance the pensions of the current generation of pensioners. Commitments have been made to future generations of pensioners which may put an unacceptable burden upon the working population and may be difficult to sustain.

*Health Services*

After the state pension, the national health service is the most important and most widely used source of assistance provided by the social services for elderly people. As a group they make more substantial calls on the NHS than any other sector of the population. The wide range of free provisions — care from a general practitioner, treatment and care in hospital and so on — have removed many fears of ill health and its financial burden. Government figures show that in 1978/79 expenditure on health care and personal social services for persons aged 65 to 74 was over one and a half times the average for the population as a whole, while the figure for people of 75 and over was four and a half times the average.[2] Evidence from the General Household Survey also shows that people over the age of 75 consulted their general practitioners one and a half times as often as persons in younger age groups, and geriatric and psychiatric patients at any one time occupy about half of all hospital beds.

Even so, not all old people are receiving as full a health care service as they need. Some of the responsibility here rests with the elderly themselves; many are reluctant to consult general practitioners because they see their health needs as less pressing than those of young children and mothers, or because they accept as incurable and untreatable what they mistakenly regard as the inevitable health problems of old age. Some general practitioners and health visitors make regular domiciliary visits to frail elderly patients to check up on the state of their health but this is far from being a universal practice. The elderly may benefit from the continuing development of primary health care teams based on group practices or health centres, providing the services of a general practitioner, health visitor and district nurse. On the other hand they may stand to lose if this means that they are deprived of a continuing relationship with a family doctor who is knowledgeable about their psychological and social problems as well as their physical ailments. The closure of many local pharmacies may also deprive the elderly of access to simple advice and medication.

The lack of adequate, accessible dental care may affect both the psychological and physical wellbeing of the elderly person. A mobile, fully-equipped dental service for the housebound and those with transport problems would be the answer, although a costly one. An important facility, which is used by one in four elderly people in any year, is the chiropody service. Minor foot complaints, if untreated, may seriously affect an old person's capacity for self-care and mobility. The extension of this service, both in the numbers of people treated and the frequency of treatment, is held back not only by cost considerations but by the acute shortage of trained chiropodists.

Criticisms can be levelled, too, at the hospital care provided for elderly patients although, to get this in proportion, it must be borne in mind that only about two per cent of old people are hospital in-patients at any time and that in many cases their stays are short. Scotland has taken the lead over England and many other countries in the development of geriatrics as a medical specialism. Scotland is also relatively well provided with geriatric hospital beds with 15 per 1000 of the population over the age of 65. Nevertheless, geriatrics is one of the less prestigious and less sought-after areas of medical and nursing practice so that staffing levels and standards of amenity in many geriatric hospitals, or in the geriatric wards of general hospitals, are below those normally provided for other patients. At the same time, owing to the shortage of geriatric beds, many elderly patients are occupying expensive beds in acute wards, to which they may have originally been admitted for intensive treatment.

A case has been made that with the ageing of the elderly population the NHS should provide on an extensive scale even simpler in-patient nursing facilities than are to be found in geriatric hospitals. This would relieve pressure on other hospital accommodation and also cope with the increasing numbers of very frail residents being admitted to local authority and voluntary residential homes who need more intensive nursing care than these are equipped to provide.[3] Such nursing homes might also cope with the special needs of at least some of the old people with mental disabilities of various kinds. It has been estimated that of the 7000 mentally frail old people who need full-time care about one half are in psychiatric hospitals. Others are inappropriately placed in acute or geriatric hospitals, large numbers are in residential homes which cannot provide all the nursing and medical care required, while those who remain in their own homes do not always receive the necessary high standard of domiciliary health and personal social services.[4]

An important part of the range of provisions for the elderly are day hospitals which provide diagnostic, medical and rehabilitative services on an out-patient basis with the aim of keeping their patients out of full-time hospital care. The number of day hospitals has been growing gradually but there are wide variations between NHS districts in the provision made, and in some cases they do not operate to maximum efficiency because of transport difficulties in getting patients to and from their homes. Day hospitals differ from local authority day centres mentioned below in that their function is primarily medical rather than social, but they perform complementary functions in the spectrum of community care for the elderly.

*Housing*

Suitable housing is another very important factor in making for a satisfactory old age. The majority of elderly people continue to live in ordinary housing which has usually been the family home for a number of years. However, this may be too large for their requirements, expensive to run and to heat and, if owner occupied, expensive to keep in a reasonable state of repair. Nearly half of pensioners in Scotland live in council housing but this is not always suitable. There may be difficulties in obtaining a transfer to a smaller council house although such an exchange would release a unit large enough for a family as well as providing the older person with more appropriate accommodation. Owner occupiers, who make up about 30 per cent of the elderly population, may find great difficulty in getting a suitable council tenancy or in purchasing a smaller house if they decide to sell their existing home because of its size or because they wish to move to be nearer relatives. Both local housing authorities and the private housing market have been slow to respond to the need for small housing units suitable for elderly occupants. But the poorest housing conditions are found among those who live in privately rented accommodation, about one in five of elderly households. This section of the housing market is notorious for its lack of basic amenities, such as an indoor WC, a bath or a hot water supply, and for the poor standard of maintenance and repair. A good deal of progress has been made in recent years, however, in the rehabilitation of formerly privately rented accommodation by housing associations in housing action areas, where many of the residents tend to be elderly.

In the light of evidence from the 1971 census of the far from satisfactory housing conditions of the elderly, central government drew up guidelines in the mid-1970s for a more flexible approach to meeting their needs.[5] Three types of housing were distinguished: 'mainstream' dwellings, that is ordinary housing stock; 'amenity' housing, that is small units with central heating and various built-in aids for the elderly; and 'sheltered' housing, which is amenity housing with the addition of a resident warden, a call-system and possibly other services such as communal dining, laundry or recreational facilities. It was envisaged that the majority of the elderly would continue to live in small mainstream houses but that the supply of amenity and sheltered housing should be greatly increased either by conversion or new building. Sheltered housing, if well designed and if backed up by adequate domiciliary services, can often delay the necessity for entry to a residential home or hospital. Ideally, flexible use should be made of different types of housing and residential care to meet the requirements of individual elderly people.

A target of 25 sheltered units per 1000 of the population over 65 seemed reasonable in the early 1970s, although subsequent research suggests that 50 places per thousand would not be excessive.[6] At the same time, about 100 amenity housing units per 1000 people over 65 was suggested as a broad guideline. Some local housing authorities have shown considerable initiative in developing these schemes but there are wide variations between areas and progress overall has been slow. The present supply is only about a third of the way to meeting the original target in the case of sheltered housing and the provision of amenity housing is only about a tenth of the guideline. Doubts have also been expressed about the validity of claims that are made for sheltered housing. Do local authorities achieve the appropriate mix of ages and states of dependency in selecting occupants so that they can be of mutual assistance to each other? What role is the warden expected to fulfil? Is too much expected of her in the way of services? What happens to tenants as they become more frail and more dependent? This is an aspect of housing provision to which more attention needs to be paid, and which calls for close collaboration between housing departments, social work departments and the voluntary housing associations which are active in this field.

*Personal Social Services*

If old people are to live independent lives in their own homes for as long as possible then they may need assistance to do so, either as a substitute for family care or to relieve the burden on relatives. It is the responsibility of social work departments to provide such assistance either as a specific duty, as in the case of the home help service, or under their general responsibility 'to promote social welfare' in section 12 of the Social Work (Scotland) Act, 1968. In obtaining access to these services old people may be in contact with a social worker who will give advice, guidance and support as well as ensuring that clients receive all the benefits to which they are entitled. The elderly have been making increasing calls on the social work departments. One in three of social work clients in 1976-77 were people over the age of 65, and the elderly made up half of the recipients of services such as home helps and meals-on-wheels.[7]

The most widely used and highly valued of the domiciliary services is the home help service, which provides not only assistance with a wide range of household tasks — cleaning, shopping, cooking and the like — but also invaluable social contacts for housebound or lonely old people. About one in ten of the elderly population in Scotland are receiving the services of a home help but there is evidence that provision is far from reaching all who would like or would benefit from it. Furthermore, many of those who do receive it would like more than the two or three hours a week which is the present average level of service. Local authorities may make a charge provided that it is 'reasonable' with regard to the income of the recipient and the cost of supplying in the service. Charges are subject to a means test in practice. The means tests and the charges themselves may deter some old people from applying for a home help or restrict the amount of service which they are willing to purchase. In Scotland local authorities are not, however, allowed to charge people on supplementary benefit for the home help service. A domiciliary meals service — meals-on-wheels — and lunch clubs are available in most areas, and again are valued for the social contacts as well as the actual meals. Potential demand, however, exceeds supply both in respect of the numbers receiving the service and the frequency with which meals are supplied which may be as few as one or two per week. The meals themselves are generally supplied by school kitchens and there are doubts about their suitability for the nutritional needs of elderly people. The meals services are interesting examples of collaborative effort on the part of the statutory authorities which provide the meals and the volunteers who deliver them (generally members of the Women's Royal Voluntary Service), or run the lunch clubs.

Small numbers of elderly people — about 4000 out of more than 700,000 people over 65 — are cared for during the day at centres run by social work departments which provide services such as meals, chiropody and recreational facilities, as well as being valuable sources of social contacts and providing some relief for families. Day clubs run by voluntary organisations provide similar facilities. Attendance, however, may only be possible on a few days a week because of excess demand and in some areas transport may be difficult and expensive. Some social work departments use their welfare powers to provide a range of other services which include subsidised holidays and outings, home visiting schemes, library services and the like. Here the voluntary organisations, large national bodies like Age Concern, the churches and local old people's welfare committees, have an important role to play. This could be extended if more assistance were forthcoming from social work departments in the way of training and back-up support for the volunteers, and the loan of premises and transport facilities.

There are wide variations as between areas in the facilities provided and the amount of money spent on them. In Scotland there is the further complication that services may be difficult to organise for scattered populations in rural areas but this by no means accounts for all the local variations. Thus, for example, in the late 1970s expenditure on the home help service in relation to population size was six times as high in the Western Isles as in the Highland region, areas which have much in common, and expenditure on meals services was 15 times as high in the Central region as in the Highland region. On some of the islands and in the Borders region there are no day centre facilities, partly, no doubt, a result of organisational difficulties, while in the Strathclyde region expenditure on such facilities is, at least in comparative terms, substantial.[8] Some facilities involve heavy capital and running costs but others, like the home help service appear to depend as much on local initiative and political will as on financial resources.

*Residential Care*

Although the great majority of elderly people are able to live in their own homes, the time may come when this is no longer possible and residential care is necessary unless their disabilities are such as to require admission to hospital. The need for residential care may of course be precipitated by the lack of suitable housing or domiciliary services. Social factors such as these, rather than infirmity, were found to be the reason for one in four elderly people being in residential care in a survey carried out in the early 1970s, and similar findings were made in a study of elderly hospital patients in Glasgow and the west of Scotland.[9] Where for reasons of age or infirmity people are unable to remain in their own homes it is the statutory responsibility of the social work department to provide alternative accommodation. If a person is in need of care because of self-neglect but refuses to enter a residential home then the department may exercise compulsory powers of admission but such cases are rare.

The social work department may itself provide residential homes or may place elderly people in registered homes run by voluntary organisations, mainly the churches. There is residential accommodation for fewer than 20 people per 1000 aged 65 and over although as early as 1963 central government set a target of 25 places per 1000 elderly. Scotland has more places in relation to the size of the elderly population than England, and more of these are in voluntary homes but, conversely, domiciliary services are less well developed. Charges have been made for residential care since the present arrangements came into operation in 1948, the intention being to preserve the pride of the old person. In most cases this means the transfer of the state pension to the home, leaving a small amount of money for personal needs. In the case of two out of five residents in voluntary homes social work departments subsidise what the old person is able to pay from his own income.

There have been a considerable number of new homes opened over the past two decades, in part to replace the large institutions inherited from poor law days by smaller, better equipped and more home-like accommodation, and in part to provide more places. Good design and up to date equipment should make for better quality care but there are still shortages of skilled staff and much remains to be done to humanise the hospital-type regimes found in some homes. The availability of beds to a large extent determines the criteria which social work departments use in deciding whether or not residential care is desirable. Again the number of beds in relation to the size of the elderly population varies from area to area. In some areas there are long waiting lists for admission while in others there are enough residential places to give some old people a spell of intensive care to rehabilitate them for independent living, or to give families a respite from their caring duties.

Overall there are considerable gaps in the provisions made for elderly people. State pensions are low although improvements are likely over the next two decades. The NHS has brought health care within the reach of all elderly people but standards of caring often compare unfavourably with those in other branches of medicine. The personal social services vary in quantity and quality from area to area, and demand on the whole is greater than supply. We must not, however, paint too bleak a picture. The majority of elderly people live independent lives in their own homes and large numbers have sources of income in addition to their state pensions. Surveys show that the majority of old people express a considerable degree of satisfaction with their living standards although it must be borne in mind that the current generation of pensioners have lived through the depression of the 1930s and two world wars so their expectations may not be high. Future generations of elderly may be less easily satisfied.

THE PHYSICALLY HANDICAPPED

One of the difficulties in describing and attempting to assess the adequacy of the services provided for the physically handicapped is that of defining handicap and ascertaining the numbers of people who as a result of their handicaps need special attention from the social services. A very clear and comprehensive investigation of the extent of disability in Britain was carried out by the Office of Population Censuses and Surveys in the late 1960s, the result of which were published in 1971 as *Handicapped and Impaired in Great Britain*.[10] The author, Amelia Harris, made a useful distinction between *impairment*, which is the physical fact of having 'a defective limb, organ or mechanism of the body' (few people are without some impairment be it only less than perfect eyesight, hearing or teeth); *disability* which is 'the loss or reduction of functional ability' to see or hear or move around; and *handicap* which is 'the disadvantage or restriction of activity caused by disability'. The borderline between the three categories is obviously blurred and in what follows the terms will not always be used in their strict sense.

Whether or not a disability becomes a handicap depends not only on the severity of the condition but also on the personal strengths of individuals, their perception of themselves and their expectations from life, the support which they receive from their families and if necessary from the social services and the attitudes of the communities in which they live. Harris estimated that in Scotland in 1970 there were some 108,000 severely or appreciably handicapped people over the age of 16 who were living in their own homes; an estimated 16,000 were very severely handicapped and of these a considerable number were elderly women living alone. There must be added children with physical handicaps and handicapped people living in hospitals or other residential care. Furthermore, the estimated numbers varied from area to area with a range between 25 and 40 per 1000 of the relevant population.

The handicapped population has grown very considerably over the past quarter of a century. Advances in medical science keep alive many people who would once have died as a result of their abnormalities, diseases or injuries. The vast increase in road accidents has added to the numbers of young handicapped people. An ageing population is more prone to disabling conditions like blindness, deafness, strokes and arthritis, and the elderly are by far the largest section of the handicapped population. A further complication is the wide range of disabilities which may cause handicaps. These include sensory defects of sight and hearing, disabilities which affect mobility like muscular dystrophy and multiple sclerosis, and conditions which affect total functioning such as cerebral palsy or heart and chest complaints. Some impairments are stable like limb amputations, some may improve and some may become progressively worse. Considerable numbers of people have multiple disabilities, and mental and physical impairment may go together. The needs of the disabled vary widely but they also share some common difficulties: loss of income, the extra expense of being handicapped, problems of self-care and fewer social contacts. Many disabled people are known to a wide range of different authorities, both statutory and voluntary, as being in need of assistance in finding work or requiring personal social services of different kinds, or as being the recipients of cash benefits available to the handicapped. It is, however, a very different question whether all the handicapped people needing help are known to the relevant agencies and are receiving all the assistance needed.

The state has accepted some responsibility for the disabled since the poor laws of the sixteenth century, but the involvement of the churches and private philanthropists dates from much earlier than this and continues to play a large role. State and voluntary activity alike gained in impetus during the nineteenth century. The blind were the first to benefit and have continued to be the pace-setters for services for what are known as the 'general' categories of handicapped. The two world wars drew attention both to the needs of the war disabled and other disabled persons for rehabilitation, and to the potential contribution which the handicapped could make to the economy, particularly in times of labour scarcity. The handicapped benefited perhaps even more from the general improvement in health, education, income maintenance and other social services which followed the second world war than from services directed specifically to their needs. The late 1960s and 1970s saw increased interest in the needs of the handicapped, in part as a result of pressure from organisations of the disabled themselves.

This renewed interest manifested itself in the provisions of the Chronically Sick and Disabled Persons Act, 1970 and also led to extensions in the financial support available to handicapped people and their families. Although there is considerable criticism of the services and cash benefits available to the handicapped, there is no doubt that considerable improvements were being made before the economic constraints of the late 1970s put a stop to further developments. The stated objectives of our present day provisions have come a long way from the segregationist policies of the nineteenth century which sought to protect the handicapped from the rigours of everyday living, shutting them away in large institutions remote from the centres of population. Now the aim is to integrate the handicapped into society as fully as possible and to enable them to live as near normal lives as their incapacities will permit.

We now look at various provisions for the physically handicapped, and the point may be repeated that reference should also be made to the other chapters in the book which deal with specific services.

*Health Care*

The NHS plays a large part not only in keeping alive many disabled people but also in making available the continuing medical care which many need in order to cope with their disabilities. General practitioners are central figures in the lives of handicapped people of all ages in diagnosing, treating and helping individuals to manage their disabilities. Access to the various services, however, largely depends on self-referral by disabled people or their families, and many of the handicapped, particularly among the elderly, either find difficulty in visiting their doctors or are reluctant to trouble them with chronic and perhaps incurable conditions.

The hospital services are responsible for acute treatment in the case of serious illness or accident, rehabilitative services for those who can return to normal or near-normal life and long-term in-patient care for the severely and permanently handicapped. Acute care is generally of a high quality but there is a shortage of rehabilitation units where the disabled person can receive the wide range of medical, paramedical, employment and personal social services which are essential for recovery. Nor are NHS prosthetic aids — artificial limbs, wheelchairs, hearing aids and so on — which can help the disabled person to achieve a considerable degree of normal living, always of as high a quality and sophistication as could be desired. The Scottish Hospital Advisory Service in its report for 1980 was particularly critical of the standards of hospital provision for the young physically disabled and pointed to the need for more small hospital wards providing active rehabilitation plus the proper environment if long-term care is necessary.[11] Physical handicap and rehabilitative medicine have not received the attention from the medical profession which they merit, although these areas were singled out in 1976 for priority treatment in the plans put forward in *The Health Services in Scotland: The Way Ahead.*[12]

*Education for the Handicapped Child*

Lack of suitable education may be as much of a handicap as the disability itself. The responsibility to provide for the education of handicapped children has rested with the local education authorities as part of the general duties laid upon them by the Education (Scotland) Act, 1946 to provide for every child's education 'according to his age, aptitude and ability'. Wherever possible the needs of the handicapped child were to be provided for within the normal school structure but in the case of severely handicapped children special schools were to be provided with high staff/pupil ratios, and specially qualified staff. The provision of such schools underwent considerable expansion from 1946 onwards, and here the voluntary organisations, with local education authorities' financial support, played a large part. By 1979 some 2000 children, the majority of those found to have special educational needs, were attending special schools, 80 per cent of them in schools run by local education authorities and 20 per cent in voluntary schools. There were particular difficulties in providing special education for children in the less densely populated areas such as the Highlands and Islands.

The special schools, however, were increasingly criticised because of their emphasis on social rather than academic education, the lack of provision for secondary education and the segregationist policies which they implied. During the 1970s the debate about the respective merits of integrated and special school education for handicapped children gathered momentum. The Warnock Committee in its report published in 1978 endorsed in principle the concept of integrated education but laid stress on the quality rather than the location of such education and saw a continuing role for special schools both in catering for the severely handicapped and as resource and advice centres for ordinary schools coping with handicapped children.[13]

Provision for children with special educational needs is now covered by the Education (Scotland) Act, 1981. The vast majority of such children will continue to be educated in ordinary schools with such extra attention as is required in the form of remedial education, adaptations to course content and so on. The legislation is largely concerned with children having 'pronounced, specific or complex' educational needs whatever the cause. The local education authorities are to assess these children by medical and physical examination, and to keep records of their needs (including those of children over school age) and how it is proposed to meet them. Parents will be involved in such assessment and will have the right of appeal against any plans made by education authorities with which they are not in agreement. Special schools will continue to cater for such children where necessary. The Secretary of State for Scotland has recommended that handicapped children should be given priority for pre-school education and should be able to stay on at school after the official leaving age.

The transition from school to work presents particular difficulties for handicapped teenagers and the discontinuity of service which we mentioned at the beginning of the chapter is obvious at this time. If teenagers take up further education they remain the responsibility of the education authority, which also has responsibility for careers advice, training and job placement. If, however, they enter a local authority or voluntary training centre for the more severely handicapped they come under the oversight of the social work department or of a voluntary agency. All too often, however, the young person, without adequate guidance, falls out of education or the employment market altogether. Some of the employment services are described below but these are geared more to the needs of the older person, in particular the manual worker who has been in employment before becoming disabled.

*Employment Provisions*

The employment services for handicapped people in their present form date from the Disabled Persons (Employment) Act, 1944. The majority of adults who become disabled by reason of accident or disease are in fact able to return to their former occupations. The Manpower Services Commission is required to maintain a register of those who are substantially and permanently disabled and require assistance in obtaining work. Not all people who are disabled choose to register. They may be doubtful about the help this would give them or they may consider it a positive disadvantage to be labelled as handicapped. In any case, registration is not necessary to obtain the various rehabilitation and employment services on offer. These include the services of a disablement rehabilitation officer (DRO) who will liaise with medical personnel in assessing the degree of handicap and the remaining work potential, and advise on obtaining suitable employment. The DRO may recommend a spell at an employment rehabilitation centre for more detailed assessment and for assistance in adapting or in readapting to employment conditions. This may be followed by a period at a skillcentre if vocational training or retraining is considered desirable.

In an attempt to ensure the collaboration of employers in taking on disabled persons, a quota system was set up by the 1944 legislation. This requires employers of more than 20 workers to fill three per cent of their vacancies from the disabled register. Two occupations, electric passenger lift operator and car park attendant, are reserved for the registered disabled. Grants are available to make adaptations to their premises and subsidies are given to employers who take on disabled workers on a trial basis. For workers too severely handicapped to be able to cope with normal working conditions the government has set up the Remploy factories, where the pace and conditions of work can be adjusted to the needs of the individual. Local authorities and a number of voluntary organisations also provide sheltered employment, in particular for the blind.

Employment services for the handicapped, which on the face of it appear fairly comprehensive, have been subject to a great deal of criticism and have been under scrutiny for some time by the Manpower Services Commission. The DROs, it is considered, do not always receive the necessary training for the difficult and delicate tasks of assessment which they are called upon to undertake. There are only four rehabilitation centres in Scotland, and people not living near them may have travel or accommodation problems. It is sometimes claimed that skillcentres are too much oriented to manual work, while training opportunities programmes, which were providing clerical training at colleges of further education, were cut back in the early 1980s. The quota system, it is widely considered, has not worked satisfactorily for many years. Many employers have evaded their responsibilities, few have been prosecuted and on average less than half the required quota of jobs has been filled from the disabled register. But meeting the quota has become increasingly difficult as the number of handicapped people on the register has declined and it has often been unable to supply sufficient workers with the skills required by prospective employers. Proposals have been put forward by the Manpower Services Commission that the present arrangements should be replaced by a scheme that would place upon employers the responsibility to give full consideration to all disabled people, whether registered or not, when filling vacancies. A code of practice would be issued to help employers in complying with the new requirements.

At the same time, places in sheltered employment have fallen behind demand and by their nature have been largely confined to larger towns. There are less than 900 places in Remploy factories in Scotland and a similar number in workshops run by local authorities or voluntary organisations. A certain level of output is required which excludes many of the more severely handicapped, much of the work is repetitive and rates of pay are low. The Remploy factories are costly to run, and there have been management problems and difficulties in finding outlets for their products. Overall the employment prospects of disabled people are poor, particularly in times of recession; their levels of earnings have been well below those of the workforce as a whole and rates of unemployment very much higher. On the other hand, a job gives the person with a handicap greater opportunity to make social contacts and the chance to lead a life more on a par with that of non-disabled members of the community. Employment generally means a higher standard of living than social security benefits, although the disabled person in sheltered employment may question whether it is worthwhile to work for a low wage, if account is taken of the effort of getting to work and the expenses involved. For some of the very severely handicapped employment may be out of the question. Adult training centres or day centres may then provide occupational or recreational interests but places are few and waiting lists are long.

*Income Provisions*

The majority of handicapped people who are unable to work are dependent on social security benefits. Benefits for the handicapped are complex which results in many people being imperfectly informed of their rights. They are also inconsistent which gives rise to different levels of support for handicapped people with like needs. The basic income which a handicapped person receives depends primarily on the cause of disability, and there is a hierarchy of different entitlements. There are relatively generous pensions and other allowances for the war and industrially disabled, and contributory benefits at lower rates for insured workers whose disabilities are the result of other causes. At a still lower level are non-contributory pensions which are available to those who have never been able to work and pay contributions. Most recipients of non-contributory pensions also have to claim supplementary benefit. During the 1970s the financial position of the latter two categories was improved, and brought nearer to that of the war and industrially disabled, by the introduction of new benefits — attendance, mobility and invalid care allowances — designed to help meet some of the additional expenses which handicap inevitably involves. Parents may also apply to the Family Fund, financed by the government but administered by the Joseph Rowntree Memorial Trust, for lump sum grants towards the purchase of equipment such as washing machines and bedding which will ease the burden of caring for a handicapped child.

Looking to the future, proposals have been made to bring industrial injury benefits into line with benefits for other disabled workers, but they have met with considerable opposition from the trade unions. The government has proposed some minor adjustments to the scheme which would favour the long-term severely handicapped at the expense of the short-term industrially disabled. The Disablement Income Group, a consortium of pressure groups for the handicapped, has advocated the simplification of the benefits structure so as to bring about parity of treatment: one income for all disabled people, assessed on degree of disability and unrelated to cause of disability or financial means. This would be costly and is very unlikely to be seriously considered in the foreseeable future.

*Housing and Personal Social Services*

Many handicapped people, especially if their handicap is severe or they are advanced in years, may need help with self-care, domestic chores, adaptation to their homes or even special housing to make independent living possible. In the majority of cases families provide the extra personal care required, and the attendance and invalid care allowances make some recognition at least of the financial burden this may involve. If such support is not available, or if the efforts of the family need to be supplemented, the responsibility rests with the social work department either under the Social Work (Scotland) Act, 1968 or the Chronically Sick and Disabled Persons Act,

1970 (which was extended by the Chronically Sick and Disabled Persons (Scotland) Act, 1972). The 1970 and 1972 legislation requires social work departments to obtain information about the numbers of handicapped people in their areas and to make known to them the services available. These might include domestic help, meals, home adaptations such as ramps to permit wheelchair access and adjustments to kitchens and bathrooms, and assistance in obtaining telephones, radios, television and other recreational facilities. The legislation also requires new public buildings to be accessible to the handicapped and to have appropriate toilet facilities. The handicapped were to be represented on the various advisory panels relevant to their needs and younger handicapped persons (under the age of 65) were not to be accommodated with geriatric patients in hospitals or in residential homes for the elderly.

The responsibilities of social work departments were loosely defined and have rarely been carried out with much energy or imagination. The statutory duties laid on the departments in respect of children and young people, which are discussed in chapters 6 and 7, have been given precedence over the needs of the physically handicapped (or the elderly or mentally handicapped for that matter). Nevertheless, some progress has been made, notably in the provision of toilet facilities and ramps for wheelchair users, and orange disc parking permits for disabled drivers. There has been some increase in the number of disabled people having access to the very useful home help service or being assisted with the cost of installing telephones or taking holidays. Places in day centres have slowly increased in number. But, overall, provision of these services is very far from meeting potential demand, local responses vary widely and access to services depends very much on the accident of where the handicapped person happens to live. The Chronically Sick and Disabled Persons Act, 1970 was hailed as a charter for the handicapped but expectations have often been disappointed. The physically handicapped have been given low priority at a time when severe restraints are being imposed on public expenditure.

Adaptations to their homes to make them suitable for disabled living may be carried out by either the local housing authority or social work department. Increasing, though still small, numbers of disabled people have benefited but there are frequently long delays in assessing what is needed and then in carrying out the work. As far as specially designed housing is concerned the lead has been taken by voluntary organisations, for example the Thistle Foundation, which have pioneered a number of experiments in residential living for the disabled. Responsibility for providing for severely disabled people for whom independent living is impossible but hospital care is not needed also rests with social work departments. There are, however, no local authority residential homes for the younger disabled in Scotland, although numbers of older people who have become disabled with age are living in residential homes for the elderly. The 1970 legislation required the health and local authorities to make annual returns of handicapped people under 65 years of age living in hospital geriatric wards or in local authority residential homes for the elderly and the numbers have gradually declined. There are few hospital wards for the younger disabled or chronically sick and residential accommodation outside hospitals is provided by voluntary organisations, such as the Cheshire Homes, the Red Cross and the Spastics Society. There are only 600 places in these homes in the whole of Scotland.

The voluntary organisations led the way in providing for the welfare of the handicapped and they continue to play a large part in supplementing or filling the gaps in local authority services. Of particular interest in the post-war years has been the development of mutual aid organisations for different sections of the handicapped population such as the Muscular Dystrophy Group, the Heart and Chest Foundation and the Multiple Sclerosis Society. These have been formed by the families of the handicapped, or by the handicapped themselves, often with the support of members of the caring professions. Their activities include practical help with transport, recreational and residential facilities, as well as advice and mutual support for the disabled and their families. Increasingly they have come to play an important role both in providing funds for research into the causes of and possible cures for various disabilities and as pressure groups pushing for improvements in central and local government services. The large contribution which the voluntary organisations already make to the wellbeing of the disabled could be enhanced by better co-ordination among the organisations themselves, and by better and more imaginative collaboration between the voluntary and public sectors.

Blaxter's study of a group of men and women of working age in the Aberdeen area who had been discharged from hospital after suffering potentially disabling injuries or accidents underlines the difficulties experienced by many handicapped people.[14] One in four were found to have difficulties with self-care, over half of those in employment had work-related problems, one in 20 were living below the supplementary benefit level, and many had personal problems of poor family relationships, loneliness or lack of occupation or recreation. Likewise, some disabled children suffer from serious educational disadvantages, while distressing poverty and loneliness is to be found among some of the elderly and people with physical and mental disabilities.

It is, however, impossible to generalise about the benefits and services which individual elderly or handicapped people receive from the welfare state. Categorisation has been a useful device in singling out sections of the population with special needs for preferential treatment, especially as this has made it possible to dispense in many cases with detailed investigations of needs. But categorisation as a tool of social policy has its limitations. Within these large categories are people with very different needs which benefits and services based on assumed average needs cannot always meet to the full. It is left to the more individualised approach of supplementary benefit and the personal social services to go some way towards filling the gaps.

More important, however, than provision for individual special needs are the overall levels at which benefits and services are made available to broad categories of recipients. Here we must not, of course, fall into the trap of making an implicit assumption that everything must be provided by the state. In the majority of cases individuals can reasonably be expected to make some provision for their old age and many in fact do so. Similarly, elderly people themselves and their families provide a large part of the personal care which is required. The handicapped may be in rather a different situation. They have had less opportunity to save and they may require more attention than their families are able to give. With certain reservations, however, it can be said that the elderly and the handicapped have derived more than average benefits from the growth of the welfare state and have shared to some extent at least in the higher standards of living which economic growth made possible in the 1950s, 1960s and early 1970s. Future prospects for the elderly and handicapped will depend in large measure on the recovery of the economy, and on the willingness of the working population to forego present consumption and to give of their time and interest. The extent to which it is possible to maintain and improve the living standards of these and other groups in need will thus be determined by a range of factors which constrain the work of the social services.

*References*

1. See for example: A. Hunt, *The Elderly at Home*, HMSO, 1978; and M. Abrams, *Beyond Three Score Years and Ten*, Age Concern, 1980.
2. *The Government's Expenditure Plans 1981/2 to 1983/4*, Cmnd. 8175, HMSO, 1981.
3. Scottish Home and Health Department and Scottish Education Department, *Changing Patterns of Care: Report on Services for the Elderly in Scotland*, HMSO, 1980.
4. Scottish Home and Health Department and Scottish Education Department, *Services for the Elderly with Mental Disability*, HMSO, 1979.
5. Scottish Development Department and Social Work Services Group, Circular (SDD) No. 120, (SWSG) No. SW/25, 1975.
6. See: *Changing Patterns of Care*, Section 4.
7. Social Work Services Group, *Social Work Case Statistics 1976-77 (SWSG Statistical Bulletin)*, SWSG, 1978.
8. *Changing Patterns of Care*, Section 3.
9. V. Carstairs and M. Morrison, *The Elderly in Residential Care*, Scottish Health Service Studies, No. 19, Scottish Home and Health Department, 1971; and B. Isaacs, M. Livingstone and Y. Neville, *The Survival of the Unfittest*, Routledge and Kegan Paul, 1972.
10. A. Harris, *Handicapped and Impaired in Great Britain*, HMSO 1971; and J.R. Buckle, *Work and Housing of Impaired Persons in Great Britain*, HMSO, 1971.
11. See also: Scottish Home and Health Department, *Health in Scotland, 1980*, HMSO, 1981; and Scottish Home and Health Department, *Scottish Health Authorities' Priorities for the Eighties* (SHAPE Report), HMSO, 1981.
12. Scottish Home and Health Department, *The Health Services in Scotland: The Way Ahead*, HMSO, 1975.
13. *Special Educational Needs: Report of the Committee of Enquiry into the Education of Handicapped Children and Young People* (Warnock Report), Cmnd. 7212, HMSO, 1978.
14. M. Blaxter, *The Meaning of Disability: A Sociological Study of Impairment*, Heinemann, 1976.

## FURTHER READING

*The Elderly*

E. Mortimer, *Working with the Elderly*, Heinemann, 1982.
An analysis of the problems of the elderly and services available to help them.

A. Tinker, *The Elderly in Modern Society*, Longman, 1981.
A comprehensive study of the literature and research evidence on the needs of the elderly. Includes valuable synopses or extracts from legislation, surveys and other relevant documentation, and extensive bibliographical references.

P. Brearly, J. Gibbons, A. Miles, E. Topliss and G. Woods, *The Social Context of Health Care*, Martin Robertson and Blackwell, 1978.
An analysis of the social and medical problems of the elderly, the physically handicapped and the mentally ill.

*The Physically Handicapped*

D.A. Boswell and J. Wingrove (eds.), *The Handicapped Person in the Community*, Tavistock Publications and the Open University Press, 1974.
Readings in the sociological, psychological and practical aspects of physical and mental handicap.

A. Morris, *No Feet to Drag*, Sidgwick and Jackson, 1972.
An account of the events leading up to the Chronically Sick and Disabled Persons Act, 1970.

E. Topliss, *Provision for the Disabled*, Martin Robertson and Blackwell (2nd edition), 1979.
A discussion both of concepts of disability and of provision for the disabled in the fields of education, rehabilitation, employment, personal social services and social security.

# Index